# DIXIE DEAN

Other Robson Books by John Keith

*The Essential Shankly*
(2001) paperback £8.99

*Bob Paisley: Manager Of The Millennium*
(1999) hardback £17.95, paperback £8.99

*Billy Liddell: The Legend Who Carried the Kop*
(2003) hardback £16.95

# DIXIE DEAN

## The Inside Story of a Football Icon

### By John Keith

FOREWORD BY ALEX YOUNG
'THE GOLDEN VISION'

ROBSON BOOKS

This edition published in Great Britain in 2003 by Robson Books,
The Chrysalis Building, Bramley Road, London W10 6SP

An imprint of Chrysalis Books Group Plc

British Library Cataloguing in Publication Data

A catalogue record for this title is available from the British Library.

ISBN 1 86105 632 X

Typeset by SX Composing DTP, Rayleigh, Essex
Printed in Great Britain by Bell & Bain Ltd., Glasgow

This book is dedicated to my wife Pat, my daughters Lauren and Isobelle, to my brother Graham and his family and to the memory of my late mother Lilian and my late father, Hal, who had the pleasure and privilege of seeing Dixie Dean play.

# Contents

# *Preface*

The preparation and research for this book included the transcription of many hours of taped interviews with Dixie Dean, some of which I had conducted and others which were kindly put at my disposal by BBC Radio Merseyside from the 1970s series presented by my late friend and colleague Bob Azurdia. As some of the events referred to and recalled by Dixie had taken place many years previously, some more than half a century earlier, this involved hours of checking and cross-checking for purposes of accuracy. Wherever possible, amendments on factual detail have been made.

In addition to expressing my grateful thanks to Radio Merseyside I am indebted to members of the Dean family, Dixie's sons Geoff, Bill and Ralph and daughter Barbara, not only for their contributions to the book but also for their assistance and support.

I also wish to offer my grateful thanks to Gilbert Upton, that esteemed Tranmere Rovers supporter, historian and author of several books about his hometown club and the early years of Dixie Dean. Gilbert's enthusiastic assistance on matters of fact, plucked from the archives, has been invaluable. He has also kindly supplied some of the pictures and illustrations, as have Alan Upton (no relation) and Frank Christian.

My thanks also to football personalities past and present, to Dr John K. Rowlands for supplying material on Albert Geldard and the 1933 FA Cup Final, to the late actor and comedian Bill Dean and to David France, Richard Whitehead, Tom Clare and Mal Scott-Taggart.

I am particularly grateful to Alex Young, himself an Everton legend, for writing the foreword and to everyone else who has helped in producing this book.

'Dixie was the greatest centre forward there will ever be. His record of goalscoring is the most amazing thing under the sun.'

Bill Shankly

# *Foreword*

## By Alex Young

Dixie Dean was unique. A legend. An icon. The superlatives rain upon him and rightly so because his feats still seem unbelievable. I feel privileged and honoured to be one of the players to have pulled on that Everton No. 9 jersey and followed in the footsteps of a football giant. Like me, I am sure that every player who wears that jersey is, to a greater or lesser degree, conscious that he is treading the path blazed by a man who could have been built to score goals.

My father, who was a coal miner in Scotland, told me about Dixie when I was just a wee boy. So when I signed for Everton from Hearts in November 1960 I was well aware of Goodison's proud centre forward tradition, enriched by Dixie and continued by men like Tommy Lawton and Dave Hickson before me and Joe Royle, Bob Latchford and Graeme Sharp who followed me. I never saw Dixie play but I am delighted to say that I met the great man on two or three occasions and I treasure a photograph of myself flanked by Dixie and Tommy Lawton which was taken at a dinner to celebrate our 1962–63 championship win. The following year I played in Dixie's testimonial match at Goodison, which was another wonderful memory.

When I first came to join Everton I had torn ligaments. I was transferred wearing a back splint! So for the first few months I was in the treatment room and I used to have long chats with old Harry Cooke, who was the trainer during Dixie's great days. Harry recounted story after story about Dixie so I got well versed in the Dean legend.

He told me that on a few occasions he had to give Dixie black coffee a couple of hours before a game because he'd been out the night before. Then, even though substitutes weren't allowed at that time, he would tell Dixie: 'If you score three in the first half we'll take you off at half time.' Sure enough, according to Harry, Dixie would go and get three! After hearing all this it was great to meet the man himself. Dixie was an ordinary man, a working class man, a modest man, a nice man, a genuine man and a man of the people. He was also a man the people idolised, right up to his dying day. Dixie told me, without boasting but just as a matter of fact, that when he was at his peak as a player and he went out in public he would stop the traffic.

When I came down to England, years before the television play *The Golden Vision* was made, I was flabbergasted at the adulation the supporters gave to players. It was much more intense than in Scotland and I think Merseyside is the hotbed of it. They love footballers and it's a special place. So I can understand why, in this kind of environment, Dixie was a superstar in his day. But he respected the fans as much as they respected him. He also told me that he would sign little squares of paper before he went out because he didn't want to disappoint anyone who asked him for his autograph. I wonder what these highly paid guys in football today would think of that? Sometimes I think they look down on the supporters. They should thank their lucky stars and take a leaf out of Dixie's book.

Dixie's goals record is incredible. Some say that the change in the offside law just after Dixie joined Everton made it easier for forwards to score goals. It was long before my time but apart from the fact that teams developed tactics to counter the change, it must not be forgotten that, unlike today, defenders were allowed to tackle from behind and kick right through the ball. Don't forget, either, that Dixie scored all those goals using the old style lace-up balls – which weighed a ton when they were wet – and on pitches that were like cowfields compared to today's bowling green surfaces which the light ball just skips over. Even when I started with Hearts, playing wide right as a young lad in 1955, when you took a corner kick your concern was getting the ball past the first post! Never mind bending them and curling them like David Beckham today! The ball and the pitches started to get better only in the later stages of my own career. So to score 60 League goals in a season, as he did, as well as all his other feats, was just unbelievable.

He and I were very different types of centre forward. Apart from the fact he was dark haired and I was blond, Dixie was a powerhouse and I certainly wasn't. His game was in stark contrast to mine. Although it was in the 1960s when I first met him you could see why he must have been a fearsome opponent for defenders. He had a bull neck and looked a really strong, powerful figure. I could imagine him playing in today's Premiership. Once he adjusted to the pace, you would see him whacking in the goals the way the lighter ball is swerved in from the flanks. Just think of him getting on the end of the crosses we see now. He did the business in his own day and I am sure someone of his talent would do it in today's game.

What struck me about Dixie the person was that there was no sense of arrogance about him. Like myself, he came from a working class background and if you had ideas above your station you were soon dragged back and put in your place. The message that came through to me from talking to Dixie was to give supporters their due respect

A trio of great Everton centre forwards . . . Tommy Lawton, Alex Young and Dixie Dean at Everton's 1963 League championship celebration dinner (copyright *Daily Express*)

and show humility. My wife Nancy and I have also met Dixie's charming daughter Barbara on a couple of occasions. We get on great and it was enjoyable listening to her recalling memories and anecdotes of her father.

Dixie Dean was a man who, quite simply, will never be forgotten. His story is an amazing one, his deeds weaved into the fabric of Everton Football Club and the heritage of British football.

# CHAPTER ONE

## *Dixie's Land*

He was a son of the early years of the 20th century, when a big mac was a long raincoat and logging-on meant queuing in the job line to earn a few shillings as a woodcutter. Yet the subsequent technological and social revolution, now spilling into the 21st century, has done nothing to dim the deeds of William Ralph Dean, the man they called Dixie and whose name means one thing . . . goals. Football has changed dramatically since Dixie Dean was terrorising defences in the 1920s and 1930s. Even the game that he knew when he died in 1980, a dozen years before the advent of the Premiership began generating huge amounts of money and wall-to-wall multi-channel televised action, is almost unrecognisable. Britain's national sport is now a mega, global business. It is quoted on the Stock Exchange, clutched to the bosom of governments, politicians and corporate interests and subject to the vagaries of the financial market. The game of the cloth cap belongs to a bygone age.

One cynic observed that only two terrestrial features are visible from outer space: the Great Wall of China and the average Premiership player's wage packet. Football has become the chic universal product of the new millennium, its importance embracing every nation from tinpot dictatorships and struggling Third World countries to affluent Western democracies. The clamour for a piece of the action within the corridors of power of the game's world ruling body FIFA, testify to that. Yet the game's hard, common currency has remained unaltered by time, technology or finance. Goals remain football's priceless commodity and the master of the scoring art was Dixie Dean, the greatest centre forward of them all, the working class hero who became his own era's version of a pop star. He was, in a sense, the archetypal Roy of the Rovers. Yet Dean achieved in reality what still seems a flight of comic strip fantasy. He was the supreme embodiment of sporting dreams, the ultimate hero. Wonderful testimony to Dean's status was provided by a confirmed Second World War incident in the Western Desert when an Italian solider spat in the sand in front of his British captors and cursed in broken English: 'F—— a ya Weenston Churchill and f—— a ya Deexie Dean!' It was witnessed by a British serviceman called Patrick Connolly, later to break into show business, adopt the stage name Bill Dean in honour of his idol, and become famous for many roles including Harry Cross in the television soap Brookside.

Today, clubs will pay a king's ransom to players who can put the ball in the net with some regularity. The best of them reach a total little more than half Dixie Dean's record of 60 League goals in a season. Yet today's Premiership breed are paid many times more in a week than Dean earned throughout his entire 16-year professional career. Dean was in his pomp in the Roaring Twenties, the dawn of the Jazz Age. But his own Dixie melody was a constantly repetitive refrain of goals, goals and yet more goals. His haul of 60 in a League season stands alone as a towering feat, the Everest of goalscoring and a peak that has defeated all challengers through the generations. It is a record etched in stone in the annals of football.

Great strikers, ranging from Bill's own Everton and England successor Tommy Lawton and including Nat Lofhouse, Jimmy Greaves, Arthur Rowley, Roger Hunt, Bob Latchford, Gary Lineker, Ian Rush and John Aldridge right through to Michael Owen, Andy Cole and Robbie Fowler, as well as other celebrated marksmen, have never even come close to equalling it. And with as much certainty that can be applied to boundaries of sporting endeavour and achievement, Dean's record will surely remain unsurpassed as one of football's enduring yardsticks of excellence, even when interplanetary travel becomes as common to the man in the street as taking a ferry across the Mersey has become to citizens of Birkenhead, the town that was home to Dixie Dean. He was fiercely proud of his roots and was quick to remind you that people from his side of the river were *Wackers* while those from the Liverpool side were *Scousers*, a little known piece of Merseyside demographic demarcation about which he was passionate.

The rich potential that alerted a batch of clubs to the young Bill Dean at Tranmere blossomed brilliantly at Everton where he launched his assault on opposing defences to leave the record books in tatters and secure a place in football immortality as the game's prototype centre forward, a giant of his craft for club and country. His 349 League goals for Everton between 1925 and 1937 is an all-time record for one club, as are his 37 senior hat tricks in a Goodison jersey. He also struck 18 goals in 16 England appearances. In addition to his remarkable 60 League goals in 1927–28 he also scored three in the FA Cup, four for England, six for the Football League, eight in FA Trial games, nine on an FA tour and a further 10 in friendlies and charity games to reach an incredible total of 100. A century of goals by an individual player in one season! It is barely credible even in the cold print of statistics. It is more than most clubs total in a single campaign today.

I had the poignant privilege of taking Dixie Dean to Goodison Park as my guest for the game at which he died – a testy Mersey derby in March 1980. The universal impact of his death reminded us all that he fulfilled one of the searching tests of an icon in achieving recognition beyond the confines of the sport at which he excelled.

The change in the offside law in 1925 – amending the 'fewer than three players between the attacker and the ball' stipulation to 'fewer than two' – provided the platform for Dean to open a new, ground-breaking chapter in goalscoring.

As defences grappled with the new situation, forwards made hay. The year prior to Dean's 60-goal season. Middlesbrough's George Camsell scored 59 in the old Second Division. But the rule change must not be allowed to detract from the excellence of Dean nor diminish his pre-eminence among goalscorers, as his contemporaries, both fellow professionals and observers, have powerfully attested. He possessed unequalled heading power, so forceful it matched the shooting strength of some players, complementing his scoring ability with both feet. What made his deeds even more amazing was that he had to overcome the massive handicaps of two serious injuries, one before the first brick in the Dean legend had been laid, and the other threatening his life and Everton career.

As a 17-year-old during his initial season at his first League club, Tranmere Rovers, he lost a testicle after an agonising incident during a reserve match at Prenton Park. The mental scars might have run even deeper than the physical ones as he was ruled out of action for more than a month. The surgery required was the first of 15 operations he would undergo in his career. Yet, showing the unquenchable determination, courage and humour that were hallmarks of his character, he shrugged off that loss to his anatomy both professionally and personally. A year later he joined Everton and his football career soared. Later, after marrying his beautiful sweetheart Ethel Fossard, he fathered four children, three boys and a girl.

Perhaps that early battle against pain at Tranmere proved an ally to Dean when early in his Everton career a life-threatening motorcycle accident left medical opinion pronouncing he would never play again. He sustained a fractured skull and shattered jawbone and was unconscious for 36 hours. To aid his recovery he had to have a metal plate inserted in his head. But within four months of receiving his horrific injuries Dean proved the doctors wrong by plunging back into football combat, displaying even more awesome heading power than before his road crash. He was football's original Bionic Man.

William Ralph Dean, the man destined to become a legend, a by-word wherever football is played, was born on January 22, 1907 at 313 Laird Street in the north end of Birkenhead. The arrival of a bouncing baby boy delighted his parents, William and Sarah, who had already produced five girls and thought they were destined to have a sixth daughter. A son was highly prized by working class families in that Edwardian era when Britain was governed by the Liberals under Sir Henry Campbell-Bannerman and women were officially second class citizens. It would take another 11 years and a world war before a campaign by the suffragettes would earn the right for women – at least those over 30 – to vote.

Dean's native Birkenhead, situated on the south bank of the River Mersey on the Wirral Peninsula and famous for its docks, shipbuilding and repairing, had once been in competition with its big neighbour Liverpool across the river. So intense was their rivalry during the 19th century that Liverpudlians raised the ire of their Birkonian neighbours by bestowing the title 'one-eyed city' on Birkenhead, the origins of that insulting soubriquet lost in the mists of time. They did, however, have joint cause for celebration over the substantial engineering feat of building the Mersey Railway, linking Birkenhead and Liverpool through a tunnel under the river, which opened to commuters in 1885 as an alternative to the ferries. Two world renowned road tunnels, Queensway and Kingsway, would follow during the next century.

Earlier in the 1800s Birkenhead's prosperity, rising with every ship that moved down the slipway and the arrival of rich merchants, stoked the town's ambitions and it stole a march on Liverpool by having Europe's first street trams and creating the world's first park built for the public and by the public, through subscription, 'to serve the urban poor.'

Birkenhead Park, first mooted in 1841 and rising from a drained swamp, opened in 1847 fronted by magnificent Grecian-style pillared gates. And although Liverpool doused Birkenhead's dreams by officially becoming a city in 1880 their splendid park proved the inspiration for the creation of New York's famous green oasis Central Park, meaning that a part of the Big Apple will be forever Merseyside.

William Ralph Dean, fiercely proud of his roots until his dying day, was to become Birkenhead's most famous 'export', raising the goal standard in football to unseen and unprecedented heights. His birth completed a notable January treble in the annals of Merseyside sport. A year earlier Nel Tarleton, later to find boxing fame as British and British Empire featherweight champion and twice world title challenger, had been born. Like Dean, Tarleton would also appear in front of a massive crowd at Anfield, home of Liverpool Football Club, where more than 30,000 packed in to see him valiantly outpointed for the world crown by the German-American southpaw Freddie Miller in September 1934. Twelve months before Tarleton's birth saw the arrival of another January baby set for the fight game, the popular lightweight Dom Volante, of Anglo-Italian descent.

The sport that attracted Dean's father, William, was football, and the team he supported was Everton. He took his son to Goodison only once, to watch a game when he was an eight-year-old during the club's title-winning 1914–15 campaign, which preceded League football's closure because of the First World War. But first impressions counted and young William vowed on that single trip that one day he would play professionally for Everton.

William senior came from Chester and was an engine driver with the old Great Western Railway – once even having the honour of driving the Royal train – before switching to the Wirral Railway to be closer to his future wife Sarah. She had been in domestic employment for a wealthy family in the Rock Ferry district prior to marrying William in 1892, ironically the year that a rent dispute between factions within Everton Football Club led to a row, a split and the formation of Liverpool FC. The Deans eventually moved a few yards down the street from the house where their only son was born to live on the premises of the family's fish and chip shop.

Young William was gripped by football from a tender age and in this modern era, which has spawned schools of soccer excellence and heavy financial investment in facilities for young players, it is worth pondering on the fact that the wall of the nearby Wesleyan Chapel was to form the foundation rock of Dean's football development, necessity proving the mother of invention. His yearning to improve and hone his football skills is evident in these recollections of his childhood:

I had six sisters. No brothers. They kicked me arse, pulled me, told me to shut up. I went to Laird Street School but when I was about 11 or 12 I used to go at night to sleep at the Albert Industrial School, with the permission of Mr Williams, the old Scottish governor.

It was a borstal but I wasn't a convict or anything like that. I went there because we didn't have room at home and, also, I could play football for the Albert School!

With having five sisters – the other one Elsie moved out when she got married – as well as my old woman and old feller living above the family's fish and chip shop it was a question of space.

There were only two bedrooms and a small room where you could fit just a single bed.

I was born a bit further up Laird Street from the shop. But we moved to the shop when I was very young and I've seen myself peeling spuds at midnight more than once.

Just before we moved to the shop I remember being in the house one day when I was about five and my mother giving me a wash in the bowl on the table under the window.

Suddenly we saw this feller come into the yard to pinch something or burgle the house. He wasn't entitled to be there. I saw him and made a bit of an effort to chase him and I fell through the bloody window and ended up in hospital.

From about seven or eight I was continually playing football, both for Laird Street and the Albert Industrial School. I used to practise heading by throwing a ball on to the roof of an old chapel at the back of our house. I'd already marked out a goal on the wall of the chapel and when the ball came down off the roof I'd head it against the wall.

That wall was a great thing for me. I enjoyed every minute of it. As well as using it for heading practice it was also good for passing. You didn't need to worry about having someone to kick the ball back to you. I could run the length of the wall from about 10 or 12 yards hitting the ball against the wall and receiving it with my foot, my thigh or my chest and thumping it back. It was very good practice.

I never had any proper coaching. I can honestly say that what I learned I taught myself, either from practising on the chapel wall or any match I could get fixed up with. We'd just pick two teams and put the coats down for goal posts.

I remember one day going up to a place called Nanny Goat Mountain which was near the bottom of Bidston Hill and which got its name because there really were nanny goats walking around.

A game was going on there this particular day and they were short of a player. As I was taking my sister for a walk in her pram at the time I joined the game and used the pram as a goalpost!.

When the game was over and I got back home one of my older sisters asked me: 'Where's the baby? You took her out for a walk.' I'd forgotten her! I had to go running back a mile and a half to get my sister who was still in the pram we'd used as a goalpost!.

Just down below where we lived, in the Upper Brassey Street School in Birkenhead, there was another boy coming along called Ellis Rimmer. He was their star turn. We both went on to play for Tranmere and later we were capped together for England against Spain at Highbury (Dec 1931, won 7–1).

I was never a great schoolboy at anything except football. I'm afraid I got no further at school than giving out the chalks and the ink. I suppose I was a dunce.

I could just about write a bit but I was no good at doing sums or anything and I used to sag school quite a lot. In fact, the headmaster warned me if I stayed away again he'd give me a good hiding.

One day I got a bit of a fright when all the boys were ordered into the main hall and a man from the Education Committee stood up in front of the whole school and said: 'Come forward, William Ralph Dean'.

I said to myself 'here we go'. I thought I was going to get punished for something. But this education chap said: 'Congratulations on being selected to play for the Birkenhead Schoolboys football team'. Then he presented me with a commemorative medal. It was the first medal I ever got.

I asked the headmaster if I could go home early and show the medal to my mother. He let me go – and I stayed away for three days celebrating!

The Laird Street School played in blue jerseys, like Everton, and the night before a match I'd sleep in my jersey because it meant so much to me.

The Albert Industrial School was at the back of Laird Street and I had to have a tale to tell in case anyone asked me on the field during matches why I was put into the borstal!.

My yarn was that I stole a duck from Bidston Hill and brought this duck home and, because someone had snitched on me, I was chased by one or two coppers. So I took the duck in the lavatory and tried to put its head down the pan. But the duck quacked and the coppers caught me! That was the story I made up!.

The Albert School was a great thing for the boys who were sent there. They could learn any profession they wished, from making shoes to engineering.

I played football for the Albert School on the Wirral Railway field, which was a beautiful ground. It had lovely turf. We'd also play over in Liverpool against the likes of St Edwards Orphanage and other games in Cheshire.

Although the Albert School was a borstal I've met a lot of very good fellers all over Britain who were sent there and who've done well for themselves. Some of them have become good musicians and other have built their own businesses.

I left school at 14 and played for Birkenhead Schoolboys for two seasons instead of the usual one because I was picked for them a year earlier than normal.

Young Dixie (front row with ball) in the 1920–21 Birkenhead Schoolboys team (copyright unknown)

I played outside right for the first year and centre forward the second season. Even in those days there was only one result I looked for in the paper and that was Everton's. I never looked for Liverpool. I never bothered about them. Just Everton.

One day when I was thirteen I scored 18 goals in three matches on the same day. The first match I played in was a Birkenhead Schoolboys trial game at Prenton playing fields and I scored six. Then I borrowed a bike so I could get down to Birkenhead Park to play for my school team, Laird Street. I scored six in that one, too.

That afternoon I played for a team called Melville and got another six. So it was a good day's work. They were all 90 minute matches with schoolboy goal posts.

My mother had two fish and chip shops and I was pretty lucky in that respect because it helped me develop broad shoulders turning the spuds for her. The quicker you got them done the sooner you got out to play football.

I also had another lucky touch from the fish and chip shop in the way of free passes for the picture houses. We got them for putting the cinema bill up in the shop window.

I also enjoyed myself dancing. My sisters encouraged me to go to classes and I turned out quite a decent bit of a dancer, especially tap dancing. I loved tap dancing and right up to my last operation I'd still have a go.

There was many a time during my Everton days, particularly when we were away on special training, I'd start performing my tap dancing for the lads.

During the First World War my father stayed at home because he worked for the Wirral Railway, which was a reserved occupation. I remember the war days very well.

The people next door to our fish and chip shop had a milk round and I got a job delivering it. I used to get up at four o'clock in the morning and go up to Burgess's Farm outside Birkenhead, get the milk, bring it back and deliver it round Birkenhead. I was allowed an extra hour off school to do it.

When I was a bit older I finished delivering milk and used to go across to Liverpool early in the morning by tram and train to buy fish at St John's Market for my mother's fish and chip shops. The customers knew our fish was fresh. By sending me as a youngster my mother would save money on the tram fare. There were no buses. Up to the age of 14 I could travel on the tram for a halfpenny.

But I was quite a big boy and at least three times I had to go to the tram depot with my mother after they'd refused to believe my age. She played hell with them. So I used to carry a letter from my headmaster at Laird Street School to prove that I was still under 14.

During wartime we also had an allotment. We had to grow our own potatoes and vegetables to help the war effort. I remember one time during the war when the rumour went round that two or three Jerries had been dropped on Bidston Hill and were on top of a house. But we found out the next day that they were three chimneys, not Jerries!.

From where I lived the main North West army camp was only about a mile and a half away at Bidston. There was where all the 'drafts' used to go from.

They'd walk right down Laird Street to the river and either board their ships there or get the ferry to Liverpool and sail from there. That was them on their way to France.

We enjoyed life a lot more than the youngsters do now. Many of them today are just young hooligans. I don't know how they do enjoy themselves but we certainly did, even if it was only making a swing round a street lamp post with someone keeping watch to make sure a copper wasn't coming.

We also had games of pitch and toss, again with two or three good 'keepers' on the look out for coppers. Our childhood was very happy and I'd have played football for the love of the game.

My mother bought me my first pair of boots when I was nine or ten. She took me out and had me fitted for them. As I grew I think my mother and father could see that football was going to be my career. Both of them were keen for me to do it.

But apart from one trip to Goodison as a kid I never managed to see Everton or Tranmere because I was playing every Saturday afternoon. I wouldn't miss. Even if I turned up for a game and found out I couldn't get in a team I'd be a linesman, anything, as long as it was football.

On one occasion when Dean played for Birkenhead Schoolboys against the powerful Liverpool Schoolboy side his father promised him a shilling for every goal he scored, which turned out to be a bizarre 'bob a job'.

Birkenhead lost 5–0 and young Bill, forced into defence by the weight of Liverpool's pressure, put through his own goal. When his father asked how many he had scored he replied: 'I only got one today'. His father duly paid up but when he read a newspaper match report and learned it had been an own goal he tackled his son about it. 'You never said anything about who I had to score the goal for,' replied young Bill, whose plea persuaded his father that he should keep his prize money.

Mainly, though, it was opponents who were on the receiving end of Bill's burgeoning goalscoring skill and power. In another schoolboy game, an English Trophy match between Birkenhead and Bootle at Tranmere's Prenton Park ground in 1920, the visiting goalkeeper Ryder had to have treatment from St John Ambulance men after stopping a Dean shot with his fists.

Later, he got in the way of another Dean blast and had to be taken off with a fractured arm, the Bootle centre forward Allman going in goal. Birkenhead won 4–0 with Dean scoring all four.

As a teenager in Birkenhead, Bill Dean's charisma as well as his talent was evident. Elsie Holcroft, then a nine-year-old, said: 'In the early 1920s I remember Dixie playing on top of Gallaghers Hill at the top end of Price Street. There was a big pond below the hill, where we girls used to watch the boys fishing for eels, and beyond that was a large playing field. That's where we used to watch Dixie play on Saturdays. He just lived for football.

'To us he was a hero and even though he was only in his early teens you could see he was a star in the making. He scored a lot of goals and every time he did we used to cheer like mad. He was a handsome boy with a mass of very curly hair. He cut a very romantic figure. Everyone around knew Dixie.'

His schoolboy opponents certainly did. 'I played centre half for my school team from 1920 to 1922,' recalled Len Kirkham. 'On a few occasions we played against Laird Street School with Dixie at centre forward. Even in those days he was full of confidence, drive and enthusiasm, the result being that I might as well have stayed off the field as try to stop him.

'In the 1921 season I was chosen to play in the town trials between the Probables and Possibles at Prenton playing fields. I was centre half for the Possibles playing against Dixie. I did not get my place in the town team but I followed his career closely.'

Dixie also played for Lingholme in the Claughton and District League and Reginald Birkett, who died in February 1980, was the man who claimed to have been the first person to sign Dean on an official football form. He was secretary of the alliance of local teams of Birkenhead North End District, the records of which were destroyed in the blitz during the Second World War. Birkett revealed that the young Dean's burgeoning career survived an early pre-meditated drenching! 'Our family lived at 54 Clifford Street, Claughton, which was an end terraced house. The end of the house, with a chalked-up goal, made an excellent playing area, well used as an early stamping ground for Dixie and his companions.

'The force of the ball from the youthful but powerful Dixie, who sent it crashing against the wall, and the rattling of the railings of the wall when being used for rest periods, constituted a further source of annoyance.

'On one particular Sunday afternoon Mrs Birkett, a hard-working lady, was wont to retire for a well-earned rest. A preliminary warning to the young Billy Dean being disregarded, the youthful sportsman was eventually dispatched from the field of play with a well directed cascade of water from above!'

He was also adept at other sport and once, representing the Boys Brigade company he had joined for its football opportunities, he took part in an athletics meeting and won the 80, 100 and 200 yard sprints as well as the high and long jump competitions. He also played cricket in matches on Leasowe Common and struck up an early interest in golf, motivated originally by the chance to make extra pocket money. He used to caddy at the upmarket Wirral Ladies Golf Club but soon developed a life-long liking and talent for the game which dovetailed with his football commitments. By the age of 15 he had honed his handicap to two, became a scratch player by 20 and in addition to his success in footballers' golf tournaments his skill on the greens and fairways was crowned when he won the Wirral Amateur Championship.

Long before a football career loomed into view for Bill Dean he had already been given the nickname that would become universally famous . . . or almost. In later life Dean said that he had acquired the soubriquet Dixie because his swarthy appearance and black curly hair was reminiscent of people from the southern states of America. In fact, his contemporaries who played in childhood street games with young Bill reveal a totally different reason. Gilbert Upton, himself a native of Birkenhead and a Tranmere Rovers supporter, historian and author, offers compelling evidence on the origins of English football's most famous nickname.

'Quite clearly, Dixie himself always went with the version that he got his nickname because of his appearance and the link with the Deep South of the United States,' says Upton. 'And it was a wonderful name for him to have, one of the greatest any footballer has ever had. It's perfect. The alliteration of the double 'D' rolls off the tongue. 'Dixie' means goals and every Dean potentially is known as 'Dixie'.

'But if you speak to the people from the north end of Birkenhead where Bill came from – and I've been lucky to speak to a couple of his contemporaries from that area – they don't remember him at all as 'Dixie'.

'They definitely remember him as 'Digsy', apparently because of the strength of his hands when playing tag in the street. I have this written in two letters, one from Bill Houldin and another from a Mr H.G. Trace, now living in Ashford, Middlesex.

'They once lived very close to Bill Dean, Mr Trace in Crocus Avenue and Bill Houldin in the Dock Cottages. They both say that Bill was called 'Digsy' when they knew him and, clearly, he was a well-known young man around north Birkenhead.'

It was Dean's move to Tranmere that would establish once and for all the spelling of his nickname. But, first, he followed his father into the employ of the Wirral Railway after leaving school at fourteen in January 1921.

I left school on a Friday and my old feller had made all the arrangements for my mother to take me to the shops at Grange Road in Birkenhead. She bought me a nice new pair of overalls. They were the first long trousers I ever wore.

On the Monday I started serving my time on the Wirral Railway as an apprentice fitter. I was interested in working for the railway because I liked the Wirral Railway football ground.

All I had to do was climb two fences and I was there. I'd get in a kit for someone, sometimes to play in a match, even if it was a Thursday afternoon team who'd found they were one man short. I could always wriggle in that way.

The reason I could do it was that the two other apprentice fitters didn't like the night job, the 10 to 6 shift. So I took if off both of them. They'd work the 2 to 10 and 6 to 2 shifts and I'd do the night job from 10 to 6 so that I could play football during the day.

The engine shops were plagued with rats and during my night shifts I'd try to get rid of as many as possible by taking a kick at them as they ran past. You had to be quick but I got a few each night! . . . At the football ground I could always get some sleep by having an hour's doss and that suited me down to the ground. I got paid 12 shillings a week for the night job. I used to save what I could of it in a lemonade bottle after giving my mother some money. She'd be satisfied with about 7s 6d and I'd have the rest.

I'd served as an apprentice for just on two years and my old general manager then was a man called Martlew. His two sons were both doctors and they were both directors of New Brighton Football Club . . . They'd asked me several times if I'd like to go and have a trial with them. But I couldn't see eye to eye with that . . . I just had one ambition then and that was to get to Everton.

Eventually, though, I went to play for Pensby Institute, which at the time was out in the country from us. If you missed the bus you had to run out there. I used to get a nice little bit of tea and two shillings from them . . . Of course, the two shillings was supposed to pay for the bus but I used to use Shank's Pony. After one match at Pensby I was just getting stripped when a chap came up to me and said: 'How would you like to have a trial with Tranmere?' . . . I thought it was a bit of a stepping stone so I said: 'Yes, I wouldn't mind.' He said: 'If things come off they'll sign you professional.' It was a chap called Jack 'Dump' Lee, who was Tranmere's main scout.

Dean's scoring exploits were bound, sooner or later, to attract the attention of Lee, a former Tranmere player from the 1890s and early 1900s, but it is thought that a glowing testimony to Dean's talent was given to Lee by a representative of the Tranmere programme printers, Wilson & Jones, of Hamilton Street, Birkenhead, who had seen Dean in impressive scoring action for Pensby. After the rising young star missed his pre-arranged trial at Tranmere to fulfil a commitment at a local boxing club it is believed that when a new date was fixed the printers' man travelled with young Dean in a taxi to Prenton Park to ensure that this time he kept his appointment with destiny.

# CHAPTER TWO

# *Rovers Ticket To Goodison*

As if to underline the wisdom of Tranmere's avid interest in his talents Bill Dean signed off for Pensby Institute by hitting four goals in a 6–1 win over Upton in the Wirral Combination, stoking his rapidly growing reputation. He signed amateur forms at Prenton Park on November 27, 1923 – eight weeks prior to his 17th birthday – before being registered as a professional on April 19, 1924. And it is now that his nickname 'Dixie' becomes established, as Tranmere chronicler Gilbert Upton revealed: 'When Dean's signing for Tranmere was reported in the *Birkenhead News* they refer to Dixie Dean. He was still only 16 so, clearly, he had acquired the nickname "Dixie" from a very early age.

'I would have thought that somewhere along the line it changed from "Digsy" to "Dixie". Perhaps the *Birkenhead News*, on first hearing the soubriquet "Digsy", wrote it down as "Dixie" and unwittingly committed it to history. We will never be quite sure . . . Dixie always believed his nickname was due to his appearance and even in his later years, when he was lionised, he still signed his autographs as "Dixie". We know this because people have told me they have menus from this, that and the other dinner which Bill signed as "Dixie" . . . Yet there are stories one hears that if a new, young player came into the dressing room at Goodison and called him "Dixie" he would very quickly be put in his place and told: "Please call me Bill." Perhaps players had to earn the right to call him "Dixie" in the dressing room.'

Fittingly, Dean scored on his debut for Tranmere reserves in a 3–1 Cheshire County League defeat by Whitchurch, a team that included

**Young Blood for Rovers.**

TWO YOUTHS SIGNED.

During the last few days Tranmere Rovers, following their recent signing of Edwards, the Bebington youth, have added to their list two seventeen-year-old players who have been distinguishing themselves in local junior circles.

One of the new signings is C. Millington, a cousin of Joe Mercer, the old Rovers centre-half, who has been assisting Ellesmere Port in the West Cheshire League. He fills the central position in the half-line, and although only seventeen years of age he is 6ft. 1in. in height and weighs 11st. 4lb.

Dixie Dean, the other signing, a former Birkenhead Schoolboy, capped his season's performance on Saturday last by scoring four goals for Pensby Institute.

How the *Birkenhead News* reported Dixie's signing by Tranmere Rovers in November 1923, when he was still only 16 years of age.

his Birkenhead Schoolboy team-mate Ellis Rimmer, a butcher's son who could carve open defences at will and supply menacing crosses from the left flank.

Tranmere secretary manager Bert Cooke, a man who would later incur Bill Dean's enduring wrath, signed Rimmer the following season when he provided much of the ammunition for Dean's prolific goal output, a combination that would later also be called on by England. Dean's debut display, at the age of 16 years and 313 days, was recorded in glowing terms by the *Birkenhead News*. Their match reporter 'C.D.A.' might not have realised he had witnessed the birth of a legend and surprisingly referred to Dean being 'tall' when he stood a hardly gigantic 5ft 10½in. But he was clearly impressed and wrote: 'Dean was every inch a complete success. Though only young, he is tall and unusually well built and carries his 12 stone with ease and grace . . . He showed himself to be a bustler and an opportunist – but not that alone for he fed his wings and plied his partners in a style which suggests that with the right encouragement he will flourish into a player who would be an asset to any side . . . Dean received from Rothwell and went right through and, from a sharp angle, put the ball into the net. Towards the end, Dean went down on his own and, going at a great pace, sent in from a difficult angle. The ball hit the upright with a force that seemed to suggest that it was trying to uproot the woodwork.'

A further *Birkenhead News* report hailed Dean as 'the star attraction' and added: 'Splendidly endowed physically he has height and weight and if somewhat lacking in polish this can easily be benefited by careful coaching. He has got one strong point and that is his direct shooting.'

This is how Dean recalled his arrival at Tranmere and his Prenton Park progress:

I gave up my apprenticeship and signed full time for Tranmere for £4/5 shillings a week, but not on any summer wages. At the time if you were in the first team you got a £1 bonus if you won and 10 shillings if you drew, and in the reserves in the Cheshire County League it was 10 shillings and five shillings . . . In those days that was pretty decent. But when I came to learn a little I believe that Tranmere should have been paying me £6 a week for playing in the first team. I made one or two inquiries but I didn't go any further with it and stayed on £4/5 shillings.

The Saturday after I joined Tranmere they played me in a Cheshire League match against Whitchurch. I scored on my debut and from then on it seemed to be a bit easier than playing with Pensby.

With Tranmere's reserve team you had better players, which stands to reason, and at Pensby I had been doing more 'donkeying' than I should have been. From the Cheshire League side I very soon made my debut in Tranmere's first team, in the Third Division North, before becoming a regular the following season.

The reason for Dixie's belief that he should have been paid £6 per week after becoming a full time professional and breaking into the first team is not known. Rule 7 in The Football League's 1924–25 Handbook said: 'The maximum wage, except as hereinafter provided, shall be £5 per week, with annual rises of £1 per week to a final maximum of £6 per week during the close season and £8 per week during the playing season . . . A recognised reserve team player, who by his meritorious play obtains a place in the first team, may be paid a further sum of £1 for each first team match in which he takes part.' So it could be argued that Tranmere paid him within the maximum standard starting wage for a league player and Dixie's schoolboy colleague Ellis Rimmer, who signed his agreement with Tranmere less than a year later, had a contract which revealed that his wages were lower than Dixie's. It stipulated Rimmer's earnings as: '£2.5s 0d per week from September 12, 1924 to May 2, 1925; £4.0s 0d per week when playing for the first team; Bonus – First team £1 0s 0d for a win, 10s 0d for a draw; Second team 10s 0d for a win, 5s 0d for a draw.' But had something been said to Dixie to support his claim that he was entitled to a higher wage than he was paid? He was not a mercenary man. Indeed, he declared more than once he would play for the love of the game. Or was he the victim of leg-pulling by much senior but less dedicated professionals who, as Dixie has observed, preferred a few pints and cigarettes in the Halfway House pub to honing their fitness on the training ground? The answer to those questions, ultimately, was academic, because Dean was an instant success at Tranmere.

While the twenties began to roar with new jazz sounds from exponents such as Louis Armstrong, Joe 'King' Oliver and the Creole Jazz Band and the flappers performed the Charleston, the dance craze sparked by the black musical *Runnin' Wild*, Dixie Dean did his own roaring with his craze for scoring goals. His first nine appearances for Tranmere reserves brought him eight goals and even at his tender age he began shouldering the responsibility of penalty taking, a role which many of football's greats have shunned over the years. His first team debut came on Wednesday, January 9, 1924. He was named as inside right in the Liverpool Senior Cup tie at New Brighton and scored one of the goals in a 4–2 win over the club whose overtures he had rejected a couple of years earlier. The following Saturday, January 12, Dean made his first entry in the record books when he became, aged 16 years 355 days, the youngest player to appear for Tranmere in a Football League game, a distinction he held for 76 years until Iain Hume went on as substitute at Swindon on April 15, 2000 at the age of 16 years 168 days. Dean lined up – again at inside right although there were no shirt numbers in those days – in the Third Division North game against Rotherham County and although he played well Tranmere lost 5–1. After this initial Football League taster Dean returned to the reserves to help his development, which was painfully interrupted by injury in February 1924. Dean lost a testicle in a challenge by a centre half he recalled as Davy Parkes of Rochdale, an

**TRANMERE ROVERS F.C. 1924-25**

One of the first cartoons to feature Dixie, which appeared in the *Birkenhead News* on October 11, 1924.

uncompromising stopper with whom the teenage Tranmere centre forward did come into contact during his Prenton Park career. But records show that Parkes could not have been responsible for the damage to Dean's anatomy and that the culprit was a defender out of the same stable as Parkes, a player called Molyneux, forename unknown.

Tranmere super sleuth Gilbert Upton, having painstakingly trawled through the archives, explained:

'I am 100 per cent convinced that Davy Parkes had nothing to do with Dixie's injury which kept him out for five weeks. It happened in a Cheshire Senior Cup tie against Altrincham on February 9, 1924. If you look at the record Dixie played for Tranmere against Rochdale three times and each time he played in the next match. In fact, two weeks after his last outing against Rochdale he was playing for Everton . . . When you study Dixie's career record at Tranmere you do come across a five-week gap and this was after the Altrincham game in 1924. Little bulletins on his progress appeared at the time in the local press so it is documented he had an injury problem . . . I've always assumed from Dixie's comments about his injury that after it had happened he had gone off the field and been taken straight to hospital. But I studied the match reports of this particular Altrincham game, both in the Birkenhead and Altrincham newspapers, and there is no reference to Dixie going off the field despite the obvious agony he said he was in when he went into hospital . . . I pondered over this long and hard and never came up with a satisfactory answer until I was suddenly hit by what you might say was a blinding glimpse of the obvious. Perhaps he didn't go off the field. If he had the press would have reported it. So I raised it on a medical level with my own GP. I told him I was perplexed over why someone with a bad injury like this did not leave the field . . . The doctor said it was very feasible that Dixie had finished the match but that the problem had worsened during the week to the extent that Dixie then had to go into hospital . . . This also fits in with the local papers saying he was due to play the week after the Altrincham game and when he didn't appear they referred to the fact that he had been taken to hospital with a rupture but was making good progress . . . So, having cleared Rochdale's Davy Parkes of any involvement whatsoever in the incident the player who may have been responsible for Dixie's injury is a man called Molyneux. Newspaper reports of the match list Molyneux as the Altrincham centre half. They didn't have shirt numbers in those days but if anyone is going to have the finger pointed at him it's this chap Molyneux, whoever he is or wherever he went.'

There was no doubt, however, about the agony Dixie's opponent inflicted. He recalled:

I went down the middle a couple of times and got two early goals and as I passed the centre half he said to me: 'Tha'll get no more bloody goals today. You've finished.' So I replied: 'By the looks of you, you're finished, you've had it.' Well, I'm afraid he was a great tipster that feller because when I did come sailing down the third time he kicked me where I didn't want kicking.

If the ground had have opened that day I only wish it would have swallowed me. The pain was terrific. They took me to the Borough Hospital and I had to have a testicle out. They strapped me down on this here flat bed affair and the anaesthetist was behind me. Then they give you a touch of the old gas lark, ether . . . I said to them: 'How long will I be here?' This feller said: 'You've got to wait until the swelling stops.' I said to him. 'It's already like a Lewis's balloon. If I was you I'd get out of this theatre because if this goes off it'll blow this bloody hospital up'? . . . This Doctor Davies bloke said that losing that member of my orchestra could affect me in having a family later in life. Well, the other bugger held up well because I fathered four children, three lads and a girl . . . It didn't affect me in any way in later life. At Tranmere we used to play charity games against the Society of Oddfellows. Now I'd joined them! It took about five weeks before I was playing again. Obviously, I was now a stone lighter . . . I could sprint a bit! . . . I've never wished anyone any harm but I always said to myself that I'd come across that man somewhere, somehow and I'd get a bit of revenge. And I did. I met him in Chester, about seventeen years later. He sent me a pint across the bar. When I asked the barman who'd sent it he pointed to him. I couldn't quite place the face for a time. But then I did. And I thumped him . . . They took him to the hospital. So we're evens. As a matter of fact, I promised to see him later on in the afternoon if he did come back. But he didn't come back. He was kept in the hospital for a while . . . I had fifteen operations during my football career but that was the only time I've ever retaliated. The only thing I used to do, while I was laying there, was to say to the man who'd give me a broken rib or a broken shoulder blade. 'Has this done you any good?' and that was it.

Gilbert Upton reflects: 'Was Molyneux, not Parkes, the man Dixie met? What was a fellow from Sheffield who played for Rochdale doing in a pub in Chester? It is far more likely to have been Molyneux from Altrincham. It's like a who dunnit? But as Dixie is a legend you've got to have a bit of mystery! . . . Perhaps Dixie had memories of Parkes from another match, even though there is nothing documented. One contemporary report in the *Birkenhead News* includes the telling appraisal of Parkes as one of the most vigorous centre halves in the League, whose destructive work, valuable to his side, too often endangered the limbs of his opponents. So there's no doubt this fellow Parkes, who had a few years on Dixie, was a fearsome Third Division centre half in a very traditional English style! . . . In other words he was a menace. Anything that moved he kicked! So there's no doubt Parkes roughed up Dixie a bit but he didn't inflict the damage that must have been traumatic for a young man of just 17 . . . Dixie was such a hugely physically gifted, athletic, good looking young fellow that the injury must have sent a few tremors through him. You can tell when he was recalling the injury late in his life that he was re-living the pain of it.'

Dixie resumed playing in March 1924, scoring in five of his remaining sixteen games that season, which included a five-goal haul in a 7–0 Cheshire League hammering of Middlewich, the club's best individual total since Harry Fishwick's six in 1908. He also made two more Third Division appearances, first as an emergency left half against Rochdale – and Davy Parkes – in April and then a goalless draw at home to already promoted Wolves on May 3, his first outing in a League game at centre forward. The game was watched by a crowd of almost 12,000 and the Tranmere team was: Mitchell; G. Jackson, Stuart; Buchan, Leary, Campbell; Moreton, Sayer, Dean, Littlehales, Cartman.

Dixies's first summer as a Tranmere professional was dominated by Britain's success at the Paris Olympics, featuring 100 metres winner Harold Abrahams and 400 metres winner Eric Liddell, and recreated more than half a century later in the Oscar-winning film *Chariots of Fire*. The haul of eight British gold medals in Paris was unequalled until the Sydney Olympics in 2000. Dean's own athletic prowess found full expression in Tranmere's training regime:

The week's training at Tranmere started on Tuesday, although you'd be in Sunday and Monday if you had any injuries. On

Tuesday morning you'd run ten to twelve miles from the Tranmere ground, straight up Borough Road, across over the Thornton Road and back through the Prenton playing fields. That was your morning's road work . . . In the afternoon you'd lap once or twice and then I'd go on to 30 yard sprints, which I wanted to do to make me quick off the mark. You were there again on Wednesday morning and Thursday morning and afternoon and on Friday morning you'd go in and do a few sprints. Then you'd rest up for the match the next day . . . I was always one of those lads into keep fit. I used to play a lot of golf. I learned my golfing tricks at the Wirral Ladies Golf Club. I used to go caddying there and you were swinging clubs all day long . . . And, of course, when I got into the football game the first thing I did was buy myself a set of golf clubs. I got down to scratch and won quite a few competitions. I really loved golf . . . I also used to go dancing a lot. I learned ballroom dancing but I'd never had any special partners or anything like that. I wasn't what you'd say over keen on girls as a youngster. Not really . . . I just might meet one at a dance and have two or three dances with her – well, they used to think they were courting you or something. I also used to go to the pictures in those days, just before the talkies began. I liked cowboy pictures or something like that. No love stories and all that caper. No, it used to be the Westerns . . . I had a good time while I was with Tranmere because I used to go to all these here different functions at the town hall. The Police Ball, the Farmers Ball. Quite a lot of them . . . They had quite a number of characters at Prenton in those days. The forwards included Jackie Brown, then a current Irish international inside forward, and Stan Sayer. The centre half was Fred Halstead. Those lads could go on the ale a little bit and they certainly used to . . . We also had a chap named Frank Checkland, who was a teacher across in Liverpool, and during this time we also had a young Pongo Waring taking chocolates and cigarettes round the ground . . . Pongo used to tell the supporters that he was as good as me and that he'd prove it to them one day. Which he did. It was about five years later but

he'd done what he said he would do . . . Also at this time there
was outside left Ellis Rimmer, who'd played with me for
Birkenhead Schoolboys. He came and signed for Tranmere
while I was there . . . I didn't play a great deal with Ellis because
my transfer was coming off. But later on he moved to Sheffield
Wednesday and we played together for England against Spain at
Highbury when we won 7–1 . . . Tranmere certainly had a tough
side in those days. It was a tidy side. But I never got any advice
from any of them. There was nothing like that at Tranmere then.
They'd rather stay in the 'Halfway House' those fellers! They
had no time for such things. No, I can say, really, that I taught
myself.

Dean, still only 17, made a massive impact for the launch of the
1924–25 season. He scored six times in three pre-season public trial
games and after a blank against Port Vale reserves in the Cheshire
League he scored four and five respectively in his next two second team
outings, at Nantwich and home to Whitchurch. The clamour for his first
team recall became irresistible and at Doncaster on Saturday,
September 13, 1924 he took over at centre forward from injured Stan
Sayer. The game also marked the debut of newly signed Ellis Rimmer
and although Tranmere lost 2–0 Dean would hold his place when fit
until his move to Everton six months later. Seven days later Dixie broke
his League duck by scoring in a 1–0 home victory over Southport. It was
the first of a torrent of League goals, 379 in all over his career, that
would establish William Ralph Dean as a football icon. And once his
first for Tranmere was in the proverbial onion bag it fairly bulged under
the weight of his subsequent strikes. In his first ten Third Division North
outings that season he hit nine goals . . . and the Dixie legend was born.
   With clubs the length and breadth of the country enviously eyeing
Tranmere's boy wonder the young scoring prodigy rifled his first
League hat trick on October 25, 1924 in a 4–3 home win over
Hartlepool United. Once again it was to spark yet another assault on
the game's record books because Dixie was to amass an unrivalled 43
senior hat tricks over the glorious sweep of his career. Typical of the
rave reports Dean was receiving across the land came in the *Halifax*

LEAGUE — DIVISION III. — Northern

# Tranmere Rovers v. Hartlepools United

AT PRENTON PARK

KICK-OFF 3-0 P.M.

TRANMERE ROVERS
1
MITCHELL

2
JACKSON

3
STUART

4
CHECKLAND

5
HALSTEAD

6
CAMPBELL

7
MORETON

8
SAYER

9
DEAN

10
BROWN

11
CARTMAN

Ref : Mr. I. JOSEPHS, Durham

HARDY
12

RICHARDSON
13

SMITH
14

COOK
15

BUTLER
16

NICHOLSON
17

STORER
18

FOSTER
19

OSMOND
20

ALLEN
21

COWELL
22

HARTLEPOOLS UNITED

*Any changes will be notified on Alteration Board.*

Teamsheet from the programme which marked Dixie's first
Football League hat-trick on 25 October, 1924.
*(George Higham)*

The Tranmere Rovers programme team sheet for the match in which Dixie scored his first Football League hat trick on October 25, 1924.

*Daily Courier and Guardian* who said in December 1924: 'Rovers are the most watched team in the country for quite a crowd of League clubs have sent their scouts on the trail of young Dixie Dean, the youthful centre forward of the Rovers who this season has sprung into the limelight with meteoric brilliance . . . Town's defence crumbled in front of the swift thrusts of Dean and his men. Dean dribbled half the length of the field to equalise . . . he is without doubt a coming star.' Frenzied speculation about Dean provided Tranmere with plenty of food for thought with their prized asset's future now a constant topic on the Birkenhead club's agenda. Said Dixie:

A chap named Bill Gaskill was in charge of the team and then Jimmy Moreton, who used to play outside right for Tranmere, also went on the training staff. Bert Cooke was secretary-manager. And this man took everything on his own shoulders. Took the lot, as regards signing players on, paying players, diddling players. I know that because he diddled me . . . I knew things were happening regarding my transfer because Newcastle were interested in me. We went to the North East to play Ashington in a Third Division game and stayed in Newcastle overnight.

On the Saturday morning Cooke took me to St James' Park where we were met by the Newcastle chairman and directors who took me all round the ground. They told me how I'd fit in there and so on . . . But it never impressed me at all. I just said 'yes' and 'no' and 'thank you very much' and 'I hope I'll see you again some time' which I did, later on. This Cooke asked if I would care to be transferred to Newcastle. I said: 'No, thank you very much.' He then said: 'It's not only Newcastle who are interested. There's also Aston Villa, Bolton and the Arsenal. You can go to any of them.' I said: 'If you don't mind, I don't wish to go to any of them. I'm quite alright where I am, at present.

On January 10, 1925, twelve days before his 18th birthday, a kick on the ankle in the game at Walsall forced Dixie to miss the second half and hampered him for the next two games, which he struggled through. One of the matches was at Southport on the day of the January 24 eclipse, when it went dark at Haig Avenue at half time. Fortunes never brightened for the visitors who lost 1–0, prompting a cartoon in the local paper which featured a caricature of Dixie in the gloom. But he was back among the goals with a brace against Ashington and proceeded to hit another two hat tricks, against Barrow and Rochdale, the latter achieved against his familiar foe Davy Parkes in what was to be his last Tranmere game at Prenton Park. A week later he scored in Tranmere's 2–1 defeat at Darlington but was forced to limp off 20 minutes from the end with another ankle injury. His premature exit was to prove a permanent farewell to Tranmere and a framed article recording that fact, which still hangs in the boardroom at Darlington's Feethams ground, emphasises the stature Dixie was to gain. He scored 27 goals in 27 League games that season, including a bountiful run of 18 in his final 17 appearances, and Gilbert Upton observed: 'Dixie was brilliant in the air for a man who stood less than six feet but also superb on the ground.

A *Southport Guardian* cartoon reflecting on Dixie's eclipse-affected appearance for Tranmere at Southport in January 1925

'At Tranmere they used to say that his great goals started on the halfway line. He was not seen as a goal poacher hanging around the penalty area but as someone who could create goals for himself . . . At Tranmere he would get the ball and go through the defence and unleash his powerful shooting. The cry "give it to Dixie" began at Tranmere.

'If I had a time machine I would go back to Prenton Park in 1923–24 and 25 and just watch Dixie. And I'd stay as long as Dixie was there . . . In those days centre forwards were highly prized and Tranmere, quite remarkably, produced three distinguished ones in a four-year span: Dixie, his fellow England international Pongo Waring and Bill Ridding.'

Monday, March 16, 1925 was a day off for Tranmere's players. It was also transfer deadline day. Dixie Dean, now the hottest property in English football, went to the cinema, believed to be The Scala in Argyle Street, Birkenhead, to see *Rupert of Henzau*. But outside the celluloid world the curtain was going up on events that would ensure it was going to be 'Dixie of Everton', as the young man himself discovered when he returned to the family's fish and chip shop.

I went to a matinée at the pictures and when I got home my mother told me that Mr Tom McIntosh of Everton wanted me to go down to the Woodside Hotel to have a word with him and off I went. I didn't look for a tram . . . I got shifting, running. It must have been the quickest two miles ever! When I arrived, there was Mr McIntosh, the Everton secretary, waiting. We shook hands and he said to me: 'I'd like you to come to Everton.' I hardly believed it. It was the greatest delight of my life . . . I agreed right away. As a matter of fact I didn't even ask 'How much are you going to give me?'. I had no idea until I got paid on the Friday. It was six pounds a week plus a two pounds win bonus in the First Division and a pound for the draw . . . To join Everton was all that I'd been waiting for. I'd refused quite a few offers, just waiting for Everton to come. I signed on the Wednesday and Mr McIntosh said to me: 'You'll be playing against Arsenal at Highbury on Saturday.' 'Oh, blimey,' I thought, 'that's a bit of a jump!' The previous Saturday I'd played in the Third Division at Darlington. But, any rate, on the Thursday I went over to start training . . . I met the Everton players, got introduced to them all, and I felt quite at home right away. They had a few hard knocks there and two were centre forwards. One was Jack Cock, who Everton had bought from Chelsea, and the other was Jimmy Broad . . . They looked over at me and one of them said to the other, 'It looks as though we'll be away from here pretty soon, now.' As matter of fact they were – Cock within two or three weeks and Broad before the end of that year – and I took over from them . . . Anyway, on the Friday after signing for Everton I packed a little case and off I went to London for the game at Highbury. And I scored a good goal, as I thought. And so did the goalkeeper. This ball came over and I headed it into the top corner of the net . . . The goalkeeper just caught the ball as it fell and threw it upfield to be kicked off. But the referee was pointing that the ball hadn't gone over the line or something or other. So I didn't get the goal . . . The Everton team at that time included

England international Sammy Chedgzoy at outside right, Scottish international Alec Troup at outside left and several other Scotsmen including Hunter Hart at left half, Billy Brown at right half and Jock McDonald and David Raitt at full back . . . They'd bought Alec Troup from Dundee. He was a great little player, that. He could put the ball within an inch of my head while Sammy Chedgzoy could send a good ball over,

## DEAN'S DEPARTURE.

### Transferred to Everton at Record Fee.

**By "R.E.T."**

While it was generally felt that Tranmere Rovers would sooner or later part company with their youthful talented leader, W. R. (Dixie) Dean, the fact remains that the official announcement of his transfer to Everton on Monday has come as a severe blow to the more ardent supporters of the local club. The deal was completed at the Woodside Hotel on Monday evening, and I can with authority state that the figure obtained was, as near as makes no matter, £3,000. This, of course, is a record figure paid for a player who is only 18 years of age, and moreover

How the *Birkenhead News* reported 18-year-old Dixie's transfer to Everton in March 1925.

too. We worked well together and old Sammy seemed to take a great fancy to me. He gave me a little bit of tutoring and demonstrated one or two things in training.

There are varying reports as to the exact amount Everton paid Tranmere for Dean. The Tranmere accounts that year stated £2,270 in transfer income, which is likely to be a net figure. The *Birkenhead Advertiser* gave the fee as £2,900 while the *Birkenhead News* said it was 'as near as makes no matter to £3,000.' The latter sum has become the accepted figure, then a record for a Third Division player and for an 18-year-old. Everton were delighted to pay it and the club's official history published in 1928 said without undue modesty: 'Everton are to be congratulated on their acumen in securing Dean from Tranmere Rovers in the face of competition from 20 clubs.' The Football League transfer record at the time stood at £5,500, the sum Sunderland had paid South Shields three years earlier for Warney Cresswell, later to become a team-mate of Dean's at Goodison. The income just about cleared Tranmere's overdraft but Dixie always believed that he should

Dixie (right) with his Everton friend and mentor, Sammy Chedgzoy (copyright unknown)

have received £300 as his cut rather than the £30 he was paid, which was donated by his mother to the cash-strapped Birkenhead General Hospital. Dixie, who was earning £4/5 shillings at the time of his Tranmere departure, claimed that secretary manager Cooke had broken a promise:

> Bert Cooke promised my mother and dad that I'd receive £300 of the fee Everton paid. He said he'd kick me off with a bank book and I'd have 300 quid in it. When I received a telegram about a fortnight after joining Everton I went along to the Tranmere ground and Cooke handed me a cheque for £30.
>
> So I turned round to him and said: 'You've made a mistake here, you've left an "0" off.' He said: 'I'm sorry Dean, but that's all the League would allow you.' And I knew very well that he'd made these conditions with my people . . . So I went across to see Mr John McKenna, who was president of the Football League and a former chairman of Liverpool FC. I asked for an interview, went in to see him and told him what had happened . . . His only words to me were: 'Dean . . . you've signed lad, haven't you?' I said: 'Yes, sir.' He said: 'Well I can't do anything for you now. I could have done. But I'm afraid not now you've already signed.' And that was that.

Once again, just as with the wages issue, we are not privy to any promises or assurances from Tranmere that might have been given to Dean officially or unofficially, although Rule 10 of the contemporary Football League Handbook stated:

> When a player is transferred the club transferring him may, with the consent of the (League) Management Committee as a reward for loyal and meritorious service, pay to such a player in lieu of the amount which the club has guaranteed, or would have been likely to guarantee such player for a benefit, reckoned upon the playing season of service in proportion to the qualifying period for a benefit with such club.
>
> A club, through any of its responsible officials, either promising

or leading a player to hope for any payment in excess of Rule will be regarded as guilty of breach of Rule.

The rule clearly links any payment to length of service and accrued benefit and not the size of the transfer fee. Tranmere historian and author Gilbert Upton reflected: 'I now believe that, in all probability, when Dixie first signed professional forms in the 1924 close season Tranmere had contracted to pay a benefit of £300 after 10 years. Was Dixie, unfortunately, under the mistaken impression that he should receive the £300 on his transfer to Everton? . . . Dixie obviously felt short-changed over his transfer. He really believed what he said and he didn't just set out to malign Bert Cooke. My own view, though, is that it was simply a misunderstanding . . . There's no doubt in my mind that under League regulations his wages were pretty well spot on and he was getting more than Ellis Rimmer, who had joined Tranmere at about the same time . . . When Dixie left his share of the transfer fee was based on time not on his salary. I have discovered, for instance, that when Pongo Waring left Tranmere for Aston Villa three or four years later – a player many rated at the time as better than Dixie – his share of the transfer fee was exactly based on how many years he had been at Tranmere . . . He got nothing like the £300 Dixie felt he was due. In fact, Pongo's transfer fee was almost £5,000 so if Dixie had been right Pongo would have been entitled to something like £500. I think that somehow Dixie had been misled but, clearly, he deeply believed he was due more . . . Bert Cooke must have realised from very early on that in Dixie he had a hot property on his hands, with a posse of scouts coming to watch him. The story goes that Bert attended a representative game at Goodison between the Football League and the Scottish League . . . And for once in his life this man from the little club on the other side of the river found himself being the focus of attention for chairmen, directors and managers from the country's famous clubs . . . After the match one rather pompous chairman approached Bert, waved his cheque book in front of him and made an unspecified offer for Dixie that he felt Tranmere just could not refuse . . . Bert, for once in his life holding all the aces, replied: 'I'm very flattered by your offer . . . for that sort of money you can have a photograph of the lad.'

For William Ralph Dean, joining Everton had been the thrilling fulfilment of a dream and the realisation of the vow he made to himself when he had been taken to Goodison by his father as an eight-year-old.

I didn't feel really terribly sad about leaving Tranmere because I did always want to get away and get to the one and only club . . . Everton. That's been my club since I was a kid. So that's it. I'd have played for nothing there.

I just knew I'd come off at Everton. It had been there since I was a child. I just seemed to know that I could do something and, of course, it didn't take me long to prove it.

The fact that Dixie's Everton debut happened to be at Arsenal only days after his arrival from Tranmere forged a chain of connections between Dean and the London club. They would provide the opposition when he set his incredible 60-goal record in May 1928 and it would be against Arsenal that he would score his final League goal for Everton in August 1937. But that was a long way off from that weekend in 1925 when Dixie Dean first donned an Everton jersey. Saturday, March 21 was the date. It was hardly an auspicious start, the disappointment compounded by his disallowed 'goal'. Everton lost 3–1 at Highbury and the official club history published in the 1920s states: 'Unfamiliar with his associates it was not surprising that Dean did not shine on that occasion.'

Yet Dixie took it badly. Robin Bailey, a well known contemporary writer, revealed: 'The first time I met Dean he was in tears. He wept bitterly over what he thought had been his hopeless failure. It was after his first game for Everton against Arsenal at Highbury that I sought an interview with the expensive new forward just transferred to Goodison Park . . . He did not think he would be able to hold a place in First Division football. But the 'old soldiers' in the side gave me that footballer's wink which signalled: "The boy's good. He's downhearted about missing a chance or two but he's the right stuff." 'Yet the Everton chairman, W.C. (Will) Cuff, voiced his concern over newspaper comment about Dixie's debut display at Highbury. Said Cuff: 'William Dean was described in a Liverpool paper as "a passenger". That was not exactly kind or constructive criticism of a boy of 18 who had never seen a First Division match, had never seen London and couldn't sleep a wink at night through nervous strain . . . I mention these facts because I feel spectators and press critics should take every consideration with players, and especially with new players, lest they spoil a career.'

Curiously, though, Arsenal had gone to extraordinary lengths to claim that they had not been among the pack of clubs pursuing Dean's signature which, in addition to already spurned Newcastle, included Everton's arch rivals Liverpool, Manchester United, Aston Villa, Birmingham, Huddersfield, Middlesbrough and Chelsea. Tranmere received a remarkable telegram from a legendary figure within Highbury's marble halls, which was later to hang framed in Everton's boardroom. It stated:

'TO COOKE stop TRANMERE ROVERS stop NOT INTERESTED IN DEAN stop HERBERT CHAPMAN stop ARSENAL stop'

Everton's £3,000 signing of 18-year-old Dean prompted a plea to supporters by the *Liverpool Daily Post* which said: 'It is probably the heaviest transfer fee that has ever been paid for a mere boy. Everton once had another boy on their books who started well but eventually fell through the frailty of human nature and the sickly adulation of the crowd . . . It is to be hoped the crowd will not make a 'god' of Dean. He is very human and has many boy-like touches. It is not so much what he has done but the way he has done it. He is a natural footballer with a stout heart, a willing pair of feet and a constitution that will stand him in good stead.' The newspaper's concern was unwarranted. Dean's temperament was perfect and his physique able to withstand severe buffeting by defenders. Indeed, if it were possible to create a robot centre forward for the rigours of the English game the design model would be William Ralph Dean.

A week after his Highbury debut he had his Goodison baptism, tasted victory in an Everton shirt for the first time and scored his first goal for his life-long idols.

The Saturday after my debut at Arsenal I scored on my first appearance at Goodison. It was against Aston Villa and we won 2–0 . . . On the Saturday morning before home games my mother, even before she brought me a cup of tea, would always bring me in a spoonful of Phosphorine. Then I'd have an egg or something like that . . . Around about 12 o'clock I'd have a bit of boiled fish and toast and then I left to go to Goodison for the match, down Park Road North to Duke Street and Park Station. The crowds were starting to go across as well . . . In those days of the trams in Liverpool there were queues and queues of people waiting, either in Water Street or down at the ferry or wherever the 'specials' ran from. Then I'd be going up to the ground with the supporters, in these old 'jam jars' as they used to call them . . . The lads included the gang off the railway, my old man's crowd. They must have had about 25 or 26 tickets a week – buckshee! But there was a good atmosphere. It was all good patter and that sort of thing . . . But once or twice I did get held up in the crowd when there was a real good match on. I was always told by the Everton board that if anything like that did arise I was to jump in a taxi. Well, I had no money for taxis then, really. But that's what they always told me.

Dean made a total of seven first team appearances that 1924–25 season when Everton finished a dismal 17th in the old First Division. His last outing of the campaign was in a 4–1 April defeat at West Ham, when he scored his side's goal, after which he was drafted into the reserves. His step down was to be only temporary.

# CHAPTER THREE

# *Face To Face With Elisha*

In fulfilling his dream of becoming an Everton player Dixie Dean had joined a club that was a pillar of the English football establishment. Everton were one of the Football League's founder members in 1888, a decade after their formation as St Domingo FC. After the 1892 rent dispute which led to the formation of arch foes Liverpool their new Goodison Park home became one of the most imposing theatres of English football and by 1909 boasted two double decker stands, a third being added during the Dean era in 1926. In these days of multi-million pound state-of-the-art new stadia it is worthy of note that those three Goodison 'double deckers' cost around £70,000. It seems small change now but was a massive outlay in its time. Everton are also believed to be the first professional club to produce match programmes and to erect goal nets at their ground after their invention by Liverpool city engineer John Brodie, who also designed the first Mersey Tunnel and helped plan the Indian capital of New Delhi. He devised and patented the idea of nets after watching an amateur match in 1889 in which the referee disallowed two 'goals' and had to be rescued, with Brodie's assistance, from angry spectators.

Everton were also to gain the grandiose but fiercely protected label of the 'School of Science' with their venerable chairman William Charles Cuff setting out their football creed by declaring: 'It has always been an unwritten but rigid policy of the board, handed down from one generation of directors to another, that only the classical and stylish type of player should be signed. The kick-and-rush type has never appealed to them.' Cuff, a solicitor and Everton's secretary manager for seventeen years prior to becoming chairman, was a man of vision which ultimately earned him the presidency of the Football League. He backed the player's union, the Professional Footballers Association, in its long struggle for a provident fund, and warned about inflationary transfer fees. But one deal to which he was fully committed was the signing of Dixie Dean and gave unstinting support to secretary manager Tom McIntosh in landing the country's hottest football talent.

By the time of Dixie's arrival Everton had twice won the championship – in 1890–91 and 1914–15 – and the FA Cup in 1906 and evidence that their aims set out by Cuff had been met was provided by that much respected publication *Athletic News*. It pronounced quite simply: 'No team in the country has served up more delightful football than Everton.' One of the players, the England right winger Sam Chedgzoy, who became Dixie's first Goodison mentor, co-operated with a local journalist to force the FA to rewrite one of the laws of the game just before Dean's arrival at Everton. Ernest Edwards, sports editor of the *Liverpool Echo* who wrote under the name 'Bee', found a loophole in the re-wording of a rule in the FA statutes permitting a goal to be scored direct from a corner kick. The phrasing of it, he spotted, allowed the kicker to touch the ball more than once. He discussed it with Chedgzoy and they hatched a plan to expose the loophole in the law in Everton's home game with Arsenal on November 15, 1924. When Everton won an early corner Chedgzoy placed the ball but then dribbled it through to the goalmouth before unleashing a shot that went wide.

He was lectured by the referee but, previously primed by Edwards, the winger insisted: 'There's nothing in the rules to stop me doing it, ref!'

Edwards wrote: 'Some weeks ago I told how it was possible to dribble with a corner kick. Instantly my decision was challenged. I reiterated that a corner kick could be touched twice by the taker of the kick and a deputation from the Referees Society said that I was wrong and that they had a unanimous decision against me . . . The comma and the word OR in the newly worded rule to permit a corner kick taker to score from the corner spot had broken the spirit of the rule but the rule as it stands can only be read one way . . . Today, the sequel. Sam Chedgzoy determined to try out the rule. He was entrusted with a corner kick in the first minute but instead of centering the ball took the liberty of pushing it up some yards and, running on, drove in a shot.

'Chedgzoy deserves thanks for his help in this matter. The governors of the game will, I suspect, alter the rule next season.'

Chedgzoy and Edwards did not have to wait that long. The FA called an emergency meeting at which the corner kick law was clarified. But it was another similarly-timed rule change that was to have a profound effect on English football as Everton unleashed Dixie Dean on opposing defences in his first full season at Goodison.

On June 12, 1925 the International Board changed the offside law so that the number of opponents required to be between the attacker and the goal-line was reduced from three to two. The immediate effect was a massive rise in the number of goals scored, from 4,700 in the Football League in 1924–25 to 6,373 the following campaign. And the season after that George Camsell set a new English record with 59 goals for Middlesbrough in the old Second Division. It was into this situation that Dean stepped but it would be churlish to claim that his phenomenal goals output was due to a law change. He had, after all, scored prolifically at all levels under the old rule. And he kept on scoring even when, within a short time, teams devised methods of combating the new offside rule and preventing forwards from exploiting it. Arsenal led the way when manager Herbert Chapman and one of his players, Charlie Buchan, launched the 'third back game.' This meant that their centre half – initially Jack Butler followed by Herbie Roberts – dropped back to operate between the full backs with one of the inside forwards, in turn, falling back into a deeper role. The 'stopper' centre back had been born along with Arsenal's enduring reputation for being a counter attacking side. Whenever the change in the offside law was mentioned later in his life, Dixie would offer a forcible reminder about other differences, too. 'Don't forget that the ball we played with was much heavier than the balloons they have today. I suppose they've got to have them lightweight now because they play in bloody carpet slippers! Don't make any mistake, in my day when the ball was wet it was like a lump of rock. Defenders were no fairies and they soon got wise to the situation. So don't tell me that goalscoring was easier then.'

Dean began the 1925–26 season in Everton's reserve team but with a burning appetite for scoring goals. He had managed two in the First Division after his arrival from Tranmere a few months earlier, one of them at Goodison against Aston Villa.

I got it at the Stanley Park end and I can still see it now. The ball had been taken down the left wing, little Alec Troup squared it back and I ran in and hit it. It flew into the net . . . That was the start of the goalscoring lark! I had so much confidence in myself. I knew that somehow or other this was for me. There was no other thing for me . . . I would never turn back. This had been sort of drilled into me. Sammy Chedgzoy kept telling me not to worry. He was a father to me. I owe a lot to Sammy. He was a great old China, that feller . . . After going into the reserves and scoring seven against Bradford – five with my head – I got four in another reserve match and got back in the first team. After that I was never left out through choice for almost 13 years, after Tommy Lawton had come to Everton.

Dean was restored to League action in Everton's fifth game of the 1925–26 season, a 1–1 home draw with Tottenham on September 12. After drawing a blank in that game and in a 4–0 home drubbing of West Brom, he was on the mark in a 4–4 deadlock at Manchester City, his first senior goal of the season and third overall for Everton. From then on he was an automatic choice. His hometown newspaper, the *Birkenhead News*, had seen fit to chide Everton for not using Dixie to best advantage immediately after his move. They reminded Tom McIntosh and the coaching staff that their prized new capture was no goal hanger and that he liked to make his own goals as well as cash in on the service of others. Any necessary tactical adjustments had clearly been made by the time he scored his first Everton hat trick, in a 3–1 win at Burnley on October 17, 1925, a week after he had scored in a 7–3 drubbing at Sunderland. The following Saturday, as Britain prepared for the first white lines to be painted on its roads in a bid to cut accident figures, Dixie went down a one-way street towards goal by collecting his first Goodison treble in a 4–2 defeat of Leeds United, watched by a crowd of 28,660. The Everton team was: Menham; McDonald, Livingstone; Brown, Bain, Hart; Chedgzoy, Peacock, Dean, Kennedy, Troup. His first goal – a shot off an upright – came just three minutes into the match and his second off a Chedgzoy cross from the right, which Dean headed in. Chedgzoy was again the creator for Everton's third goal, driven in by Kennedy eight minutes before half time, and the skilful winger plotted the completion of his friend Dixie's hat trick 10 minutes after the interval with a cross that Dean diverted into the net with his outstretched foot. His name was now the first to be pencilled on Everton's team sheet and the cry 'Give It To Dixie', which had originated at Prenton Park during his Tranmere days, rose from the throats of Evertonians the length and breadth of the land.

Dixie ended that season with a scorching output of 32 goals from 38 League appearances as Everton moved up to finish in mid table limbo in 11th place. He also scored in the FA Cup against Fulham, who won in a third round replay. That season had also marked the launch of one of football's great rivalries, now elevated to folk story proportions . . . that of Dixie's duels with the majestic Liverpool goalkeeper Elisha Scott, the Ulsterman rated by those who saw him as the greatest British keeper of all time. They first faced each other at Anfield on September 26, 1925, a derby day that ended in gloom for Dixie and Everton . . . vanquished 5–1 by their arch rivals in front of a crowd of just under 50,000. But in the ensuing years there were to be many smiles for Bill at his fellow legend's expense. Scott played 467 games for Liverpool over a 20 year span, won two championship medals and earned the last of his 31 Ireland caps as he approached his 42nd birthday. Such was his brilliance that Everton even tried to sign him in 1934 . . . but the uproar from Liverpool supporters meant that the Anfield club had to squash any possibility of the move taking place. Because of injuries Dean and Scott were on opposing sides in derby games just eight times plus three international meetings, one of which Ireland won in Belfast, when Scott kept a clean sheet, and the others ending in England wins, with Dean scoring once. Their rivalry was committed to sporting folklore, spawning the apocryphal story of Dixie walking down the street, nodding to Elisha in recognition and the great Irishman diving full length in the gutter to save!

In their eight Mersey derby confrontations Dixie put nine goals past the celebrated Irishman including a rapid hat trick at Anfield in September 1931 as part of his overall haul of 19 goals in 17 outings against Liverpool. It was a Mersey derby record that stood until Ian Rush surpassed it more than half a century later when meetings between the clubs were far more frequent than in Dean's day. And in Dixie's view Scott was the supreme master of his craft.

He was the greatest goalkeeper I've ever seen that bloke. There's no getting away from the fact that he was the greatest . . . I used to send Elisha a little tube of aspirins before each Mersey derby. He'd get them the day before the game at his house in Wallasey with a note saying: 'Get yourself a good sleep tonight because I'll be there tomorrow.' And just before we went onto the pitch he'd say to me: 'You'll get none today, you black headed bastard.' I'd say: 'I'll be there. Don't you worry.'

In one derby at Anfield (September 1931) I scored a hat trick against him in the first nine minutes. When the third one went in I went up to Elisha and said to him: 'How would you like your eggs poached now, sonny?' You should have seen his face! If looks could kill I'd have been a gonner! There was a funny story about the last of my three goals that day, concerning the Liverpool left back Jimmy Jackson, who was actually a church minister and nicknamed 'Parson'. Our winger Teddie Critchley saw Jimmy hesitate and managed to swing the ball across and I was there to meet it and nodded it into the net. The worst part about it for Elisha is that the ball went between his arms and the crossbar.

The next thing I knew was Elisha giving Jimmy some choice Belfast language! Don't forget, Jimmy was a parson! As I was walking back to the centre circle – there was no hugging and kissing lark in those days – Jimmy came up to me, put his arm around me and said: 'William I feel like I never want to play in front of that man again!'

After matches Elisha would make his way down to the Lisbon pub in Victoria Street and so would I. We used to go down the steps into the bar. Elisha would have his usual bottle of Guinness and I'd have the old pint of bitter. We'd talk about all sorts of things but there would hardly be a word about football.

On that field we were great rivals. I wanted to beat him and he wanted to beat us. Off the field it was different. We were good friends. He was the greatest goalkeeper I've ever seen. I admired Gordon Banks and I like Ray Clemence. But Elisha was the best . . . There is a story told that we were supposed to have met each other walking down Lord Street in Liverpool and when I nodded my head Elisha is said to have dived through a jeweller's shop window! . . . We played together in a team in a charity match for St Edward's Orphanage and Elisha very nearly signed for Everton at a time when goalkeepers were in short supply and we had two or three injured . . . Everton made sure Elisha knew they were interested. And I think he would have come over and signed for us. Just think . . . he might have been playing behind me in the Everton team by following his brother Billy to Goodison. Billy had played for Everton many years before I arrived . . . But the story of Everton's interest in Elisha got into the papers and the protests from supporters were so strong that it put a stop to it. Liverpool sent for Elisha and the directors gave him three or four hundred quid and he went back to Ireland to become player manager of Belfast Celtic . . . He became a very wealthy man and towards the end of his life he used to come to stay with us in Chester when I ran the Dublin Packet pub. He was a great feller that! God bless him. He was a good 'un. The best goalkeeper I have ever seen.

With the help of a journalist, Dixie later committed his thoughts on goalkeepers to print in a *Liverpool Echo* article published in 1931:

When I am old and grey I hope to be allowed to go into goal and spend my declining years therein! That is how I feel about it. Have you ever studied the position of goal? The men who play there are allowed to warm themselves by walking up and down, and if you go near them the tear-falls can be heard miles away.

Actually, goalkeepers are the best friends I have got – outside the field – but inside the field they are the people I have always hated.

For some strange reason the goalkeeper is given a special dispensation. He of all men must be cloaked. In the old days they used to haul them in the dressing room every week. Judging by the stories our secretary tells me. But all that is changed. Today be assured that if you are a centre forward and you try to connect a boot with the ball when the goalkeeper is in possession, the 'bird' is a certainty.

Enough on that line, however. The purport of my chat isn't so much the way goalkeepers are treated, but about the goalkeepers I have played against, found hard to beat, and why they are hard to beat. I want to talk about some of the best men of my time: their methods. You can pick where you like, but for sheer intuition and ability and agility rolled up into one little piece commend me to 'Leesh' Scott. He plays for a club that has been made famous by its string of goalkeepers – none of them cost more than a tanner or so, but they run along this line with rare success: Doig, Hardy, Campbell, Scott, and sometimes Riley. What a collection of stars.

I never played against Sam Hardy, but it is sufficient to know that he himself tells me there was never one quite so good as Scott. I ought to know something about what he can do. I had my first Derby day against him, and could not score. This may sound selfish criticism, but I certainly thought him uncanny. If I drew up a chart of goalkeepers in order of merit, as far as my judgment is concerned, I would place them this way:

(1) Elisha Scott, Liverpool FC
(2) Harry Hibbs, Birmingham
(3) John Thomson (the late), Celtic.

(with the belief that Thomson would have gone to the top in due course but for his wretched accident and death).

Hacking of Oldham, in his greatest mood, was a very able goalkeeper, and one of the few who doesn't display nerves. Oh, yes, we who often stand quite near the goalkeepers, can tell you readily the goalkeepers who are bundled by bustling forwards into a state of nervousness that shows itself on the face and particularly in the eye.

Hacking was strong and rousing, whereas a man like Hibbs adopts a very natural style, and a beautiful action. In fact, I reckon Hibbs should be taken slow-motion for the purpose of the future generation of goalkeepers. Hibbs has a dive method to take a cross-grained shot and is alone in reaching those going-away shots, but Scott seems to be best with a point blank charge. It can't be luck when a goalkeeper goes on saving penalty kicks. Scott saved one at Chelsea the other day that they reckon Odell drove in at a furious pace. Don't tell me it was a lucky save; Scott does these things uncannily, and I think one of his means towards saving is that he is never still. So soon as the attack against him crosses the half-way line watch Scott jump.

As showing how easy goalkeeping is – joke over! – one has only to remind you that when a team goes away they never think of sending a goalkeeper as reserve; it is always a half-back, forward, or full-back. Never a goalkeeper! Standing between the goalposts you begin to wonder how some of them reach the point of the ball, but having seen the able Coggins and Sagar of our club pounding the balls out I have ceased to wonder how they do it and why goalkeepers are in the ascendency. I have come to the conclusion that it's a gift. Otherwise how could you explain the work and worth of the continental goalkeepers.

Everywhere the cry is for new styles – save in goalkeeping. This phase goes on growing better and better; yet we forwards keep getting a goal or two, and thus the game is saved from the stalemate that would arise if forwards were unable to score and goalkeepers stopped everything.

Everton's heady optimism about their swiftly rising scoring star, following Dixie's first full season at Goodison, dramatically evaporated in a few life-threatening moments on a sunny Sunday afternoon in North Wales. In June 1926, Dixie took a girlfriend, Evelyn Jones, who was also his tennis partner, for a spin on his motor bike. As they travelled along the St Asaph Road a motorcycle combination that had been darting in and out of traffic moved out to pass another vehicle . . . and ended up colliding head on with Dixie's machine, throwing both him and his passenger off the bike. Dixie and the two men on the combination sustained serious injuries and were taken unconscious to hospital. The girl riding pillion on Dixie's bike was also taken to hospital but discharged the following day. The three injured men had been taken from the scene of the accident on the back of a lorry to Lluesty Infirmary, near Holywell. Dixie was unconscious for 36 hours. It was revealed that his jaw bone was fractured in three places and that he also had a suspected fractured skull. But the Welsh infirmary, a hospital cum workhouse, did not have x-ray equipment to make a definite diagnosis and it was more than a week before he was well enough to be moved to hospital in Liverpool where fears of a fractured skull were confirmed. Dixie's life, thankfully, had been saved. But his football career seemed in dire danger. The stardom that beckoned him was in peril of being snuffed out. Even Everton's club doctor, J.C. Baxter, pronounced after seeing Dixie several times that he would never again play football.

Dixie recalled his accident and its aftermath thus:

The season had finished, it was the summer of 1926 and I bought a new Imperial motorbike, one of the latest models. I was taking a young lady to have a run out and went into Wales . . . We were just going through Holywell when a combination coming towards us kept cutting in and out of the traffic. Then it hit us head on. It was just as well I came off the way I did. If I'd come off on the left I'd have gone down a mountain side . . . I finished up in hospital with a fractured skull and pretty well patched up. Then they moved me from Wales to Liverpool and put me in the Sir Robert Davis Nursing Home in Eaton Road, West Derby . . . My head was parcelled up in a splint and bandages and God knows what. They'd put a metal plate in my head which later had to be removed. They also strengthened my jaw, which was left with a hole in it caused by the crash.

# The Birkenhead News

PUBLISHED every WEDNESDAY & SATURDAY.

WEDNESDAY, JUNE 23rd. 1926.

## "DIXIE'S" DISASTROUS DRIVE.

◆

### JAW FRACTURED IN HILLSIDE CRASH

——

### Woman Pillion Rider Injured.

——

#### WILL DEAN PLAY NEXT SEASON?

Alarming reports have been spread that "Dixie" Dean, the idol of football fans, who was injured in a motor crash on the St. Asaph-road outside Holywell on Sunday, will not be able to play football during the coming season, but medical reports are reassuring, and the "News" understands that all being well, he will be as fit as ever in a few weeks' time. His jaw, which was fractured in three places is mending rapidly, and there ...

How the *Birkenhead News* reported Dixie's 1926 motor cycle accident

The seriousness of his injuries were underlined in a contemporary report from Everton's official history which stated: 'Doctors were afraid he could not live for many hours. His survival astonished them.'

The report continued: 'He was removed to a West Derby nursing home and for months he wore silver plates in his head, the club meanwhile ensuring he had the best medical care and treatment. When recovery was assured the medical pronouncement was: 'This man will never be able to play football again.' 'But,' the official history went on 'Mother Nature often deceives the doctors.' The accident and the recovery period were days of high anxiety for Dixie, his family, the club and the supporters. But Dixie's steely determination was a powerful ally in his remarkably swift recovery. He recalls the moment when his football career began to re-awaken:

One day at the nursing home I was up a tree and somebody shouted from down below: 'Hey, if you can climb up there getting those apples you can come back and start playing again.' It was old Tom McIntosh from Everton. So, good enough, I came down that tree and said: 'When can I go?' While I was there I was a porter and I used to wheel those who had passed away down to the morgue. So when Tom McIntosh came that day it was the start of a new era for me.

Astonishingly, he made nonsense of the best medical opinion by returning to action just 15 weeks after the accident in a reserve game at Huddersfield Town on October 9, 1926.

The ground was very heavy and so was the ball. Everton told me to go on, try it and then come off . . . But Teddy Critchley sent this ball over, I headed it and it flew into the back of the net. Everyone, including me, was delighted. They kept shouting to me 'come off, come off' but I shouted back: 'I'm not coming off. Blimey. I've just headed that in there and there's a pound bonus here!' So I stayed on and that was it.

Such was the public joy that Dixie's career was back on track that when he made his home re-appearance in a reserve game a crowd of more than 30,000 packed into Goodison, which that year saw the opening of the Bullens Road double decker stand to replace the stadium's original old grandstand. On October 23 at Leeds, Dixie finally returned to Football League combat and celebrated with a goal in Everton's 3–1 win, their first away victory of the season. It surely ranks as one of the game's great personal comebacks and set the tone for Dixie's career-long battle against injuries, some deliberately inflicted by opponents. Dixie revealed that his battle scars and injuries prompted a bizarre rite of passage for Everton recruits:

> Our trainer Harry Cooke seemed to spend half his life in hospital with me. I had broken bones, bones taken out of my ankles, broken ribs, broken toes and two cartilage operations . . . Harry put the bones and the cartilage in pickle (preserving fluid) and when new fellers joined the club the first thing Harry did was to show them the jars. The big difference then was that we played in real boots not the carpet slippers they wear today . . . If somebody put the boot in you didn't go down and start rolling over the ground and then get up to take the free kick. If you were down you stayed down because that meant you were really injured . . . In those days there were some really hard men, especially in Yorkshire, and because of the number of injuries clubs had to have a big playing staff, sometimes between 40 and 50 professionals.

Everton's immense relief and gratitude over Dean's recovery from his motorcycle accident was revealed in the original *History of the Everton Football Club* which gushed: 'The romance of Dean's recovery and the amazing increase in his skill are psychological, physiological and supernatural occurrences. They are striking witnesses in favour of the aphorism that fact is stranger than fiction . . . His future and its achievements will be watched with absorbing interest by the football world. May the fates be kind, may he be another of Everton's long service men, a devoted attaché of the club in which he rose to fame, to the club which is proud of him.'

Dixie meets a group of admirers, circa 1935 (copyright unknown)

The writer, the late Thomas Keates, offered an intriguing contemporary assessment of Dixie's heading ability. 'Ordinary players,' he said 'butt the ball with the crown of their heads and it usually goes over the bar . . . Dean artistically glides it downwards with the side of his head. In this respect he excels every other famous centre forward. His head-play is the primary contributor to his success, although as a ball hunter and ground shooter, forceful yet cool and deliberate, he seems to have nothing to learn . . . His most conspicuous associate in the team as a scientist is Cresswell (that's Warney Cresswell, the skipper signed from Sunderland in February 1927) whose low driving and placing are captivating.'

Once Dixie's comeback was underway there was no stopping him. He finished the 1926–27 campaign with 21 goals from 27 First Division outings and bagged another three in the FA Cup before Everton bowed out to Hull City in a fourth round second replay. And emphasing how brilliantly he had recovered from the accident Dean was called up for his first full England cap that season, scoring twice on his international debut in a 3–3 draw with Wales.

In those days they used to have Probables v. Possibles trial matches for the England team and I played in two of those in the 1926–27 season, came off pretty well and got a number of goals . . . I got my first cap in the February, against Wales at Wrexham. One of the *Liverpool Echo* paper boys shouted to me as I was going home to Birkenhead one night: 'Alright, Dixie. I see you're playing for England.' He knew before me. I didn't know. That's how good the FA were in those days. Good enough, I got a paper off him and there it was. I made my England debut at Wrexham and scored twice in a 3–3 draw. After the match had been going for about 20 minutes one of the Wales players said to me: 'If you don't get moving yourself, you'll be getting the boot stuck in.' Naturally enough I turned round and said: 'I don't think you'll be able to do it. You're not good enough for that.' He said: 'Oh, you wait and see.' . . . It turned out to be my cousin, Alfie Jones, one of my Aunt Annie's lads and I didn't even know him! He chipped back at me: 'If you don't behave yourself I'll tell your mum!'

When you reported for an international match you were asked: 'Do you want a medal or the money?'. The money was £6. For my first England appearance against Wales in that match at Wrexham I took the medal. But after that I took the money . . . For years the Wales skipper was Fred Keenor. I nearly choked him. That feller would kick his own mother for a couple of bob. All he could do was kick or try to cripple somebody. He'd set himself out to do it. That's a thing I never believed in. That wasn't my game. The game was football . . . not foot-man . . . This Fred Keenor tried it on with me in an international at Turf Moor, Burnley. He called me a 'black headed bastard' and I caught him at half time under the gangway as we were going into the dressing rooms. Somebody pulled my right hand back. Otherwise one of us would have been taken to hospital and the other one – me – would have been sent off . . . It was a policeman who'd got hold of me but when the authorities knew the full strength of what Keenor had said to me I was let off and Keenor had to write an apology, which he did and that was that.

Dixie's second England outing was felt like a hammer blow in Scotland. His two goals at Hampden Park on April 2, 1927 ended a tartan dominance over the English on home soil that had stretched back 23 years since Steve Bloomer's only goal of the game at Parkhead on April 9, 1904.

My second England appearance was against Scotland and that was when we quietened the Hampden Roar. The FA asked the England players to make their own way to Scotland. Two Everton directors travelled up with me on the Friday and we stayed at the St Enoch Hotel, Glasgow . . . We were all sitting in the hotel lounge after arriving in Scotland when Tom Paton, who was a cotton millionaire from Bradford, sent his valet down to see me . . . He said to me: 'Would you ask the lads if they'd come upstairs to see Mr Paton?' I said OK and up we went. When we got there this Tom Paton said to me: 'I've been travelling about with the England team for so long and I've never seen them win in Scotland. I'll tell you what I'll do. I'll give you a tenner a man if you win. And whoever scores gets a tenner a goal . . . Jack Hill, the Burnley centre half, was the England skipper. After we'd come down from Tom Paton's room I said to Jack: 'He's crackers! Blimey. Ten pound a goal. I'll be a millionaire tomorrow night.' . . . At that time we only got six quid for playing for England. And it *was* six pound. You couldn't pinch a halfpenny off them. When you told the FA where you'd travelled from to meet up – in London it was the Euston Hotel – the treasurer feller knew to a halfpenny how much you were due . . . We got paid eight pound a week by the club who, under the terms of the contract, had the right not to pay you when you were away on England duty, although I still got paid by Everton . . . The attendance that day at Hampden was more than 111,000. Just think. We were getting six quid apiece out of that from the FA! So Tom Paton's offer was a big incentive for us . . . We won 2–1 and I got both goals. You've heard all about the Hampden Roar. Well, when our first one went in you could have heard a pin drop. And when I got the second in the old onion bag I thought I was playing in a cemetery!

It was England's first win at Hampden, all the more creditable and sweeter because it was achieved after Alan Morton had put Scotland ahead and following visiting skipper and centre half Hill's departure for stitches in a head wound, before his return as a passenger on the wing. Despite their bitter disappointment, Scots supporters gave an unprecedented standing ovation to two-goal Dean, who was also the toast of his team-mates.

One man though, made an astonishing remark to Dixie in a joyful England dressing room:

We were all celebrating our win when this selector came over to me and asked who I was! I told him my name but it didn't seem to register with him. 'I'm the player who scored the two goals' I added. 'Oh, yes,' he replied, the penny dropping at last. 'But you didn't do much else did you!' I walked away quickly and never felt the same about him again. But it didn't spoil what was a great day.

Our lads were very happy and when we got back to the hotel we quickly changed and got down to the lounge to wait for Tom Paton. When he got back he invited us up to his suite, which had a huge old-fashioned mantelpiece. And all along this mantelpiece were the little heaps of money. I could see mine. There was 30 quid in it. I put it into the share-out and we were all well satisfied . . . The next time England won at Hampden – in 1939 – my Everton successor Tom Lawton scored one of the goals. He went up there and cured them!

But when I made my first appearance in a Wembley international it was against Scotland's 'Wee Blue Devils'. What a day. I was on point duty! I never got a ball played to my head, my feet nor anywhere else. They beat us 5–1 and that team was rightly called the Wembley Wizards. And they had a great forward line: Alex Jackson, Jimmy Dunn, Hughie Gallacher, Alex James and Alan Morton . . . After that game Everton asked me about Jimmy Dunn and I recommended him. He was one of the greatest little inside rights I'd ever seen and we ended up signing him from Hibs . . . Wembley had only been open a few years but the ground or the crowd made no difference to me. I was there to play football and wherever I went that's what I was there to do, although in my case a lot of people think it should have been called 'head-ball' because of the number of headed goals I scored . . . But I'd say it was about 50–50, half of my goals with my feet and the others with the old nut. For me the heading trick was a gift . . . an absolute gift . . . I could time it to practically a second and, of course, you had to have keen eyes watching these balls sailing over. You had to be able to jump at the right time, make sure your timing was right when you went up . . . I remember once at Ewood Park a Blackburn centre half who I think was called Barker touched me in the middle of the back as a corner kick was coming over and tipped me off balance. But the ball hit him on the shoulder and went into his own net . . . 'You didn't get that bloody goal,' he said to me.'

'No,' I said. 'You did. Thanks very much!' I used to get plenty
of those because they knew very well I had the heading trick.

Dixie's instant impact on international football, at the age of 20,
was startling. In his first five games for his country between February
and May 1927 he scored 12 goals including hat tricks in a 9–1 rout of
Belgium in Brussels and a 5–2 victory in Luxemburg. Overall, he
scored 18 goals in 16 England appearances and a further nine in six
Football League outings. Yet despite Dean's formidable presence
Everton slumped to 20th place in 1926–27, just escaping relegation.
Apart from 21-goal Dixie, Al Dominy and Bobby Irvine, with 12 and
11 respectively, also reached double figures for League goals to help
preserve Everton's top flight status. Even so, the club's total of 64 was
less than both relegated sides Leeds and West Bromwich Albion.

Earlier that season Dixie had said goodbye to his close friend and
mentor Sam Chedgzoy, who retired from the game and emigrated to
Montreal after making a significant contribution to Dean's development. The Everton captain and England outside right had figured in an
eye-opening experience for the young Dixie the previous year,
although not quite as he anticipated. Dean revealed:

> I got an education on my first visit to Old Trafford to play
> Manchester United. Sammy Chedgzoy warned me about one of
> the United players and said: 'Whatever happens today, William,
> don't put a boot near this man. Don't go near him. Don't upset
> him' . . . He was talking about a feller called Frank Barson. Now
> this Barson was also head of the razor gang from Sheffield. They
> were going round the country in the racing lark demanding
> money with a razor. And Sammy was telling me not to upset
> him!

Barson was a Sheffield-born centre half and former blacksmith,
who won one England cap with Aston Villa, where it was rumoured
he had once threatened the manager with a gun. Manchester United
paid £5,000 to sign him in 1922. Dean continued:

The game starts and before I know it I'm on the deck. The ball's gone down our way and this Frank Barson hit me right on the side of the chin. God, blimey, I thought! . . . Bobby Irvine, the Irish international who played next to me at inside right, came over, picked me up and asked what had happened. 'He hit me,' I said. 'Did he,' said Bobby . . . Well, that was the last feller Barson did hit throughout his football career. Bobby was a real good, hard kid who would have a go at anybody. The next time Barson came near he got the lot done . . . Bobby got him in the ribs and finished him off with the jaw lark with his foot. The next thing the stretcher comes to take Barson off and United switched their outside right Joe Spence to centre half . . . Spence comes up to us and says: 'I'll shift you bastards.' He reigned about four or five minutes. The ball comes down between the two of us and I said 'Get in'. Spence just stood there and his head opened just like the Red Sea, right down the middle. Blood! You've never seen anything like it! . . . We were the School of Science but we played United at their own game on their own midden. If you're going to do them, do them properly. But after the match Sammy Chedgzoy still wasn't convinced about this here Barson. Sammy said: 'Now look, William, he might come into the dressing room' . . . By Christ, he did. He came in on two crutches and came right across to me. I was going to take my boots off. Instead I left them on. He came straight over to me, I stood up, he put his hand out and said: 'You're going to be a great player one day.' I said: 'Thank you very much. It's very kind of you. Are you alright now?' He said: 'Oh, yes, I've broken this and broken that.' That was the type of man Barson was. Big enough to do and say that. But old Sammy Chedgzoy alongside him was still shivering and shaking!

The 1926–27 campaign brought a new phenomenon to English football, in the form of radio commentaries of matches. The first Football League match to be broadcast by the BBC was Arsenal's 1–1 draw with Sheffield United in January of that season and the first match to be transmitted on Merseyside was Everton's 2–1 win over

Leeds on March 12, when Tony Weldon scored on his debut and Dean collected the other goal. The commentator was Ernest Edwards, 'Bee' of the *Liverpool Echo*, and in those days a chart divided the pitch into squares so that when the square number was called by the commentator the listeners would know in which part of the field play was taking place. Everton chairman Will Cuff could not resist the pun when he reflected on this watershed development of wireless by saying: 'This was the city of Liverpool's first insight into football by ethereal measures. 'Bee,' vowing that the listener would know which square a player was in by the way the play was proceeding, cut out the squares and by half time had a peremptory note from the BBC saying: "Put the squares into your round holes of commentary." He was before his time, I fear. The square has useless life.' The same season that radio reached its new football frontier also saw the formation of the Harlem Globetrotters basketball team and the manufacture and sale of the world's first box of matches.

The following season the exploits of Dixie Dean, leaping like a Globetrotter and with more strikes than several boxes of matches, would command the airwaves and prove the subject of a torrent of newsprint. Frank Barson's prophecy was about to come true.

CHAPTER FOUR

# *Heading To A Blue Horizon*

Goodison fortunes were to change dramatically, thanks to the man who fashioned a new art form in heading a ball and scoring goals. Dixie Dean would take his specialised craft to new horizons in a watershed season for himself, Everton and English football, one he would climax by taking a tram ride to immortality. The summer of 1927 had seen Charles Lindbergh make the first solo flight between New York and Paris, the 3,600-mile trans-Atlantic journey in his monoplane 'Spirit of St Louis' taking 33 hours 39 minutes. There was also a total eclipse of the sun – the last one until 1999 – but Dean's feat in that 1927–28 season eclipsed all that had gone before and left every goalscorer who has followed in a permanent shadow. He was now more than an Everton and England centre forward. To a country still racked by austerity and unemployment, a year after the debilitating General Strike, he was an heroic, star personality, his football prowess blending in the public perception with the human interest of his comeback from the motorcycle accident. Dixie spent the summer relaxing by playing his usual pursuits of tennis, cricket and golf, at which America's professionals emphatically defeated Britain in Massachusetts to win a new competition called the Ryder Cup, a gold trophy sponsored by wealthy St Albans seed merchant Samuel Ryder. Dean was no slouch himself on the golf course, with a style and an eye many thought would have made him an excellent professional if fate had decreed for him a different sporting career.

As a kid I used to caddy and collect lost balls at Wirral Ladies

Golf club, and it was a game I just took to. I got my handicap right down to scratch. I used to play and do well in competitions organised for professional footballers.

I used to play quite a lot with Cecil Ewing, who was later runner-up in the British Amateur Championship, and Dick Burke. I managed to win the Wirral Amateur Championship and wherever I went and whatever course I played I always liked to play with the professionals, such as Harry Rimmer at Bidston and Bill Davies at Wallasey.

Dean's appearance in golf tournaments, many of them charity events, drew big galleries eager to watch the young man who admitted he had a premonition about the new football season of 1927–28.

Once I'd got back in the first team the previous season after my accident things started to happen for me. The stars started to shine a little brighter. The accident never played on my mind. Once I was back playing I never thought about it . . . Anyway, my jaw and skull had healed and were actually stronger than they were before my crash! In fact, a lot of people thought the metal plate was left in my head. But it had been removed . . . Right from the start of the following season, from the very first kick-off, I simply knew I was going to do something.

That was a masterly understatement. Dean, who opened the new season having already amassed 55 goals in his 72 League outings for Everton since his arrival from Tranmere, proceeded to blitz his way through the campaign on a scoring spree unprecedented in English football. He scored in 29 of his 39 First Division appearances and his record-setting haul of 60 goals comprised eight singles, 14 doubles, five hat tricks, a four and a five. He scored 31 in 15 away games and 29 in 14 home appearances . . . 40 of his haul coming from shots and 20 from headers. After the first nine games he had already bagged 17 although there were to be many twists and turns en route to the heady drama the following May when Dixie ensured his enduring place in football folklore. Everton were transformed from relegation strugglers to champions by Dean's torrent of goals and a batch of new signings. Full back and captain Warney Cresswell had arrived from Sunderland the previous season along with wing half Jerry Kelly from Ayr United, right winger Ted Critchley from Stockport County, inside forward Tony Weldon from Airdrie, centre or inside forward Dick Forshaw from Liverpool and England goalkeeper Ted Taylor from Huddersfield, where he had won medals in the first side to win three consecutive championships. Taylor shared goalkeeping duties that season with Wallasey-born Arthur Davies, signed from Flint in the summer of 1926, and another recruit late in the title-winning season was inside right George Martin from Hull City who played in the last 10 games, scoring three goals. The ammunition for Dean's spectacular goal salvo was provided largely by wingers Critchley on the right and Alec Troup on the left. Critchley, who succeeded Dixie's mentor Chedgzoy, missed only two League games that season. Scotland international Troup, signed from Dundee in 1922, was one of only two ever-presents with left back Jack O'Donnell and was Everton's second top scorer that season with 10 goals . . . 50 behind Dixie!

Dean enthused:

Ted was a fine player and a great signing for us. He knew how to centre a ball and we harmonised well. Little Alec on the other side was an amazing feller and a great ball player . . . He stood only 5 ft 5 in but was full of bravery and skill. Because of a weak collar bone which kept slipping out of joint he had to play with a strapping on his shoulder every game . . . I think we had a perfect understanding and I think I have to thank him more than anyone else for the part he played in scoring the goals I did. I'd rate him one of the best wingers there's ever been . . . Behind us in defence we had Warney Cresswell at right back. As a captain he had our respect and he was such a great reader of the game that he was rarely under pressure. He saw things before they happened and should have won far more than the nine England caps he did get . . . Off the field he was very careful, too! I think the only time he took his hands out of his pocket was to hold his pipe or his

pint. In the pub he'd always be the last to buy a round! . . .
Sometimes he'd say: 'The beer's no good here . . . let's go
somewhere else.' He'd hope we'd forget it was his round! We
never did. But he was a great feller.

Everton raised the curtain on the season with a 4–0 home
demolition of Sheffield Wednesday on the same day that Newcastle's
great Scottish centre forward Hughie Gallacher, hugely admired by
Dean, was scoring a hat trick in a 3–1 win at Huddersfield, a result that
would carry great significance in the final title reckoning. Such was
Dean's reputation, however, that even a missed chance was highly
newsworthy, as 'Stork' in the *Football Echo* reported: 'What a
sensation. It left the spectators speechless. Everton had made an attack
through Cresswell, who had intercepted a pass in the Wednesday half
and punted it right down the middle . . . Dean, thinking he was offside,
allowed it to go by him and even Troup could hardly believe his own
eyes when he saw the referee signal 'play on'. At all events, the little
fellow did play on by pushing the ball right in front of goal where
Dean had only to touch it to make it into a scoring point . . . Here, the
sensation. Dean, to everyone's dismay, kicked right round the ball and
although Irvine came up in an effort to retrieve his colleague's error
the Wednesday goal did not fall.'
    It did, eventually, though and Dean, having set up a goal for
Forshsaw, rounded off the afternoon by scoring Everton's fourth. He
was also on the mark in Everton's second match of the new campaign
at newly promoted Middlesbrough. He was overshadowed that day
though by George Camsell, the man who had set the League scoring
record with 59 goals in the Second Division the previous season.
Camsell scored twice for the home side in the opening eight minutes
and went on to score another couple as Everton fell 4–2. Two days
later a Dean goal at Burnden Park gave Everton a 1–1 draw against
Bolton with the *Liverpool Daily Post* waxing lyrical on his performance. 'Once again,' the reporter wrote 'I have to chronicle capital
football on the part of Everton. Anyone who could see Dean working
fore and aft and not desiring or needing the ball to be placed in his
pocket; anyone seeing him win heading matches against the tall

Seddon with arms akimbo; anyone realising that here was a centre who was even introducing a feinting moment into his armour – all this without a glow of excitement. Well, he must, needs be, a dead soul. Dean was just wonderful.'

His scoring spree continued with a brace of goals in a 5–2 home conquest of Birmingham, a single in a 2–2 home deadlock with Bolton and another couple in a 2–2 draw at reigning champions and League leaders Newcastle. He scored with a first minute shot and a second half header from a Critchley cross.

O'Donnell's penalty miss at packed St James' Park cost Everton victory but Dixie was quick off the mark in Everton's next outing, a 2–2 home draw with powerful Huddersfield, whose battling pursuit of a League and FA Cup double would leave them agonisingly empty-handed as runners-up in both competitions.

Dean had limbered up for the challenge of confronting Huddersfield by bagging four goals for the Football League in a 9–1 midweek rout of the Irish League before joining millions around the world 24 hours later by tuning into the radio broadcasts of Gene Tunney's retention of the world heavyweight title against Jack Dempsey in the famous 'long count' contest in Chicago. Tunney banked almost a million dollars from the fight, making a mockery of the £8 a week paid to a superstar like Dean and his contemporaries. Perhaps that thought was foremost in Dean's mind when he took up a wager from local bookmaker and Liverpool supporter Billy Cave. For a £2 stake he was given odds of evens for one goal scored in a match that season, 5–2 for two goals and 10–1 for three goals. Cave's friend and fellow bookie, Freddie Tarbuck, father of comedian Jimmy, joined Dixie in accepting Cave's odds and backing the Everton centre forward's prodigious scoring prowess. When Dixie went into battle with Huddersfield in the last match of September he took only four minutes to score after a move launched by a Cresswell tackle and continued by a pass from left half Albert Virr. It was a spectacular strike, Dixie first heading the ball sideways and, as it dropped, smashing it past Huddersfield goalkeeper Turner. After Huddersfield had equalised Dean restored Everton's lead when he beat England full back Roy Goodall in the air to head in a Critchley corner. Huddersfield, rippling with international talent, lived up to their reputation, equalised to secure a 2–2 draw and signalled that they would be a massive obstacle to any club with championship aspirations. The same, though, applied to Everton as Dixie emphasised in his next match, against Tottenham at White Hart Lane. He proceeded to collect another brace of goals in a 3–1 win. 'Great was the joy of the excursionists and Dean was warmly applauded,' said one report. 'If Dean were a Londoner or playing for a London team they would be painting the lily of the football field. As it is, the London crowds stand in awe of him.' They were not alone.

The following Thursday, October 6, the film *The Jazz Singer* was premiered at New York's Warners Theatre. Al Jolson's phrase 'Wait a minute, you ain't heard nothin' yet!' although technically not the first words heard on screen did herald a cinema revolution: the end of the silent movie and the arrival of synchronised action and sound. Less than 48 hours later another type of action and sound was thrilling the public . . . the action of Dixie Dean putting Manchester United to the sword to the sound of deafening roars from the Everton faithful in a Goodison crowd just topping 40,000. It was a virtuoso performance from Dean, who reduced United's cynical offside tactics to rubble by scoring all his side's goals in a 5–2 mauling of the men from Old Trafford, with the *Liverpool Daily Post* justifiably gushing in its salute to Dixie's nap-hand feat. 'It is very difficult to know what to say next about this young, breezy man Dean,' the paper said. 'His five goals against Manchester United made a new figure for him in League games. To score five goals is an achievement but when he gets the whole of his side's goal list then the feat is very uncommon . . . What I saw away from home from Dean recently has led me to believe that he would one day break out into a scoring phase the like of which would startle England . . . That outbreak was registered on Saturday. Three of Dean's goals were due almost entirely to the short, sharp work of the right and bright wing pair of Critchley and Forshaw.'

Dean's quintet of goals against United completed a stunning opening sequence for the country's hottest football property. It meant he had scored in every one of Everton's first nine matches, for a total of 17, and with his four-goal Inter League salvo added, it took his haul to 21 in his first 10 games. Alas, his run ended a week later against the old enemy Liverpool, who drew 1–1 at Goodison. This time Dean could not escape the attentions of the ubiquitous Jimmy 'Parson' Jackson, who played centre half that day. Jackson, a church elder during his Liverpool career while he studied for the ministry, was deeply respected by Dixie as a man and a player:

> He was a good defender, that lad, no doubt about it, and a really nice bloke. Years later I was in the Isle of Man when I got a telegram asking if I'd meet Jimmy off the morning boat, escort him to his first church and wish him luck. So off I go to meet the boat. I met Jimmy and went up with him to the church. The next thing I know, this bloke in the church is pouring me out communion wine. And there's me, just finished two or three pints of bitter on the pier!

Dean missed Everton's next match to play for England in a 2–0 Belfast defeat by Ireland, who paraded Dean's great goalkeeping foe Elisha Scott and his Goodison team-mate Bobby Irvine. While Dixie was away, though, his clubmates rattled in seven goals without reply at home to West Ham with Tommy White standing in for Dixie and scoring twice in his only appearance of the season. But the master was at it again on his return a week later. Dean's hat trick in a 3–1 win at Portsmouth was the product of his burgeoning tactical expertise, a potential Tranmere fans had recognised during his formative days at Prenton Park. Dean operated as a deep-lying centre forward, a plan hatched between him and Tom McIntosh, a ploy entirely new to English football and years ahead of its time. Victory at Fratton Park put Everton top of the table, where they would stay until March. Dean blasted another treble in his next outing which lit the blue touch paper under Leicester on Guy Fawkes Day, November 5, the Midlands visitors being walloped 7–1, Everton's second 'seven-up' in three games. He followed up with two goals in a 3–0 win at Derby. His first came after three minutes. 'It took a second in the making,' said a report. 'Kelly made a useful push and Dean collared it, sized up the situation and blazed away.' Dixie's brace of goals at the Baseball Ground meant he had scored eight in his last three outings, a scoring burst that preceded the announcement in Paris by Jules Rimet, head of football's world ruling body FIFA, of the birth of a new World Cup competition. The fact, though, that the four British associations resigned from FIFA just a few months later, following a row over the definition of amateurism and broken-time payments for loss of earnings, and did not rejoin until 1946, underlined that the domestic game was the all-consuming passion for them and the man in the street.

League and FA Cup football offered escapism and relief from the harshness of everyday life in Britain. Although the 1920s saw the growth of suburbia and the country's infrastructure slowly being modernised, with electricity powering trains and trams and lights replacing gas lamps on city streets, they were hard times for the working man and even tougher for the unemployed, which included a significant number of miners. Against that backcloth a hero figure of Dixie Dean proportions was a magnet to the fans who, like figures in a Lowry landscape, donned their mufflers and cloth caps and paid their shilling admission to the terraces. For Everton followers, however, the visit of Sunderland to Goodison on November 19 was a tale of the unexpected. Not only did the Wearside club manage to stem Dean's torrent of goals they headed back to the North East with a 1–0 win. Dixie's response was a two-goal blast at Bury in Everton's next game, which they won 3–2, when all his menace and trickery was evident. His first goal was described thus: 'Dean was confronted by a full back but he tricked him in the most beautiful manner by digging the ball forward, racing round the back and scoring without giving Richardson a dog's chance.'

His second at Gigg Lane was also one to behold, perhaps owing something to Dixie's ballroom technique. 'As Forshaw was falling he headed forward,' reported the *Liverpool Daily Post*. 'Dean received the ball and with a two-step worthy of a dancing master he beat both backs in the space of two yards and shot in with venom.' He then had another 'blank' in a goalless home draw with Sheffield United. But his next opponents, Aston Villa, were victims not only of Dean's instinctive scoring ability but also his ingenuity as he helped himself to a hat trick and Everton to a 3–2 win. It was a wretched afternoon for home goalkeeper Tom Jackson, a trained schoolteacher from County Durham who had succeeded the legendary Sam Hardy as Villa's last line of defence. Jackson's fumble allowed Dean to hook the ball almost out of his hands into the net for the first goal. The keeper was again at fault for the second when he failed to clear a Critchley cross and Dixie gratefully applied the finish. Dean tells his own story of the goal that clinched his hat trick:

> Although it was December it was a beautiful, sunny day at Villa Park. I'd got two in the old onion bag and, naturally, I was looking for a third. Then this ball was punted upfield in my direction and I went to meet it. My first thought was to breast it down and then turn round towards the goal. But the next thing I saw was a long shadow coming right alongside me. To me, that meant that the goalkeeper had come well of his line. So instead of doing what I was going to do I jumped and back-headed the ball. It sailed into an empty net . . . Even the Villa fans applauded while the goalkeeper just looked at me. He must have thought I was 'J.C' himself! But it was the strong sunshine that got me that goal and I told the goalkeeper that. Because of his shadow I was able to anticipate that he was well out. Of all the goals I scored there was none I was more proud of than that one.

It was hailed as 'one of the most novel goals seen on the ground' but for hapless Jackson it was an afternoon to forget and he did not play for Villa again that season. Strangely, Dixie failed to get on the scoresheet when Everton walloped Burnley 4–1 at Goodison next time out. He did score in the following game but was on the losing side at Arsenal, who won a fog-shrouded contest by the odd goal in five.

Some 48 hours later on Boxing Day he was again on the goal standard, scoring twice in a 2–1 home win over Cardiff City, who were near the top of the table and had title aspirations of their own. It was an ill-tempered match, out of context with the season of goodwill. However, as well as his goals, Dean's display – he even did the wing half job of taking throw-ins – was magnificent and was hailed 'as a personal triumph for this amazing centre forward.' He also gave the supporters a big scare by going off injured, only to return after treatment ready to travel by train for the return fixture in South Wales the following day. Cardiff, though, kept the championship battle bubbling in the depths of winter by reversing their fortunes with a 2–0 defeat of Everton at Ninian Park. Everton completed their four-games-in-a-week Christmas programme at Sheffield Wednesday on New Year's Eve, when Dixie's double strike gave Everton a 2–1 victory and took his tally to a scorching 35 in 22 League appearances. Still only 20, he had the football world at his prodigious feet and head and raised the curtain on 1928 with two more goals, although it did not prevent Everton going down 4–2 at Blackburn Rovers. Dixie's third consecutive brace, in a 3–1 home victory over Middlesbrough, guaranteed him an entry in the record books. It raised his season's First Division haul to 39 and took him past England international Bert Freeman's club record of 38 (disputed in some record books as 36) in 1908–09, which was also a First Division record until Ted Harper of Blackburn scored 43 in 1925–26. But it was to be Everton's last League win for almost three months. Nine games without a victory saw their championship challenge stutter badly with Huddersfield threatening to take the title. League leaders Everton broke off from their championship pursuit to travel to Preston in the FA Cup where Dixie scored in a 3–0 win.

The early weeks of 1928 saw Jack Dempsey's retirement from the ring and the deaths of literary giant Thomas Hardy and long-serving Liberal Prime Minister Herbert Henry Asquith. But there was personal celebration for Dixie Dean, now a household name the length and breadth of the land. His 21st birthday on January 22 was commemorated by the Everton board of directors who presented him with a unique scroll, which today has pride of place on display at Goodison and is viewed regularly by the public on Everton's popular stadium tours. The scroll reads, in rather formal but highly respectful tones: 'Dear Sir, We the undersigned desire to unite in tendering to you our sincere congratulations on the attainment of your 21st birthday. As a member of the Everton Football Club, and a representative of England in the international matches, your good sportsmanship and brilliant play, together with your unfailing tact and initiative as a leader, has endeared you to the hearts of thousands of your admirers.

A rare picture of Dixie Dean at his 21st birthday party in Claughton
Village, Birkenhead in 1928. His father William is on his right (copyright
unknown. Possibly *Liverpool Daily Post & Echo*)

We hope you will enjoy health and strength, long to continue in
your present career and that your future prospects may be crowned
with all happiness and prosperity.'

As a slightly belated birthday present Dean grabbed two goals in a
fourth round FA Cup tussle at Highbury six days later. But his double
was not sufficient to prevent Arsenal winning a thrilling contest 4–3,
thus leaving the Merseyside club the sole aim of winning the League
championship, which they still led. In the preceding First Division
game at Birmingham, Dean failed to score in a 2–2 draw and although
he added another to his total at Huddersfield on February 4 to take his
total to 40 it was a day of Everton gloom as they crashed 4–1 to the
Yorkshire 'Double' chasers. A hat trick from Scotland outside right
Alec Jackson and a goal from England left winger Billy Smith moved
Huddersfield to within a point of Everton, whose struggle to win a
match was to continue until the spring.

The following midweek game Dixie rammed in five goals for
England against The Rest at Middlesbrough in a trial match for the

forthcoming collision with Scotland at Wembley on March 31. But he
was to taste no such joy when he resumed club duty three days later.
Indeed, Everton's misery was deepened when Tottenham won 5–2 at
Goodison on a sodden pitch with Dixie failing to score after receiving
little service. The anxieties of the fans were rising. Were Everton
going to blow it? Was Dixie going to fail in his record attempt? The
man himself, though, took it all in his stride and his determination was
bolstered by his delight at seeing two of his fellow Birkonians and
Tranmere Rovers players, centre forward Tom 'Pongo' Waring and left
winger Ellis Rimmer, make big career moves to Aston Villa and Sheffield
Wednesday for reported fees of £4,700 and £3,000 respectively. Not
only would they both go on to play for England but Waring, with 49
for Villa in 1930–31, would go closer than anyone has ever done in
the top flight to Dean's 60-goal record.

Everton's alarming form dip and loss of the League leadership was
hardly guaranteed to build confidence for their next outing: the three-
quarters-of-a-mile trip to Anfield to face Liverpool, who were themselves
having an indifferent season and had lost three of their previous four
League matches as well as bowing out of the FA Cup at Cardiff. To
Dixie, though, nothing stirred the blood more than a tussle with the
'old enemy' and this one was extra special. It was his 100th League
appearance for Everton, having already become the first player under
21 to score a century of League goals, a landmark he had reached at
Portsmouth back in October and a feat unequalled until Jimmy
Greaves 32 years later. Dean's great friend and foe Elisha Scott was
missing for the 56th League meeting of the Merseyside clubs and
Arthur Riley was the goalkeeper he had to face. Scott was playing for
Ireland against Scotland in Glasgow that same afternoon, although he
had been dislodged in the Liverpool team by South African star Riley
earlier in the season. There were only five minutes on the clock when
Fred Hopkin put Liverpool ahead. But the roars from the Kop in a
56,000-plus crowd were stifled by Dixie who fired Everton level after
beating 'Parson' Jackson who, it was waspishly reported, 'covered
Dean as though he were a co-pastor'. He scored another before half
time, firing past Riley after running onto a Tony Weldon pass, and
extended Everton's lead with a header on the hour from a Ted

Critchley cross to complete a hat trick. It took his League goals total for Everton to 98 overall and 43 for the season, equalling Ted Harper's record. Although goals from Tom Bromilow and renowned marksman Gordon Hodgson secured Liverpool a 3–3 draw it was a satisfying outcome for the visitors in general and Dixie in particular. Coupled with the draw against Liverpool at Goodison earlier in the season it launched an unbeaten Everton sequence of nine consecutive League derbies stretching to October 1932, although they did lose to their arch rivals in the FA Cup earlier that year.

Any success against Liverpool brought a warm glow to Dixie, who declared:

There was nothing like quietening that Kop. When you stuck a goal in there it all went quiet, apart from a bit of choice language aimed in your direction! Scoring there was a delight to me. I just used to turn round to the crowd and bow three times to them . . . Everton have always been noted for going out on the pitch to play football. We got called the 'School of Science' quite rightly. The other lot, the Reds . . . well, they were a gang of butchers! . . . They should have been working in the abattoir. McNab, McKinlay, the Wadsworths. God bless my soul. They'd kick an old woman! I had some great fun, though, with the lot of them.

However, another month would pass before Dixie scored another Everton goal and many punters and pundits believed his 60-goal quest to be beyond him. After the derby match he needed 17 goals from Everton's 13 remaining League games . . . and two of those he had to miss to play for England and the Football League. So 17 from 11 matches looked to be mission impossible, even for Dixie. Even the one goal he needed to surpass Harper's First Division total proved elusive. Everton figured in a goalless draw at West Ham in their next match, with Dean unable to escape the shackles of a pack of defensive 'minders', and he missed another barren encounter, at home to Portsmouth, to play for the Football League in a 6–2 trouncing of the Scottish League at Glasgow's Ibrox Park when, ironically, he scored twice. Dean was back in the Everton side at Manchester United only to suffer another blank afternoon for himself and the team, who lost 1–0. It was followed by a similar defeat at Leicester when Dixie pulled a thigh muscle, went off and returned on the left wing after treatment. Everton had now gone four games without scoring, they trailed Huddersfield by four points and, to set a new 60-goal record, Dixie faced the monumental task of hitting 17 goals in his eight remaining games, England duty ensuring his absence from the March 31 trip to Sunderland.

Although one bookmaker had already suffered singed digits, after Dixie had accepted his early-season odds on goals per game, others went spectacularly belly-up to reflect the public view that the season would hold only disappointment for Dixie and Everton. Everton were quoted at 1,000–1 to win the title while their club programme reported: 'With Dean requiring a further nine goals to reach the magical total bookmakers listed him at 10,000–1 to hit the mark.' Two things then happened for player and club . . . Dixie found the switch to his goal machine and the toll of Double-chasing began to hit Huddersfield. Fortunes began to change for Dixie and Everton on March 24 when he scored twice in a 2–2 home draw with Derby, to sweep past Harper's total set two seasons earlier and establish a new top flight record of 45 goals.

'Today, after weeks of suspense, Dean got the goal that gave him the honour of top record scorer in the First Division of the League,' proclaimed one report. 'The critics of the world have come to the conclusion that he is the best centre forward the game has known.' On the same day Huddersfield were beginning an FA Cup semi final marathon with Sheffield United. The Yorkshire rivals would need three games to settle the issue, Huddersfield eventually winning through to Wembley where they lost 3–1 to Blackburn.

While Dixie was on the wrong end of a 5–1 triumph by Scotland's 'Wee Blue Devils' at Wembley, his clubmates were winning 2–0 at Sunderland. When Dean resumed action for Everton at the start of the Easter programme he still needed 15 goals from the last seven games. Although the official Goodison attendance for the Good Friday duel with Blackburn was 48,521 it is believed the true figure was more than 60,000 to see Dean score twice and help Everton to a 4–1 win. The following day Dean collected another goal in a 1–1 home draw with Bury which, coupled with Liverpool's good neighbourly defeat of Huddersfield, put Everton back on top of the old First Division on goal average. Now Dixie had 48 goals with five matches to go. He knocked off another couple from his wanted list in a 3–1 win at Sheffield United and scored again in a 3–0 home victory over Newcastle, prompting a reporter to observe: 'O'Donnell takes free kicks with a sweeping half shot and Dean heads them en route – a fine, pre-conceived notion. Then Cresswell, with a simple swing of the leg, lobs the ball to the middle with the same accuracy he imparts into a golf ball. That was how Dean came by his 51st goal.'

Aston Villa's visit to Goodison was an emotional occasion for Dixie because his counterpart was another former Tranmere player, his friend Tom 'Pongo' Waring who earned the nickname from his team-mates, recalls Tranmere historian Gilbert Upton, 'because of his malodorous feet'. The same feet, though, could certainly score goals and Waring and Dean received a standing ovation when they shook hands before kick off. Two years earlier their friendship had prompted Dixie, then a big First Division star, to go to Prenton Park and sit in the stand amongst a few hundred spectators to watch Waring score twice on his debut for Tranmere's Cheshire League side. His visit also exploded the myth that he boycotted Tranmere after the acrimony with Bert Cooke over his transfer to Everton. When the paths of Dean and Waring first crossed on the big Goodison stage both played their part in a thrilling contest with Everton winning 3–2, Dean scoring two to Waring's one. On the same afternoon Huddersfield lost in the FA Cup Final. One half of their Double ambition had been crushed. The second would suffer a similar fate, with the League title heading for Goodison. By the time Everton reached their penultimate match, at Burnley on April 28, Dixie had given them the key to the championship door while Huddersfield hopes died with defeats in three of their last four League games. Yet George Camsell's one-year-old, all-time League record of 59 goals in a season seemed safe and tantalisingly out of Dixie's reach, despite his total of 53 in 37 First Division appearances. But drama befitting a comic strip was about to unfold.

# CHAPTER FIVE

# *A Tram Ride To Immortality*

Saturday, May 5, 1928 was Dixie Dean's date with destiny. It was the day on which his name would stretch beyond the legend of his own sport of football and achieve a fame given to few human beings. The day, in fact, when the name of William Ralph Dean became immortal. Arsenal were the visitors to Goodison Park. Everton were already champions, thanks to Huddersfield's defeat at Aston Villa three days earlier. Only one question hung on the lips of Everton supporters and football followers far and wide. Would Dixie score the three goals he required to overtake George Camsell's previous season's total in the Second Division and set a new, barely credible, League record of 60 First Division goals? At one stage it had looked mission impossible. Bookies, punters and pundits alike had written off Dean's chances. Even now, it was a massive task to score three goals against Arsenal, although he had already put three goals past them in Everton's League and FA Cup defeats by the Highbury club earlier that season.

There was a bit of fun attached to it. I needed 10 goals from the last four games! I thought to myself 'I'll have to get a move on here' but I seemed to just take it in my stride . . . I scored one in our win over Newcastle and then I bagged another couple when we beat Aston Villa 3–2. I still needed seven from the last two matches and it was off to Burnley for the next one . . . Big Jack Hill, the centre half and England captain, was up against me and I got four before half time. But not one of them was a header. They were all hit in. We won 5–3 but I went off before the end because I'd pulled a muscle in my leg. Old Harry Cooke, the trainer, said 'no more, come off' so I did . . . Harry came home with me and slept in our house at Claughton to try to get me fit for our last game of the season, at home to Arsenal when I had to get three goals to break Georgie Camsell's League record of 59, which he set the year before in the Second Division . . . Harry was bandaging and putting plasters on my leg right through the week. He stuck with me right to the morning of the match and we went across to Goodison together.

But the night before the game Dixie fulfilled a previously accepted invitation from a Roman Catholic priest to open a church charity fete at Prescot, Merseyside. After performing the ceremony he was among a small party of people who went to the priest's house for a meal.

I'm not a Catholic but I must say that priest, Father Brown, did have an affect on me that night. We all sat round the table as he said a prayer asking God to help me break the record! . . . The following morning I got up at my usual time at home and to me it was just another match, another day. I went up to the ground as normal on the tram with all the fans. I always caught the 44 from Water Street . . . Naturally enough, they were all asking me if I was going to break the record. I just said to them: 'Wait and see'. I got off the tram and walked along Goodison Road and into the ground. I got there nice and handy, as a matter of fact . . . As Huddersfield had lost during the week we were champions whatever happened. In fact, the trophy was sitting there at the front of the directors box ready to be presented to our captain, Warney Cresswell, after the match.

The ground admission price to witness the unique drama that was about to unfold was one shilling and four old pence in the boys pen. Threepence in old currency bought you a cup of tea and a meat pie. The match programme – published jointly by Everton and Liverpool, who finished in 16th position to beat relegation by a point – cost twopence. The programme's front page advertisement offered 'a five

The day Dixie made history . . . the centre spread team sheets from the Everton programme for the match with Arsenal on May 5, 1928 when a Dean hat trick set a new record of 60 League goals in a season

guinea overcoat for 50 shillings' and declared: 'You may not believe it but it's true!' At the nearby Lyric Theatre in Everton Valley the Lyric Players were presenting *A Sailor's Wedding Ring* with admission prices ranging from six old pence to two shillings and four pence while in the city centre Gladys Cooper was appearing at the Royal Court in *The Letter*. But the big star that day was Dixie Dean and the only matinee that mattered was at Goodison where the official attendance is recorded as 48,715. But around 60,000 people are believed to have packed into the stadium for what was also the farewell appearance for the Arsenal, England and former Sunderland inside forward star Charles Buchan. It was ironic that the Arsenal captain's swan song should have coincided with Dean's attempt on the goal record for it was Buchan who had invented the 'stopper' centre half plan honed to destructive efficiency by manager Herbert Chapman after the change in the offside law.

Buchan, born in east London, had made his Sunderland debut at Goodison in the 1910–11 season and joined Arsenal in 1925 for £2,000 plus £100 for every goal he scored in his first season, which ended with a total of £4,100 being paid from the marbled hall coffers.

Arsenal arrived at Goodison in mid-table limbo but Buchan, above everyone on the visiting side, wanted a win before hanging up his celebrated boots. The Arsenal team was: Patterson; Parker, John; Baker, Butler, Blyth; Hulme, Buchan, Shaw, Brain, Peel. The Everton side was: Davies; Cresswell, O'Donnell; Kelly, Hart, Virr; Critchley, Martin, Dean, Weldon, Troup. The official *History of the Everton Football Club*, published less than a year later, described Camsell's 59 goals in the Second Division a season earlier as 'a fly in the ointment' and added:

'Of course on a point of merit, all in, there was no comparison in the two achievements. Still, the 59 was there, an irritating numerical skeleton at the feast . . . Could Dean supplement his already staggering achievement of scoring 57 in League matches and do the hat trick against the Arsenal? If a forward scores three goals in any match he has scored above the ordinary; to score three in a specified match is a very different proposition . . . The

Some of Everton's 1927–28 League championship-winning squad. Back row left to right: Tom McIntosh (secretary manager), Jerry Kelly, Hunter Hart, Arthur Davies, Jack O'Donnell, Albert Virr, Harry Cooke (trainer). Front row: Ted Critchley, George Martin, Dixie Dean, Warney Cresswell, Tony Weldon, Alec Troup (copyright unknown)

hope that he might do it (by no means the belief that he would) packed Goodison Park with upwards of 60,000 spectators, simmering with excitement. The possibility of the doing of the doubtful, and the chance of seeing it done, were magnets. Both teams got a splendid reception, a fine sportsmanlike feeling seemed prevalent among both the spectators and players and the clerk of the weather had permitted the turf and the atmospheric conditions to be ideal . . . In a few minutes after the start a ground cannon shot from an Arsenal foot flew right to the feet of Davies, our goalkeeper; his legs were open, his hands went down like a shot. But the ball was quicker than his hands. It passed under them and, the legs being open, it was only arrested by the net . . . It seemed to grin ironically – the goal secured had the appearance of being such a soft one. It was more disheartening than a good one. The hearts of sensitive Evertonians made for their boots. 'Defeat' their fears cried . . . A goal like that has often disorganised a team. Sit still, my beating heart. It did. A few minutes later it was in its normal place. Dixie's magical head had tipped the ball into the net of the Gunners and the housewives of the neighbourhood were startled by a terrific explosion – of sound. 'Ladies it's an equalising goal for Everton.' Calm . . . Excitement – the referee (Lol Harper of Stourbridge) has awarded a penalty kick to Everton. Dixie takes it. The ball leaves his foot and, very deliberately, apparently avoiding the goalkeeper, rests in the net. Another terrific explosion. 'You really must excuse them, ladies, Dixie has equalised the irritating skeleton's record.'

The *Football Echo* reporter 'Bee' saw the early goal glut like this:

'Shaw scored in two minutes after handling the ball and getting away with it. But remarkable to relate, the ball went through the goalkeeper's hands into the net.

There was no great pace on the ball and naturally a shock such as this rather upset the preconceived notions of the Saturday celebrators. However, it was left to the man of the moment to create another sensational and memorable feat . . . Before three minutes had gone Dean had scored two goals, thus equalling Camsell of Middlesbrough with 59. The crowd's roar knew no bounds. They were crazy after this inspiring turn round in the scoresheet . . . It was all very simple in the making. The first point was from a corner taken by Critchley. Martin turned the ball on to Dean who headed it into the extreme left hand corner. This was the second chapter at the second minute. The third excelled all others. Dean was running through when the long-legged Butler crossed him . . . It was an accidental collision. To the referee it was a trip and the consequence was that Dean was able to rise from the ground and take the penalty kick successfully and well.'

Dean's first goal was Everton's 100th in the League that season and these are his own recollections:

I needed three goals against Arsenal, who were the greatest club in the land. But that didn't worry me whatsoever. I always used to think: 'I'm better than you.' . . . I didn't have to wait long for my first goal. I headed the ball from just outside the penalty area and it flew in. Soon after that I went sailing through and got into the area. I was just about to shoot when I suddenly went up in the air and ended flat on my face. Penalty . . . I took the penalty myself, which I did normally, and scored. I intended to place it. I always tried to keep them low and this was no exception. But, believe me, it went between the keeper's legs. It wasn't one of my better kicks at all. But it went in. And I could hear a voice inside me saying: 'Well, that's two you've got.'

Ten minutes before the interval O'Donnell diverted the ball into his own net to tie up the game at 2–2. Not that Evertonians were paying much attention to the score. The supporters were just willing Dixie to get a third goal and break the record. The tension was almost tangible. One man who was at Goodison that day is Sir Daniel Pettit, a lifelong Everton fan born within a mile of the stadium and later to play for the famous Corinthians, become a captain of industry and chairman of the state-owned National Freight Corporation. He recalled: 'One of my first Goodison memories is of seeing priests walking around the running track at half time. I've absolutely no idea why! But I always felt Everton had God on their side! I certainly think everyone was praying for Dixie to get his hat trick that day in 1928 . . . There was an amazing atmosphere in the ground but it was very tense. Everyone was looking at his watch. Dixie had scored twice and the clock was ticking.' Another enthralled spectator was John Gibbons, latterly of Formby, Merseyside, who recounted: 'I was about 11 at the time of the Arsenal match. The tension was unbelievable. Everyone loved Dixie . . . He wasn't the tallest player in the world. But he was barrel-chested and very strong and powerful. He'd got two goals and we were all desperately hoping he'd get a third.'

There was a bizarre contrast in attitudes between the teams after the interval, Everton single-minded in their efforts to service and supply Dixie at every opportunity and Arsenal surrounding him with a posse of markers.

The *Football Echo* reporter 'Bee' took up the story:

'Troup produced some of his fireworks which must have produced a goal for Dean had he sighted the ball. The home centre, however, lost the flight of the ball and a chance of a lifetime to make his record . . . For long spells Dean was crowded out, or received unwise passes. At the hour he broke and seemed an assured scorer when the ball swung a yard outside. Time was flying and the crowd now really got hearty over the main issue of the day – namely, Dean's need for one goal . . . One had to be present to hear the sighs of the crowd during the tense moments of the Everton attack. With nine minutes to go the crowd yearned for a goal to Dean.'

The man himself was also very conscious that the clock had become as much his enemy as Arsenal:

Time was going on in that second half and I still needed another. I was getting the ball from all angles. I was hitting them just over the bar or just wide of the post and I had two or three efforts tipped round by their keeper, Bill Patterson. The crowd were very tense . . . There wasn't long to go when Patterson tipped a shot from George Martin over the bar at the Park End. Alec Troup took the corner from the left and it came absolutely perfect for me. I ran in from outside the area to head it and the ball flew into the net. That was it. The record . . . I just bowed but the crowd went wild. Somebody ran onto the pitch and stuck his whiskers in my face trying to kiss me. Well! I'd never seen a spectator run onto the field until that day . . . Everyone started congratulating me, including the Arsenal players with the exception of one man, the great Charlie Buchan. It was his last game and he was a very jealous man, that . . . In fact the Arsenal keeper Patterson was the first to shake hands with me and congratulate me after I'd followed my header in and run into the net. So did Joe Hulme and the other Arsenal lads. But not Buchan . . . The game had to be finished, of course. So I went to the referee, Lol Harper, and said to him: 'Look, I'll be sliding off a couple of minutes before you blow the final whistle.' I thought he might say that I had to stay on but he understood perfectly. He knew and I knew what would happen if I was on the field at the

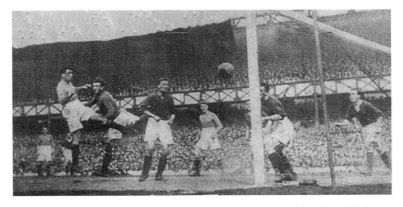

Heading into history: The only remaining picture of Dixie's record-breaking 60th League goal of 1927–28, scored against Arsenal at Goodison in Everton's last match of the season.

George Green, *Liverpool Echo* cartoonist, reflects on Everton's 1927–28 League championship win (copyright *Liverpool Daily Post & Echo*)

end . . . So I slipped off before the finish and got away from the mob. But I came back afterwards to say a few words and take my turn holding the championship trophy which Warney Cresswell had received as club captain.

A late Arsenal equaliser by Shaw to secure a 3–3 draw was purely academic, as was the strange fact that heroic Dean had scored six times in three meetings with Arsenal that season without once being on the winning side.

His feat in reaching 60 goals – his record breaker timed at 82 minutes – left an indelible impression in the memory of every spectator privileged to witness Dean's grand and dramatic Goodison denouement.

None more so than Dixie's mother Sarah, as Everton chairman Will Cuff revealed:

'Dean's mother, seated in the Press box upstairs, had prayed at the 70th minute that her only son should be granted "Just one more chance",' said Cuff. 'Many must have felt demented at the joy of their hero making a goal crop that may stand for all football's history . . . This was the centre forward beyond compare. His ability to add pace to the ball and turn it with his head was monumental. Yet Arsenal would not give him a goal. They did not want it to be said he had scored three against them to break the record. Three goals when needed and when wanted is much to expect. Players don't deliver goals to order . . . Time passed. One felt like asking the referee to order extra time if need be! Finally, the chance came and Dean, having worked more solo than in any other match in his life, had hardly the strength left in his worn-out body and limbs to take the chance. However, in it went. Goal! Dean had done it by head, by foot, by the aid of the Troups . . . meaning all his comrades who had helped him to his fantastic record . . . It was the signal for the pantomime dames and gentry to take up their stance. The crowd raced onto the field, the game appeared as if it would never be restarted. Players leapt into the air. Nobody cared a brass farthing for the remaining minutes of the match.'

Sarah Dean's prayer had been answered. The tension was shattered. Dean had headed himself into football immortality and Goodison joy was unbounded.

*Everton's Official History* also commented on the events: We made up our minds that Dixie wasn't going to get the other goal we longed to see. Good heavens, while the thought was formulating, Troup (the electric tripper), sent a nice dropping shot in front of goal, the ball hung in the air, Dixie's magical head went for it and tipped it into the net . . . You talk about explosions and loud applause. We have heard many explosions

and much applause in our long pilgrimage but, believe us, we
have never heard before such a prolonged roar of thundering,
congratulatory applause as that which ascended to heaven when
Dixie broke the record . . . The applause had some time to
indulge itself while the ball made its way to the halfway line, to
which the referee had pointed. The Arsenal goalkeeper could
have kicked the ball as it lay crouching in the net. But with feet
of lead he approached it, mechanically picked it up with his
hands, carried it out of the net and then languidly kicked it down
the field . . . Meanwhile, a very comic episode intervened. Dixie
and the players had trooped to the halfway line accompanied by
deafening shouts of 'Good old Dixie' and 'Well done, Dixie' in
a crescendo . . . While Dixie was bowing his head modestly in
acknowledgement of the idolatrous storm a low-comedy
looking chap evaded the police and, stumbling up to Dixie,
managed to shake his hand. The game had to be suspended until
he had been helped off the ground by a policeman . . . The first
comedian's turn had been such a success that a second was
frantically rushing for Dixie's hand. He got a shake and before
Dixie realised it the second comedian had kissed him . . . The
patience of the referee was exhausted. He seized the second
comedian by the scruff of the neck and bundled him off the
ground. While the unrehearsed comedy was being enacted
screams of laughter mingled with the storm of applause . . . It
really was about the most side-splitting, screamingly funny
farcical comedy and extra turn that was ever introduced to a
football match. There was no mistake about the spectators
having enjoyed the interpolation . . . The sensation of the day
was the terrific, thundering applause which greeted Dean's
accomplishment of his wonderful feat.

Dean emerged from a mass of 14 players to score his 60th goal and
Sir Daniel Pettit recalls: 'I was only 12 at the time but the moment is
still fresh in my memory. When Troup swung the ball over Dixie,
from just inside the penalty area, connected with his head and the ball
just flew into the net. The crowd went wild, mainly I suppose through

the sheer relief of seeing Dixie achieve what they had come to see him do . . . I later played as an amateur for Everton and had to decline an offer to clean Dixie's boots for five bob a week to take up a scholarship to Cambridge. I'd have loved the chance to give the great man's boots at least one polish!'

It is said that the roar exulting Dean's record-breaking strike was so loud that it scattered the flocks of sea-gulls and pigeons at the city's Pier Head several miles away. Urban myth it may be but John Gibbons was present to experience the amazing reaction to the goal that made history and transformed Dean into a football icon. 'When he headed the ball into the net it was like an earthquake,' John recalled. 'The whole ground shook. The fans were not only overjoyed. They were also relieved Dixie had done it.' Arsenal goalkeeper Patterson, who had collided with his own defender Jack Butler as Troup delivered his fateful corner, confirmed the state of frenzy inside Goodison. 'The crowd were stark raving mad,' he declared. 'I looked at Dean and he seemed shocked. I smiled and, God forgive me, I went over and shook hands with him.' Perhaps a different kind of emotion explained Charlie Buchan's failure to congratulate Dean. The former First World War guardsman revealed later that his eyes were moist at the prospect of walking off the pitch for the last time. 'I didn't exactly weep but I could just about see my way to the tunnel,' he confessed. 'There are many who believe that Arsenal sat back and allowed Dean to get the three goals that broke the record. I can assure them that nothing is farther from the truth.

'For myself I wanted to go out on a winning note, just as I'd come in back in 1910. The Arsenal players wanted to help me in this by beating the new champions. It was a memorable day, one I shall remember as long as I live. Dean was then at the height of his powers. When he got the third, the Goodison Park crowd rose to him. It was a scene beyond description.'

The championship trophy, ironically, was presented to Everton skipper Cresswell by Liverpool director and former Anfield chairman and secretary John McKenna, in his capacity as Football League president.

Ironically, while Everton were celebrating McKenna's own club Liverpool were licking their wounds at being crushed 6–1 at Manchester United that afternoon, a result that spectacularly dispelled Old Trafford fears of relegation and left the Anfield club languishing in 16th place with the same 39-point total as United. But never in football history has the feat of winning the English game's biggest prize been overshadowed as it was that day by the incredible personal feat of William Ralph Dean.

Dixie had planted his flag at the goalscoring summit with 40 shots and 20 headers, 31 of his goals coming in 20 away games, 29 of them in 19 home matches. The three top flight scorers closest to his total were Halliday of Sunderland with 36, Beel (Burnley) 35 and Chandler (Leicester) 34.

That same season Jimmy Smith of Scottish Second Division champions Ayr United scored 66 goals in 38 matches. But the gulf in standards between Dean's league and Smith's is a gaping chasm. They were simply not comparable achievements. The importance of Dean's scoring prowess was illustrated on two counts. Everton's total

Headlines in the *Liverpool Football Echo* (right) recording Dixie setting his 60-goal record in May 1928 and the *Post & Mercury* report of the occasion

of 102 First Division goals was only the third occasion in League history that the champions had broken the century barrier and it was the first time Everton had done so. Yet Everton's 66 conceded was the highest ever up to that point by any top flight title winners and, subsequently, only two championship-winning sides have conceded more – Sunderland, who let in 74 goals in 1935–36, and Ipswich, who leaked 67 in 1961–62. Steve Bloomer, a scoring legend of an earlier football generation and whose great feats Dixie was destined to surpass, inspired the Goodison club's 'School of Science' label when he wrote in 1928: 'We owe a great deal to Everton. No matter where they play and no matter whether they are well or badly placed in the League table, they always manage to serve up football of the highest scientific order. Everton always worship at the shrine of craft and science and never do forget the standard of play they set out to achieve.'

With cup, international and friendly match goals Dean, incredibly, reached a century in 1927–28 and a few days before his magical 60th in the League a different kind of record was set when the 'Flying Scotsman' exceeded 70 miles per hour on its non-stop rail journey between London and Edinburgh. And 48 hours after Dixie had re-written football history MPs gave an unopposed third reading to the Bill giving votes to all women over 21. Yet even after Man had walked on the Moon and Britain had a woman Prime Minister, Dixie Dean's feat would still be unchallenged. I wonder what the un-named reporter writing in the *Sunday Times* the morning after Dean's day of glory would say now. With one of the most astonishing miscalculations in sports journalism he wrote: 'Dean, the Everton and England centre forward, attained a record number of goals. His total of 60 in one season sets up a record which now seems destined to be broken every season.'

Well, not quite!

Perhaps Dixie himself, in his characteristic, droll manner, captured the sheer majesty of his deeds of 1927–28 when he reflected: 'People ask me if that 60-goal record will ever be beaten. I think it will. But there's only one man who'll do it. That's that feller who walks on the water. I think he's about the only one.'

George Green, *Liverpool Echo* cartoonist salutes Dixie's 60-goal record in 1928 (copyright *Liverpool Daily Post & Echo*)

How Dixie set the 60-goal League record
game by game through 1927–28

| Date | Opponents | H/A | Result | Dean's Goals | Date | Opponents | H/A | Result | Dean's Goals |
|---|---|---|---|---|---|---|---|---|---|
| 27 Aug | Sheffield Wednesday | H | 4–0 | 1 | 27 Dec | Cardiff City | A | 0–2 | - |
| 3 Sep | Middlesbrough | A | 2–4 | 1 | 31 Dec | Sheffield Wednesday | A | 2–1 | 2 |
| 5 Sep | Bolton Wanderers | A | 1–1 | 1 | 2 Jan | Blackburn Rovers | A | 2–4 | 2 |
| 10 Sep | Birmingham | H | 5–2 | 2 | 7 Jan | Middlesbrough | H | 3–1 | 2 |
| 14 Sep | Bolton Wanderers | H | 2–2 | 1 | 21 Jan | Birmingham | A | 2–2 | - |
| 17 Sep | Newcastle United | A | 2–2 | 2 | 4 Feb | Huddersfield Town | A | 1–4 | 1 |
| 24 Sep | Huddersfield Town | H | 2–2 | 2 | 11 Feb | Tottenham Hostpur | H | 2–5 | - |
| 1 Oct | Tottenham Hotspur | A | 3–1 | 2 | 25 Feb | Liverpool | A | 3–3 | 3 |
| 8 Oct | Manchester United | H | 5–2 | 5 | 3 Mar | West Ham United | A | 0–0 | - |
| 15 Oct | Liverpool | H | 1–1 | - | 10 Mar | Portsmouth | H | 0–0 | dnp |
| 22 Oct | West Ham United | H | 7–0 | dnp | 14 Mar | Manchester United | A | 0–1 | - |
| 29 Oct | Portsmouth | A | 3–1 | 3 | 17 Mar | Leicester City | A | 0–1 | - |
| 5 Nov | Leicester City | H | 7–1 | 3 | 24 Mar | Derby County | H | 2–2 | 2 |
| 12 Nov | Derby County | A | 3–0 | 2 | 31 Mar | Sunderland | A | 2–0 | dnp |
| 19 Nov | Sunderland | H | 0–1 | - | 6 Apr | Blackburn Rovers | H | 4–1 | 2 |
| 26 Nov | Bury | A | 3–2 | 2 | 7 Apr | Bury | H | 1–1 | 1 |
| 3 Dec | Sheffield United | H | 0–0 | - | 14 Apr | Sheffield United | A | 3–1 | 2 |
| 10 Dec | Aston Villa | A | 3–2 | 3 | 18 Apr | Newcastle United | H | 3–0 | 1 |
| 17 Dec | Burnley | H | 4–1 | - | 21 Apr | Aston Villa | H | 3–2 | 2 |
| 24 Dec | Arsenal | A | 2–3 | 1 | 28 Apr | Burnley | A | 5–3 | 4 |
| 26 Dec | Cardiff City | H | 2–1 | 2 | 5 May | Arsenal | H | 3–3 | 3 |

(dnp indicates he did not play)
In addition Dean scored 3 goals in the FA Cup; one against Preston and two against Arsenal

The best performances since Dean's record

| Goals | Player (Club) | Div | Season |
|---|---|---|---|
| 55 | Joe Payne (Luton Town) | 3S | 1936–37 |
| 55 | Ted Harston (Mansfield Town) | 3N | 1936–37 |
| 52 | Terry Bly (Peterborough United) | 4 | 1960–61 |
| 49 | Pongo Waring (Aston Villa) | 1 | 1930–31 |
| 49 | Clarrie Bourton (Coventry City) | 3S | 1931–32 |
| 46 | Peter Simpson (Crystal Palace) | 3S | 1930–31 |
| 46 | Derek Dooley (Sheffield Wed.) | 2 | 1951–52 |
| 46 | Alf Lythgoe (Stockport County) | 3N | 1933–34 |

(The post-war 1st Division record is 41 – Jimmy Greaves
(Chelsea) 1960–61)

# CHAPTER SIX

# *The Legacy Of Record Breaking*

Life would never be the same again for Dixie Dean now that he had re-written football's record books. His celebrity became global and the determination of opponents to stop him by any means reached a new intensity. Four days after the dramatic duel with Arsenal he and the Everton party set off for an end-of-season tour of Switzerland, which Dixie had to punctuate by appearing in two England games. But, even as they left, the impact of Dean's goalscoring deeds had made its mark across the Atlantic which led to a lucrative offer he rejected because of his passion for and commitment to Everton. His two goals in England's 5–1 win over France in Paris had a surprise after-match sequel. Dixie recalled: 'The stadium dressing rooms were below pitch level and there were no baths. They just had a row of showers which were in full view of anyone who came along. So there we were having a shower after the game with all these Parisienne women walking past. They took no notice. They didn't bother one bit.' Two more goals in a 3–1 defeat of Belgium in Antwerp and another couple in Everton's 2–0 victory over Basle in their opening tour game completed Dixie's amazing century of goals in 1927–28. The English champions returned home undefeated with further wins over Berne (5–0), Zurich (1–0) and Geneva (3–2).

Dean, instantly recognisable and a handsome, sporting hero, attracted crowds on and off the pitch, on home soil or abroad. Even in an era when the mass media was almost quaint compared to today's all-consuming bombardment of words and images he had become a superstar and a role model for youngsters. 'There weren't many motor cars in those days and the police didn't mind you playing football in the street, in fact some of the bobbies kept their eye out for talent to recommend to Everton or Liverpool,' recounted Sir Daniel Pettit. 'In those rough and ready street matches every single boy pretended to be Dixie Dean, even the lads who supported Liverpool! He was such a hero figure. I never saw him get angry on the field and he had such style. In fact, he has been an inspiration to me right through my very varied life.'

People from all classes, creeds and countries wanted to be seen with Dixie and the power of his magnetic attraction was felt by Everton during their Swiss tour. 'Floral tributes and speeches of welcome were showered on the party and the chairman's vocal chords were severely taxed by acknowledgments and responses,' observed the club's Official History. When Everton returned home on May 23 an agent was waiting for Dixie to offer him a then substantial £150 signing-on fee and £20 a week to play in America. Dean rejected it outright, insisting he wanted to play only for Everton. A few months later the British transfer record was broken when David Jack moved from Bolton to Arsenal for £10,890, a figure that was to remain unsurpassed for 10 years. If Dixie had become available the record would not have lasted 10 minutes. Arsenal swooped for Jack after being rebuffed by Dixie. Their esteemed manager Herbert Chapman had clearly revised his opinion of Dean's talents after his telegram to Tranmere, in the early days of his Highbury reign, insisting he was not interested in signing him. Dean revealed that Chapman made a personal mission to Goodison and offered the board a blank cheque in a desperate attempt to take Dixie to London and be part of what was to become one of the greatest teams in the history of English football. Dean's point-blank refusal to leave, however, prevented the directors even discussing the possibility of his departure from Goodison and disappointed Chapman returned to the capital with the money still in the bank and Dixie still a loyal Evertonian. 'He put an open cheque on the table but there was nothing doing,' said Dean, his few words symbolising his flat rejection of the idea. Professionally and socially, despite being top of everyone's invitation list, Dixie remained true to himself, proud of his humble Birkenhead roots and rejected any

notion of adopting airs and graces. For example, in Dixie's eyes the
finest wines on offer were no match for a pint of bitter:

> I used to go to restaurants and the waiters used to come with
> these here bottles of wine. I used to say to them: 'Do me a favour
> and bring me a jug of bitter . . . I've dined with all sorts of people,
> including Lords and Ladies, and I remember seeing Lord Derby
> pick up a chicken leg and eat it in his fingers. That's exactly what
> I liked to do. So I thought to myself if he can do it, so can I.

Strangely, Dean's fantastic achievement in scoring 60 League goals
received no official commemoration either by the Football League or
the Everton club. But Everton fans presented him with a large shield
– which contained 29 silver medallions representing the clubs against
which he scored his record haul – and the *Sunday Pictorial* newspaper
awarded him an inscribed trophy celebrating his feat. Opponents,
though, were intent on marking more than his talents as Dixie
painfully discovered:

> The conditions changed a little with me breaking that record and
> Everton winning the championship. Other players set out to try
> to stop me. Not only me, but also one or two of the other boys.
> We had a succession of cartilage troubles, fractured bones,
> broken shoulder blades and so on. I remember one incident,
> especially. I'd only just come out of the nursing home and we
> played the Villa who had this tall, lanky centre half. I went up to
> head the ball with him and down I landed. I was straight back
> into the nursing home that night with another chipped bone . . .
> They were all getting set for me after that record. The centre
> halves playing against me just wanted to turn round and say: 'He
> didn't get any today.' They'd try anything to try to stop me
> reaching the ball and they used to try to pull me down by
> grabbing my shorts or my shirt . . . In a game at Sunderland the
> defenders pulled two pairs of shorts off me in the first 20
> minutes! I stood there in the snow while old Harry Cooke went
> off to get me another pair. While I was waiting I covered myself

with some of the straw they kept on the track at the side to stop the pitch from freezing!

Less than a fortnight after the Olympics had ended in Amsterdam, where Britain's Douglas Lowe retained his 800 metres crown, Dixie opened the 1928–29 campaign as he finished the previous one so gloriously . . . with a hat trick. His treble against Bolton gave Everton a 3–2 win at Burnden Park and completed three consecutive League hat tricks for the England centre forward, having finished the preceding season with three goals against Arsenal and four at Burnley. The feat was equalled by Liverpool's Jack Balmer in November 1946. After a goalless midweek home draw with Sheffield Wednesday, Dean hit another hat trick the following Saturday, this time in a 4–0 Goodison demolition of Portsmouth. But the month of September, which saw the appearance of Walt Disney's Mickey Mouse in the first sound cartoon film 'Steamboat Willie', was anything but a laughing matter for Everton in their 50th anniversary season. They lost three of their next four games, including a stunning 6–2 home crash to newly promoted Manchester City. But at least Everton ended the month on an upbeat note with a 1–0 home win over Liverpool, thanks to Alec Troup's only goal of the game, and followed that with a much-awaited 4–2 home win over Arsenal at Goodison. Dean notched up another two goals, taking his haul to eight in his last four tussles with the Highbury club. But three defeats in the next four games signalled the frustration the season was to hold for Everton as the champions nosedived to finish fifth from bottom after losing at Chelsea in the FA Cup third round.

At international level Dixie found himself on home ground against his great adversary Elisha Scott. In October 1928 England played Ireland at Goodison when the Liverpool goalkeeper saved a penalty from the Everton centre forward, although Dean did manage to score the goal that gave England a 2–1 win after Joe Hulme had hit their opener. Dixie, talking to a journalist, reflected on Scott's save in the *Sunday Chronicle*, admitting: 'I've been thinking about it for some time, especially after seeing the pictures showing how the wonder man Elisha Scott got my penalty kick away . . . The pictures show two actions, one with Scott down on his knee and the ball at his knee and the other leaning to his right to pat down the ball. There have been many arguments about his save. Some say the ball was shot straight at him, which is a libel on Scott . . . Let me tell you about his latest. Scott was at the dinner after the match with the other internationals and Billy Gillespie of Ireland, not being too well through injury and wanting to catch an early train, had popped off to the station. Speeches were made by all and sundry and, finally, Scott was asked to deputise for his captain. Up rises Mr Scott and says: 'Gentlemen, I'm nothing of a speaker in any way. Any speakin' I've got to do is done on the field of play. Thank you.' Then he sat down!'

It was a winter of severe weather and the chill for Everton lasted through to Spring. In an alarming finale they lost their last six games, three of them without Dean who, despite his injury-ravaged campaign, scored 26 goals from 29 First Division appearances, which included five hat tricks. He was in sizzling form over Christmas when three of his trebles – in home wins over Newcastle, Bolton and Derby – came in a four-match spell between December 22 and January 1. Yet there were rumours that Dixie had been dropped when he went out of the team in February and missed the return derby against Liverpool when Everton completed the double over their great foes with a 2–1 win at Anfield through goals from Tom Griffiths and the ultra versatile Tommy White, who took over at centre forward. Dean, though, dismissed the gossip that he had lost his place and revealed that doctors had diagnosed rheumatism caused by persistent leg injuries. Such was Dixie's patchwork season that he came back after a two game absence in February, had to miss the next five, returned for another match and was then ruled out of the next three before resuming for the last three games.

In the midst of this he was named ahead of David Jack in the England side, although this time he could not weave his magic at Hampden in April as Scotland won 1–0 in what would be Dean's last international for two years. But if the swift removal from their championship pedestal was painful for Everton and the Goodison faithful – less than 20,000 of whom turned out for the last home game against Manchester United – there was sheer agony to follow.

Just two seasons after being crowned champions Everton, one of the original 12 founder members of the Football League, were relegated for the first time in their history. Dixie Dean would be playing his football in the Second Division. Not even Dean's feat of scoring in each of his first 12 appearances that season – rattling in 16 goals – could preserve Goodison's proud top flight status.

It was another year in which he was wracked by injury, although he did achieve the impressive figures of 25 goals in 27 outings in League and FA Cup, in which Everton ambitions were ended by a 4–1 fourth round knock-out at Blackburn. Dean's goal haul included a satisfying four against Liverpool – two in a 3–0 win at Anfield in September and another brace in a 3–3 draw in the Goodison return in January. But by the time Amy Johnson grabbed the headlines by landing her Gipsy Moth in Darwin on April 24, 1930, to become the first woman to fly solo from Britain to Australia, Everton were also heading down under.

Injury ruled out Dixie from Everton's final five games, of which they won four and drew one, ending with a 4–1 home conquest of Sunderland with Dean's replacement Tommy White scoring a hat trick, taking his personal total to seven in those last five games. It was all too late, however, and Everton had their first experience of relegation after finishing bottom with 35 points, just four fewer than 14th placed FA Cup winners Arsenal. The supporters were shocked, stunned and angry. They were also anxious about Everton's ability to reclaim their place among the elite of English football. The club, who had spent money on new players and used 29 in all in a fruitless attempt to beat relegation, reported a balance sheet deficit of more than £12,000. Yet this low point in Everton fortunes proved to be the dark before a golden new dawn. The board won a vote of confidence by 82 votes to 61 at the club's annual meeting and horizons began to brighten. Dixie admitted:

The season we went down we didn't play too well. Not by any means. There's no getting away from that fact . . . As far as I was concerned I still managed to score a few even though I was in and out of the hospital and nursing home with injuries. I spent a lot of time in those places. In fact, I saw more theatres than

Morecambe and Wise. But mine were operating theatres . . . To me, from fairly early on in that season, it seemed we were destined to go down. We couldn't save ourselves. All our injuries started to take their toll. But when we kicked off in the Second Division I'd pretty well recovered from the operations I'd had and was having a bit of luck . . . Things that hadn't come off for me started to come off again. It was like the old days a few seasons earlier. It was an absolute treat. I was playing like the tank I'd been in 1927–28. I was ramming them in all over the place . . . We were also seeing the benefit of one or two more players. We got a new goalkeeper in Bill Coggins, who'd arrived from Bristol City at the end of the previous season, and Benny Williams, a Welsh international full back, who we signed from Swansea, took over as captain from Warney Cresswell . . . I had a bit of a lark with Bill Coggins. When he first came I told him that Everton players had to dress in a bowler and plus fours to travel to away games. He fell for it hook, line and sinker! He actually borrowed money to buy the outfit. You can imagine the scene when he turned up dressed like that to get on the train at Lime Street Station. It was a riot. But Bill, a country boy, took it all in good heart. He had a great sense of humour . . . Benny Williams took over at right back with Warney Cresswell moving over to the left. Benny captained Wales and a few years later, in an international against Ireland, he had the misfortune to break the leg of his team-mate Jackie Coulter, an outside left we signed from Belfast Celtic. What made it even more unfortunate was that Benny and Jackie lodged together in Wallasey. In the international at Wrexham they tried to sell each other a 'dummy' and they each went the wrong way! Benny happened to catch Jackie and nobody was more broken hearted about it than Benny. Jackie had his leg set and recovered. But he went to a club in New Brighton, fell down the stairs and broke the same leg again. He ended up working in the shipyard in Belfast . . . After we'd been relegated we signed Charlie Gee from Stockport and he took over at centre half from another Wales captain, Tommy Griffiths, who'd been a great defender. Charlie was, too, and went on to play for England. Tommy Johnson was another new player. He came from Manchester City. Tommy and Jimmy Dunn were our inside forwards and they helped us get things going again.

Dean and his team-mates, as if stung by the indignity of relegation, laid waste to the Second Division and rattled up some huge scores. As Britain's unemployment doubled in little more than a year to top two million and the world braced itself for a slump and economic depression the crowds turned out to get an eye-witness view of Dean, the great centre forward who was now appearing at many grounds for the first time. Everton's opening Second Division fixture at Plymouth attracted more than 34,000 spectators but even Dixie was overshadowed by an early goal glut from Tommy White, the versatile product of the Southport Boys team. He scored nine in the opening seven games before being injured and having to drop out of the side. In came Jimmy Dunn who, with Dixie, also began hitting the target with alacrity to send Everton exploding into the new season with 12 wins and only one defeat in their first 16 games. The side regularly lined up liked this: Bill Coggins; Ben Williams, Warney Cresswell; Lachie McPherson or Jim McClure, Tommy Griffiths then Charlie Gee, Jock Thomson; Ted Critchley, Jimmy Dunn, Dean, Tommy Johnson and Jimmy Stein. In addition, White made 10 appearances in three positions and scored 10 goals. But the star turn was Dean, who bagged 39 goals in 37 League outings plus another nine goals in the club's stirring FA Cup run which ended with a 1–0 semi final defeat by eventual winners West Brom at Old Trafford. In the two competitions that season he scored four goals on four occasions.

However, the Cup semi final in March came close to disaster and had distinct overtones of a tragedy at the same stage of the same competition which would tragically unfold in Sheffield some 58 years later. The Old Trafford gates were locked with 70,000 spectators inside – some 3,000 below its then official capacity – and another estimated 20,000 outside the ground. That caused crushing on the stadium forecourt which left 333 people injured. The game itself was frequently interrupted by fans spilling onto the pitch and Joe Wilkinson, understudy to injured right

winger Ted Critchley, had to ask for a police horse to be moved so he
could take a corner kick. As a football match it was one to forget for
Everton, who had the chances to have beaten their Second Division
promotion rivals by a big margin. Dean, with uncharacteristic profligacy,
missed two glittering scoring opportunities and his team-mates spurned
others. To compound Everton's agony, goalkeeper Bill Coggins failed
to cut out a cross in the second half and West Brom captain Tommy
Glidden collected the game's only goal to steer his side to Wembley the
following month, where a 2–1 win over Birmingham made them only
the fifth club from outside the top division to win the FA Cup. It would
not happen again until Sunderland's triumph in 1973.

Everton built a substantial League and Cup goals collection of fours
and fives and also hit sixes, sevens and, remarkably, a couple of nines,
as they secured an instant return to the top flight. They finished as
champions, seven points ahead of runners-up West Brom, and hit a
club record 121 goals. Plymouth fell 9–1 at Goodison on December
27 – Dean scoring four – and neighbours Southport were crushed by
an identical score in the sixth round of the Cup at Goodison. It was a
record win at that stage of the competition. Dixie again claimed four
of the goals, just as he had done in the 6–0 fourth round dispatch of
Crystal Palace on their own Selhurst Park stage.

Indeed, Dean was a veritable lion in winter and created another
record when he scored in the 4–0 home drubbing of Wolves on
November 8. It was the 200th League goal of his career on his 207th
appearance for Everton and Tranmere, at the age of 23 years 290 days.
Strangely, it was the same age at which Jimmy Greaves completed his
double century more than 30 years later. Government minister Sir
Freddie Marquis – later Lord Woolton – presented Dixie with a gold
medal to commemorate his double century and the *Liverpool Daily
Post* observed: 'It is a fine record considering his comparatively short
career. No footballer in history had a record of such consistency in
League soccer or ever will, perhaps.'

Dean's other four-goal performance that season came in a 10-goal
thriller against Oldham on December 6. At noon that day a blanket of
fog enveloped Goodison with a postponement seeming certain.

But it lifted in time for the 2.15 p.m. kick off and although Oldham struck first they went home across Lancashire on the wrong end of a 6–4 scoreline, with Ted Critchley and Dunn adding to Dixie's big haul. It signalled the start of a record-breaking sequence by Dean who went on to score in 12 consecutive League games, yielding him 23 goals, a prolific run that ended with a brace against Barnsley on February 18. Of all Everton's 'victims' that season, none suffered more than Charlton. The London club, hammered 7–1 at Goodison in October when Dean scored twice, must have had a sense of deja vu in the return at The Valley in February, two days after Malcolm Campbell set a new world land speed record of 245 miles per hour in his specially-built car, Bluebird. For Charlton, it was Blue Murder. Everton rammed another seven past them, this time Dixie scoring a hat trick, with six of the goals coming in a blistering 25 minutes before the interval. Charlton did not even have the scant consolation of getting on the scoresheet, this time crashing 7–0. It put Everton six points clear of second-place Tottenham – who were destined to finish third and miss promotion – and the *Liverpool Echo* reporter 'Bee' declared: 'The Goodison men have made a meal of the London club – in fact, a four-course dinner! This, indeed, was Everton at their greatest, the pinnacle of brilliant forward play.' The game was also notable for the rare incidence of all five forwards scoring with Ted Critchley, Jimmy Dunn, Tommy Johnson and Jimmy Stein also on the mark.

Two more goals for Dixie in the next match – a 5–2 home win over Barnsley – took him on to 199 in the League for Everton alone. But he had to wait another six weeks to register that elusive 200th. He hit the woodwork time and again and when he took a penalty against Millwall on March 21 the fans were ready to acclaim another Dean landmark. Alas, he sent the spot kick against a post and although he fired the rebound into the net it was disallowed because no opponent had made contact with the ball! Goal number 200 for Dixie finally arrived as the first of his brace in a 4–2 home win against Bradford Park Avenue on April 4. Dixie achieved the feat in his 197th League appearance for Everton at the age of 24 years 72 days.

The win over Bradford also ensured Everton of the Second Division title with five games still to be played. That feat, and the inevitable easing of the pressure, probably explains why Everton lost three and won only one of those remaining matches. But it had been an unforgettable season for Dixie, Everton and their fans. It was one also marked by a string of introspective measures by the Football Association which seem barely believable in the modern age of massive cash-generating television coverage of English football and its heady cocktail of foreign imports at playing and managerial level. Television, of course, was then a medium of the future but the domestic ruling body even perceived a threat from radio, for which a licence cost 10 shillings, 50 pence in today's currency. Amazingly, they banned all broadcasts of League and Cup games and – ironic given today's cosmopolitan, polyglot state of English football – barred clubs from signing foreigners, of which only a smattering had been recruited anyway. Even when rules had been relaxed decades later there were only 35 foreign players in the Premiership when it was launched in 1992. Back in the 1930's the FA even contemplated banning players from the same club facing each other in internationals. Two other decisions they did pass were to ban floodlights and order all public clocks at football grounds to be removed. But problems are made to be solved and the BBC countered the broadcasting ban at big games by sending a batch of reporters as paying spectators, each of them leaving the ground at set times to broadcast their account of the match up to that stage so that, eventually through this teamwork, the listener was informed about the entire 90 minutes.

Thankfully, there was no suppressing the news of Dixie Dean and his scoring exploits in a season when he also had to face a charge of careless driving in his modestly small Morris car. A pedestrian alleged Dixie had knocked him down while trying to overtake a Birkenhead tram. The charge upset Dixie. But justice was done when the case was dismissed after witnesses gave evidence that Dixie had been driving at not more than 10 miles an hour and even as slowly as five miles per hour . . . and the pedestrian was not seriously hurt. But William Ralph Dean moved with considerable pace and power on the football field, his speed off the mark evident in his performance the previous summer in a 100-yard handicap sprint at Ayr in Scotland during a trip to the races. He was persuaded to run by his friend Freddie Tarbuck, father of Jimmy, despite the fact that Dixie had already drunk several sherries in the tented bar and had no kit. Unknown to Dixie, book-maker Freddie had entered him for the all-comers race at odds of 100–1. Although it was a handicap event the lateness of his entry meant that Dixie literally had to start from scratch and, because he had no shorts, compete in his underpants. He made light of all that by winning with two yards to spare ahead of the favourite, Powderhall Sprint victor and Ayr United footballer Jock Smith, who also ran off scratch. Once again, it was evidence of Dean's superb athleticism which prompted the noted athletics commentator Ron Pickering to observe that if Dixie's sporting career had taken another path he could have been an Olympic high jumper. While Dean came away from Ayr races with his prize of a canteen of cutlery, the big smile belonged to Freddie after he had collected his winnings.

As Dean was spearheading Everton's freescoring return to the top flight his friend Tom 'Pongo' Waring's 49 goals for Aston Villa, making him the country's top goalscorer, took the Midlands club to the runners-up spot behind champions Arsenal. Dixie's own celebrity massively broadened his social circles to include a host of showbusiness stars, including Tessie O'Shea, Noel Purcell, George Robey and Flanagan and Allen. One of his closest friends was Dickie Henderson senior. His son, Dickie junior, was just a small boy when his father introduced him to the Everton legend at Birkenhead's Argyle Theatre in the early 1930s and the youngster held Dixie in high esteem throughout his life. But, beyond his sublime football talent which enraptured millions, there was nothing theatrical about Dixie. He never stood on ceremony and remained true to his blunt, working class Merseyside roots. While he enjoyed himself whenever possible he was a man of the people who played for the people and was never averse to proclaiming his social and political views with a small 'p'. He was a great champion, for instance, of Bessie Braddock, the firebrand Liverpool city councillor who became Labour MP for Liverpool Exchange for 25 years from 1945 until her death in 1970. 'You couldn't fool Bessie and you'd never want to try,' said Dixie. 'She was as straight as a die and I thought the world of her.' Luke Hogan, a former Lord Mayor of Liverpool and chairman of the city's Watch Committee, was another politician who earned

Dean's admiration because of his consideration for the working man and society's disadvantaged in an era of massive impoverishment. He had no such feelings towards J. H. Thomas, general secretary of Dixie's engine driver father's union, the National Union of Railwaymen. Thomas joined the 1931 British Coalition Government and backed their decision to cut rail employees' weekly wages from 44 to 38 shillings. 'He was a railwayman who let his own people down and I had no time for that man,' said Dean, for whom the bitter issue of rail pay was very close to home. It also cost Thomas the NUR leadership and his union pension.

Dixie was always keen to help charitable causes and youth clubs and unemployed youngsters, who were all too numerous during the depression-hit 1930s. Stories are legion of him making prize presentations, arranging fund-raising matches in various sports and giving up his time to coach aspiring footballers, even making groups of youngsters cups of tea and soup. Hardly the image of a superstar. He disliked too much ceremony and after he had presented prizes at a local primary school's speech day the governors, headmaster and visitors 'lost' their famous guest of honour when they retired for drinks and refreshments. He was eventually discovered in the school playground enthusiastically involved in a game of football with a tennis ball and two teams of youngsters. One of his pleasurable off duty activities was to meet up with his friend, boxing great Nel Tarleton, and pop into 'The Widows' pub on Scotland Road. 'The pair of them would laugh and joke with the boys in the bar as if they, just like the rest of the lads, had come straight from work at the docks instead of being two fantastic sporting heroes,' recalled one regular. Dean's love of cricket also underlined that he had forgiven the Birkett family for that boyhood Sunday afternoon dousing in Claughton! Reginald Birkett, the local football league secretary who claimed to have been the first to sign Dixie on an official form, found himself seconded for cricket duty. 'I played cricket for St Mary's, Birkenhead, and one day I was walking down Lord Street in Liverpool city centre when I was hailed from a distance by the ebullient Dixie. He then inveigled me into playing cricket for Everton FC, who used to play the summer game in the football close season.'

An anecdote that brilliantly captures Dixie's down-to-earth nature contrasts quaintly with the norm today, when players at the end of their career become eager television pundits when the mud on the boots they have just hung up is not even dry. Pathe News, a hugely popular cinema newsreel feature in pre and post war years, invited Dixie for a filmed interview at their Wardour Street studio in London where a make-up artist got a lot more than he bargained for, as Dixie recalled: 'This here chap came up to me acting like a big sissy. He had a high voice and spoke all posh, as if he'd swallowed a grapefruit, never mind a plum! He asked me to sit down and then started putting this make-up on my chops. I said: "What do you think you're doing?" He said: "I'm just putting some powder on your face to take the shine off." I turned round and said to him: "If you come near me with that stuff I'll put a bloody shine on your face!"' But Dixie Dean and Everton were destined to shine brightly for the next two seasons as more glittering prizes arrived at Goodison.

# CHAPTER SEVEN

# *A Wedding Ring And Another Medal*

Dixie Dean's fame, which encompassed his life-size wax effigy being displayed at Madame Tussauds next to cricket legend Jack Hobbs, was accompanied by the inevitable rumour, gossip and tittle-tattle that goes with the territory of celebrity. His company was sought at all levels of society and young women, in particular, were known to make fanciful and exaggerated claims of undying love, engagement and even paternity after just one dance with the dashing, eligible and magnetic football personality. Dixie laughed off most of them, even telling jokes to his friends at his own expense inspired by some of the more lurid stories. But amidst the adulation for Dixie one young lady attracted his serious attention. Her name was Ethel Fossard, a beautiful girl who made a stunning first impression on Dixie when he first set eyes on her at a Liverpool restaurant. 'They met when my mother was working as a waitress at Reeces Restaurant which I'm told was a very popular venue in those days,' said Dixie's second son, Geoff, born in 1935 in the family's club house in Goodison Avenue, adjacent to the stadium. 'Reeces was the place to go and I suppose as my mum was a beautiful, fair-haired young woman my dad fell for her in a big way.' As it happened, Ethel had also worked close to Dean's Birkenhead home and was already courting a man whom Dixie knew. Fate, however, dramatically and tragically intervened. Ethel's boyfriend fell ill and died. 'My dad went to the funeral and a little while later he and my mum started going out together,' added Geoff. 'They got married at St James' Church in Birkenhead in 1931 and although the date and place of the wedding was deliberately never publicised the details leaked out and my mum and dad told me that the place was absolutely packed, with crowds around the church and down the streets. They held their wedding reception at the Blossoms Hotel in Chester and I believe their honeymoon consisted of a tour of British race courses which I think my mum thoroughly enjoyed.' Dixie was 24 when he married, his bride 20. 'She was a lovely lady, a very gentle, caring woman and she was a marvellous mother to me, my two brothers Bill and Ralph and our sister Barbara,' added Geoff.

After the honeymoon and at the start of his new life as a married man, Dixie was appointed as Everton's new captain, his qualities

The happy couple: Dixie and Ethel all smiles on their wedding day in 1931 (copyright unknown)

of leadership formally recognised as the club resumed life in the top flight of English football, following their swashbuckling promotion as Second Division champions. Not even the most ardent Everton fan, though, could have dreamed of what was to unfold for the Goodison club. When the new season of 1931–32 opened, Bill Coggins was displaced as Everton goalkeeper by a man who was to become a by-word of consistency and durability. His name was Ted Sagar, snapped up by Everton from under the nose of Hull City in 1929.

He had made his debut for Everton two seasons earlier and was to remain at Goodison until 1952–53, making a total of 497 senior appearances and winning four England caps. Sagar had his last senior outing at the age of 42, his span of 24 years at Everton being the longest any player has spent professionally with a single English club. The season opened in August 1931 just a few days after a coalition national government was formed under Ramsay MacDonald to grapple with Britain's worst ever financial crisis and spiralling unemployment. Football provided much relief from the depression and Everton launched their new campaign with a 3–2 home win over Birmingham, thanks to a Jimmy Dunn hat trick. Although injury forced Dean to miss the second match at Portsmouth, the ever reliable Tommy White stepped in and scored another hat trick to give Everton a 3–0 victory. Indeed, Dixie had to wait until the sixth match of the season for his first goals. But how sweet they were . . . a rapid hat trick against Liverpool, and his famous rival Elisha Scott, in a 3–1 conquest of the old enemy in front of a 55,000 Anfield crowd.

> I put three past Elisha in the first nine minutes and his language was unbelievable. He'd done his usual before the match by saying to me: 'You'll get none today, you black headed so and so!' I said to him: 'Listen, Leesh, if I don't score against you today I'm going back to work on the railway, where I started.' You should have seen his face when that third one went in! Me? I just bowed to the Liverpool fans, which is something I always did when I scored against them. When I got goals against other clubs I was delighted but when I got them against Liverpool I only had sympathy for them!

The *Liverpool Echo* match report declared: 'Dean went into this game like a giant. He showed he can still be the best centre forward in the world if the chances are at hand. Little room is needed by this bulky man . . . He stood by the rival captain Bradshaw and seemed a tiny tot. Yet Dean went up to head balls that Bradshaw should have had and Dean's head was the first to connect. He was inspired and inspiring and it was good to see such earnest football from this young man and captain . . . Virility and superiority stamped him throughout the day's hard toil as a natural centre forward – the best header of a ball the game has ever had – and a genius at the art of placing himself in a proper position – and away from opponents!' It was Dean's second Mersey derby treble – both at Anfield – and as football entered the 21st century and a new millennium that hat trick on September 19, 1931 still stood as the last to be scored by an Everton player against

Liverpool. The victory at Liverpool was timely as Everton had lost their two previous games, at Derby County and home to Manchester City, without scoring a goal. Following their Anfield success they won their next outing, at home to Derby, through two Tommy Johnson goals before travelling to face formidable reigning champions Arsenal, who had cruised home the previous season seven points clear of runners-up Aston Villa. The Highbury club extended their sequence of impressive results against Everton with a 3–2 win and completed the double with a 3–1 victory at Goodison the following February. By now, Arsenal boss Herbert Chapman, had refined his 'third centre back' ploy to a fine, negative art, deputing Herbie Roberts to mark Dean and nullify the menacing, scoring threat of the player he had tried and failed to sign.

Chapman was the first great manager, the forerunner of the modern breed with a progressive outlook, a flair for publicity, extravagant transfers and tactical plans. Dean recalled:

Herbie Roberts and I were great pals. In fact, we'd often have a game of golf together. But that season we were closer than we'd ever been because he just stuck to me like glue, following me wherever I went . . . I said to Tosh Johnson during the game: 'There's something going on here. This here Roberts feller is going everywhere with me. So, listen, I'm going to take him for a walk and when he's out of the way try to dart in!'

After a while being followed by Herbie I turned to him and said: 'I'm going off now.' He didn't know what to think and said: 'Where are you going, Bill?' I said back to him: 'What's going on here? You're following me all over the place.'

He replied: 'Mr Chapman told me that wherever you go I've got to go with you.' I said 'Alright, come on then. I'm going for a jimmy riddle in the lavatory. Are you coming, too!' He didn't know what to say but all the spectators standing by the line heard what I'd said and burst out laughing.

Dixie and Everton responded to their reverse at Highbury with an astonishing scoring rampage in which Dean achieved the most blistering output even of his goal-laden career. In seven consecutive home games Everton scored an amazing 46 times while Dixie's personal figures comprised a barely credible haul of 25 goals in 12 successive outings. Everton began the extravaganza with a 3–2 home win over Blackpool, which launched a nine-match run of eight wins and a draw. Dixie failed to get on the scoresheet that day but next time out two shots and a header brought him a hat trick in a 5–1 mauling of Sheffield United at Bramall Lane. United's city neighbours Wednesday were next to be put to the sword. Up to a few minutes before kick-off thousands waited outside Goodison fearing that fog would force a postponement. But the game started on schedule and the fans were thrilled by a goal glut with both sides receiving a thunderous ovation. Dean proved to be Wednesday's chief executioner with five goals in a massive 9–3 triumph, his friend and former Tranmere player Ellis Rimmer scoring one of the Sheffield side's goals. Dixie's nap hand equalled his haul against Manchester United four years earlier. Dean followed his blank in Everton's 3–2 win at Aston Villa with a brace of goals in the 8–1 home demolition of Newcastle and after injury kept him out of the goalless duel at Huddersfield he was back in searing, scoring mood a week later with another nap hand of goals in a 7–2 home crushing of Chelsea. Dixie had reason to be especially pleased with his five-goal offering:

Chelsea had signed a centre half called J. P. O'Dowd and paid a lot of money for him. Well, he started shouting his mouth off in the paper that I wouldn't get a kick against him. Right, I thought, we'll see. I'll be there. As a matter of fact, I had a few pints the night before the game and old Harry Cooke and I actually slept in the trainer's room at Goodison. We just kipped down on the skips and used the St John Ambulance blankets to keep warm. Next morning, Harry brought me some coffee and by the time I had my usual sherry and eggs before the game I felt tip top. Well, by half time I'd stuck five in the old onion bag, four of them with the old heading lark! In fact, I had a chance to get my sixth goal but my boot got stuck in the mud with only the goalkeeper to beat. I didn't see O'Dowd after the match but, funnily enough, he and I played together for England against Ireland the following year.

Those who witnessed Dean's display against Chelsea reported that it was the most masterly exhibition of heading ever seen. There was not even a half time respite for the stunned visitors because poor visibility prompted the referee to merely order a change of ends after 45 minutes and immediately resume play. Remarkably, given Dean's scorching form and the choice of venue, he was omitted from the England team that beat Wales 3–1 at Anfield four days later, with Dixie's friend and fellow Tranmere Rovers product Tom 'Pongo' Waring of Aston Villa getting the nod from selectors to lead the attack.

The romp against Chelsea was followed by a narrow 2–1 win at Grimsby before another remarkable Goodison afternoon when Leicester were overwhelmed 9–2, Dixie scoring four of them, to secure Everton's place at the League summit which they had occupied since the end of October. Archie Clark, signed from Luton the previous May to become regular right half that season, was also on the scoresheet against Leicester, his only goal in a Goodison career that embraced only 42 appearances.

Everton's unbeaten sequence was ended at West Ham a week later, the London side winning 4–2 and keeping Dixie locked out. Four days later, however, at another London venue, he had cause for double celebration. He was recalled by England and marked his return for his country with a goal on a memorable afternoon at Highbury. Spain were the visitors, only the second foreign nation to play in England after Belgium in 1923 and 1924. They were also the first foreign country to defeat England, having won 4–3 in Madrid in May 1929. In the Spanish goal that day, as he was at Highbury, was the legendary Ricardo Zamora who had been signed by Real Madrid from Barcelona the previous year for a then world record fee for a keeper of £6,000. He had just received a £3,000 benefit from Real who paid him the princely sum of £40 a week. These were stupendous amounts at a time when Dean and his English colleagues collected a weekly wage of eight pounds and a six pound fee to play for their country. Zamora, also the Spain captain, was reputedly the world's highest paid player and regarded as football's finest goalkeeper. Dean and his team-mates ensured he would never forget that winter's day in north London. The

Dixie shakes hands with Spain goalkeeper Ricardo Zamora. When they met on the field in December 1931, Dean scored one of the goals in England's 7–1 win (copyright *Popperfoto*)

Spanish keeper made a theatrical entrance in front of the 55,000 crowd wearing rubber knee pads – hardly required in the Highbury mud – and a peaked cap. As the pre-match band were about to leave the pitch Dixie ran to the bandmaster and asked if they would play something Spanish. The band duly obliged, striking up the march from Bizet's 'Carmen'. Zamora, to the dumbstruck reaction of the spectators, responded by goose-stepping to his goal and bowing to the crowd. He then proceeded to leap acrobatically around his goalmouth during the kick-in to produce a series of grossly over-spectacular saves. And while that was going on Dixie turned to his Everton and England team-mate Charlie Gee and bet his six pounds international fee that they'd put more than five goals past Zamora, a wager Charlie accepted. And just three minutes into the game the myth of Zamora's invincibility was exposed when Dixie headed the ball to the feet of John Smith and the Portsmouth forward's low drive went straight through the Spaniard's grasp into the net. Another three minutes elapsed when Dixie's Goodison team-mate Tommy Johnson, who had been signed from Manchester City in 1930, fired in a less than menacing shot which posed no apparent threat. But Zamora stood rooted to the spot as the ball passed him for England's second goal. At that moment of personal agony the celebrated Spanish star must have reflected wistfully on the absence of his wife, a regular spectator at Zamora's matches and whom he regarded as talismanic. She also acted as his food taster to help quell his fear of being poisoned! This time she could not attend because of the Spanish FA's refusal to allow wives to accompany players on the trip. Perhaps her absence haunted him. Certainly the game became a calamity for Zamora and his team. Smith scored again before the interval and in the second half Sammy Crooks scored twice, Johnson added his second and Dean scored his 18th –

Dixie challenges Spain goalkeeper Ricardo Zamora during England's 7-1 rout of Spain at Highbury in December 1931 (copyright unknown)

and what was to be his last – England goal to make it 7–0. A last minute reply by Spain left winger Gordstiza was merely academic and the imposing figure of Zamora walked off the Highbury stage in tears. His career continued for a further five years in which he appeared in another dozen internationals and completed 1,000 first class appearances. But he could never erase the memory of the day Dixie Dean and England rained goals past him.

Dean was on the mark again when he resumed League action with Everton at home to Middlesbrough three days later, scoring a single in a 5–1 win. He also scored at Bolton a week later, although Everton lost 2–1, before embarking on two Christmas games in 24 hours against Blackburn. Dixie scored once in a 5–3 Christmas Day reverse at Ewood Park but the following day bagged a Goodison hat trick as Everton extracted revenge with a 5–0 conquest of their Lancashire rivals. However, an emphatic 4–0 reverse at Birmingham in their first fixture of 1932 was Everton's fourth defeat in six games and their title ambitions were now wobbling. They received no comfort, either, when they switched to FA Cup action, being drawn at home to Liverpool in the third round.

A 57,000-plus crowd packed into Goodison for this eagerly awaited derby collision. Admission prices of one shilling in the ground, one and six pence in the paddock and four pence in the boys pen generated receipts of £5,047. This is how the teams lined up: – Everton: Sagar; Williams, Bocking; Clark, Gee, Thomson; Critchley, White, Dean, Johnson, Stein. Liverpool: Scott; Steel, Jackson; Morrison, Bradshaw, McDougall; McRorie, Hodgson, Barton, Wright, Gunson. Bill Bocking came into the Everton side in place of former skipper Warney Cresswell, ruled out for the first time in almost two years because of ankle damage. Interestingly, the celebrated full back was given the role of press box steward for the day – and the football writers had plenty to occupy them. One of them who was present, well known Merseyside sports journalist the late Don Kendall, reflected: 'This match marked one of the best recoveries in derby history. Everton, then Second Division champions, were leading the way in the First while Liverpool were an ordinary, nondescript team but ambitious, as usual . . . Everton, playing towards the Gwladys Street

A proud Dixie Dean after winning his first England cap against Wales in 1927.

A young Dixie Dean in a picture thought to have been taken during his early career at Tranmere.

"Thanks for looking after me".... Dixie leaves the nursing home after yet another operation, this time for an ankle injury.

Time to relax off duty.
Wedding guest Dixie
enjoys a beer and a
cigarette.

Bridging a football
generation; Dixie (centre)
with his Everton
successor Tommy
Lawton (right) and team-
mate George Jackson
during a club tour of
Denmark.

(Picture appeared in Lawton's book
'Football Is My Business' published by
Sporting Handbooks Ltd in 1946).

Skipper Dixie stepping
out ready for action.

**ABOVE**: Time for refreshment; Dixie and some of his Everton team-mates slake their thirst.

© F.A. Fyfe, 1 Hollytree Road, Woolton, Liverpool

**RIGHT**: Behind the wheel for charity; Dixie in a one horse-power car at Liverpool's Paramount Theatre in January 1931 to promote the students' magazine '*Pantosfinx*', sold in aid of hospital funds.

© Morath's Pictorial Press Agency, 44 Whitechapel, Liverpool

Dixie in FA Cup action against Crystal Palace in 1931. He scored four goals in Everton's 6-0 win.

Elegance personified – a sharp-suited Dixie pictured on the Goodison pitch.

ABOVE: Welcome, señor ... England centre forward Dixie shakes hands with Spanish goalkeeper Ricardo Zamora before Everton's game at West Ham in December 1931. Four days later Zamora, whose £6,000 transfer fee made him the world's most expensive keeper, was reduced to tears as Dean and his international colleages rained goals past him in England's 7-1 hammering of the Spaniards. © Central News

BELOW: Dixie races in ready to pounce as Spanish goalkeeper Ricardo Zamora grabs the ball during England's 7-1 win at Highbury in December 1931.
© The Topical Press Agency Ltd., 10-11 Red Lion Court, Fleet Street, London

**ABOVE**: The Everton team that lost 2-1 at Aston Villa on March 25, 1933.
Back row; Tommy White, Warney Cresswell, Ted Sagar, Cliff Britton, Jock
Thomson. Front row; Albert Geldard, Jimmy 'Nat' Cunliffe (who scored Everton's
goal on his debut that day), Dixie Dean, Tom Johnson, Jimmy Stein, Billy Cook.

**BELOW**: Dixie, with his arm around his mother Sarah, among a wedding party in the
1930's. Others pictured include some of his aunts and uncles.

Signatures of the victors ... the autographs of Everton's 1933 FA Cup winning team.

**ABOVE**: Dixie (at the back in train doorway) and the Everton players and officials on their departure from Liverpool's Lime Street Station in May 1934 to become the first Football League club to play matches in the Canary Islands.

**RIGHT**: Tommy Lawton, Dean's successor for Everton and England, pictured training with a punch ball as a 16-year-old Burnley amateur shortly before his Football League début in March 1936.

Dixie in a heading duel with Arsenal's George Male at Highbury in August 1936, the opening day of the season.
© Central Press Photos Ltd.

BELOW: The 1937-38 Everton squad. Back row left to right: Theo Kelly (secretary), Cliff Britton, Jimmy 'Nat' Cunliffe, Ted Sagar, Charlie Gee, Tory Gillick, Harry Cooke (trainer). Middle row: George Jackson, Albert Geldard, Billy Cook (who has signed the picture), Dixie Dean, Tommy Lawton, Alex Stevenson, P.G. Dougal. Front row: Gordon Watson, Jack Jones, Joe Mercer.

Dixie at work in Littlewoods supply stores, Liverpool, October 1970.

A Rovers Return; Dixie Dean attends a celebrity dinner at his first Football League club, Tranmere Rovers, flanked by (left to right) Dave Russell, Kenny Campbell, Noel Kelly, Joe Mercer, Billy Liddell, George Yardley and Jackie Wright.

Dixie's daughter Barbara and son Geoff alongside their father's portrait which has pride of place at Goodison Park.

Dixie's son Geoff (left) shakes hands with sculptor Tom Murphy after the unveiling of the bronze statue of the Everton legend in May 2001.

© John Keith

Geoff Dean alongside the statue of his father.

The glitter of silverware and the smile of
success. Triumphant Everton captain Dixie Dean
shows off the FA Cup as the team's train leaves
London Euston for an amazing Merseyside
homecoming in 1933.

(picture given to John Keith by Dixie)

The boots of a legend; the footwear in which
Dixie dispatched a fusillade of goals.

end (the stand was not built until 1938) had a dream opening. In the first attack Dean streaked through the Liverpool defence and from just inside the box struck a terrific shot. The ball went all along the floor and flashed into the corner before the Irish international Elisha Scott could reach it. That was after only 25 seconds! Dixie had once again proved the real bogey man to Scott . . . It took Liverpool a long time to get over that early shock. But the immaculate 'Tiny' Bradshaw and the inspiring Jimmy 'Parson' Jackson, Scotsmen both, gradually brought back into the Liverpool team their genuine, 100 per cent spirit which for so long has thrilled supporters and struck fear into enemy hearts . . . Liverpool began stifling those diagonal cross-field passes which Tommy Johnson and Tommy White featured. Into the game with genuine power came Gordon Hodgson and Dave Wright. It was Wright who, shortly before the interval, made the vital pass which enabled Gordon Gunson to cut in and crash home the equaliser. Curiously, both Wright and Gunson had been signed by Liverpool from Sunderland . . . Everton lost confidence and skill as Liverpool resolutely took charge. Buoyed up by thoughts of their comeback after such an early setback Liverpool became the dictators . . . After 75 minutes Gunson swept down the wing before making the perfect cross onto which Hodgson swooped to head the dramatic winner, a tremendous victory which even Evertonians admitted the Reds had earned.'

The official time of Dean's goal has now been accepted as 32 seconds, the fourth fastest in more than a century of Mersey derby combat after those by Liverpool's Jack Balmer (10 secs, February 16, 1938), Everton's Peter Farrell (12 seconds, December 24, 1949) and Liverpool's Kenny Dalglish (20 seconds, September 21, 1985).

However, the *Liverpool Echo* reporter 'Bee' presented a different view of Dean's goal. He said that Scott was deceived on an icy pitch when Dixie saw his shot heading for the opposite corner of the net from the one he intended and that the goalkeeper 'went down tardily'. He also reported that the conditions prevented Dean putting Everton 2–1 up, the Everton captain sliding on his back as he was shaping to shoot. If the game had been drawn man-of-the-match Jackson would have missed the replay at Anfield the following Monday afternoon as he had to return to Cambridge to continue his studies for the ministry. Liverpool's Wembley ambitions that season were ultimately ended by Chelsea, who won 2–0 at Anfield in the sixth round, and Everton soon tasted revenge on their greatest rivals who finished 10th in the First Division.

Dean was again on the mark in Everton's next match, a 4–2 home win over Sunderland, which was followed by a 1–0 defeat at Manchester City prior to a swift resumption of Goodison combat with Liverpool, this time with crucial championship points at stake. Jackson was missing from the Liverpool side and although the visitors managed to prevent Dixie scoring, a goal apiece from Ted Critchley and Tommy White reversed the Cup scoreline with Dave Wright replying. It completed a League double for Everton over Liverpool but Dixie and his colleagues, who then suffered a 3–1 home defeat by Arsenal and a 2–0 reverse at Blackpool, were soon deposed from the League summit they had occupied for three months. They were replaced at the top by Sheffield United when they beat Manchester City 2–1. But just four days later the Sheffield side went to Goodison and returned to Yorkshire smarting from a 5–1 hammering, with Dean scoring one of the goals. It was a repeat of the score at Bramall Lane in October.

United's city neighbours Wednesday were next in the firing line and a brace of goals from Dixie helped his side to a 3–1 win at Hillsborough. It completed four wins out of four for Everton over the two Sheffield clubs that season with 22 goals for and six against. Those two victories over United and Wednesday launched a decisive 10-game unbeaten run, including eight wins by Everton, which proved too hot for their main challengers Arsenal who lost during that period to Bolton, Sunderland and Liverpool. Dixie collected 14 goals in those 10 matches to help clinch his second championship medal. With Cresswell and Critchley he was one of only three survivors as regulars in the Everton team from the 1927–28 title-winning side. Tommy White, who had 23 outings this time, had made only one appearance in the previous championship team.

Everton took the title with 56 points, two ahead of runners-up Arsenal and six in front of third-place Sheffield Wednesday. In the process, they scored 116 goals and set a top flight record by scoring

84 of them in their 21 home games. Dixie was the country's top scorer, with 45 goals in 38 League outings, but also created many more for Tommy Johnson, who scored 22, and Tommy White, who hit 18. Everton had clinched the title before their home defeat to Portsmouth in the last match of the season at which League president John McKenna of Liverpool, who had presented the championship trophy to Warney Cresswell four years earlier, this time handed it to Dixie.

If winning runs had been a significant feature of Everton's triumph, home runs were also on Dean's sporting horizon as a talented baseball performer. The 1930s was the golden age of English baseball, which was the forerunner of the American version, with Merseyside a hotbed. Dixie played for Liverpool clubs Caledonians and The Robins and went on to represent England against American side The Yankees at London's White City. One report of his appearance for Caledonians in a match at Harringay, London said: 'He made three hits and took two splendid catches, pleasing all the critics with his display.'

Alf Duffy remembers being a baseball team-mate of Dixie's: 'I played for Liverpool Caledonians and when we won the Liverpool and District League championship in 1936 we were invited to play down south against the top London club at that time, Harringay. Dixie was invited to guest for us.

'The Harringay side usually attracted a crowd between 4,000 and 5,000 but on this occasion 17,000 turned out to see the great Dixie. Bill played in the outfield that day and took two very good catches. We lost the game to this crack team but that was secondary to Bill's popularity. After our opponents had treated us to a very nice dinner some of us, including Bill, made our way to Jack Bloomfield's pub in Leicester Square where he introduced me to those great Arsenal players Alex James and Cliff Bastin.' Albert Finnis has an equally fond memory of being Dean's baseball opponent on one occasion: 'Dixie signed for Caledonians and I was a pitcher for Littlewoods. During a match between the two clubs Bill came up to bat. As I was almost ready to pitch to him, someone in the crowd shouted: 'Why don't you head it, Bill?' Bill just smiled and to everybody's amusement went through the motions of heading the ball. A couple of nights later I was watching a baseball game at the Hawthorns, Bootle, when Bill came into the ground. He saw me and, although we had met only on the one occasion, he came over. 'Hello, Bert, how are you doing?' he said. We managed only a few words before he was surrounded by his many fans.'

The greatest exponent of the baseball art was Babe Ruth, who hit his record 60 home runs for the New York Yankees in the same year, 1928, that Dixie was tearing up football's record book on the other side of the Atlantic.

The two legends met when Everton were playing Tottenham at White Hart Lane and Dixie recalled:

There was a lot of talk at the time about baseball becoming big over here and I think that's why Babe Ruth had come to England. He came to the match and was brought into our dressing room. As he walked in he said in a loud voice: 'I just gotta meet this Dixie Dean guy!' . . . We were introduced and I shook hands with him. He said to me: 'Your name's well known in the States even though we don't play your sport much.' I turned round and said: 'Well, we certainly know all about you in England even though football and cricket are our big sports.' He asked me what cut I got of the game from that day's match. I said: 'I don't get anything apart from eight pounds a week and another few bob if we win. That's what all the players are paid. I don't think he could believe that and he said: 'See that crowd out there . . . it's as many as we get for a world series game. I'd demand two thirds of the gate if I was out there.' I just said: 'You must be joking, mate.'

The contrast in earning power between the two sporting icons was stark. Dean's modest wage was dwarfed by Ruth's weekly basic of £315, although in 1930 and 1931 he earned around £40,000 a season, a massive sum in that era. He retired in 1935, founded and bankrolled a children's charity and the Yankee Stadium became known as 'the House that Ruth built.' Closer to home, though, there were political stirrings in Germany that would eventually plunge the world into another war and Dixie and Everton had their own brush with Adolf Hitler's henchmen.

# CHAPTER EIGHT

# From A Nazi Snub To Wembley Magic

Everton's crowning as champions of England coincided with Hitler's ominously burgeoning power base in Germany. That summer of 1932 his national socialists became the country's largest party by winning 37 per cent of the general election vote. Into this maelstrom of the rapidly building Third Reich stepped Dixie Dean and his Everton colleagues for a four-match tour of Germany. Ostensibly, they were friendly games although there was not much amity evident. Everton's visit was four years before the Berlin Olympics, at which Hitler was infuriated by the quadruple gold medal triumph of the great American negro athlete Jesse Owens and the British competitors refused to give the infamous Nazi salute. And Everton's tour occurred some six years before the England football team went to the same Olympic Stadium and did give the 'Heil Hitler' salute before defeating Germany 6–3. England skipper Eddie Hapgood told his team that merely standing to attention during the German anthem would be sufficient. But the British ambassador, Sir Neville Henderson, anxious not to offend the Fascists, recommended the salute should be made out of courtesy. This was endorsed by the FA and thus the English players lined up and thrust their right arms into the air, watched by Hitler's cronies Goering, Hess, Goebbels and Von Ribbentrop.

'It was the worst moment of my life, one I would not willingly go through again,' Arsenal full back Hapgood wrote in his book *Football Ambassador*, adding: 'We were all pretty miserable about it.' What, I wonder, would have happened if Dixie Dean had still been playing for England on that May day in Berlin. He detested Hitler and his acolytes and I doubt that he would have been so acquiescent to the overriding concern not to upset the Nazis.

During Everton's trip to Germany their captain's strength of character, evident in so many ways, shone through both morally and physically:

We kicked off our German tour in Dresden and all the top Jerries were there at the match, including Herman Goering. People had been talking about this salute before the game but there was no way we were going to stick our hands up! . . . While the band was playing one of our lads looked as if he was going to put his hand up so I just grabbed hold of him and stopped him. The Jerry crowd didn't like it. They started booing. But it made no difference to me. They could boo all they liked . . . Well, when it came to the match itself the Jerry captain brought his ball over, a size four. We played with a size five. He puts his ball down on the spot. I said to myself: 'I'm not playing with that bloody thing . . . it's like a kid's garden ball to us, that.' . . . So I slid it to one side and put our ball down. So he came up, spouting the Deutsch, and knocked mine away. This went on a couple of times. In the end I threw our ball to the lads, picked up his ball and said to him: 'We play with this.' 'Ja. Ja,' he said. So I said: 'Come with me.' . . . I took him right to the touchline, bounced his ball, then kicked it right over the bloody stand. 'Now we'll play with this one,' I said. And we did . . . We'd arrived in Dresden overnight and Warney Cresswell was rooming with me. But when I woke up Warney had gone. 'What's up with him?' I wondered. 'It's only half past eight.' . . . So I got up myself and soon found out where he'd gone. The River Elbe ran right in front of the hotel and there were all these birds with nowt on. Warney was down there. And I soon caught him up! . . . In another game I had to tip off our right back Ben Williams about a German international winger called Hofman. I'd played against this feller and I warned Benny, who had captained both Everton and Wales, that if Hofman got through he'd have no chance of stopping him. I said to him: 'If he comes down a bit awkward catch him a bit awkward.' . . . Benny missed him the first time. So Bill Bocking, who was a good, big strong lad, put his hand up. The next time Hofman came through he went down and was carried off on a stretcher. I didn't fancy those German stretchers, either. They had barbed wire and everything round them. The Germans did Jimmy Stein in the same game . . . The first floodlit match we ever played was against a local team at a place called Kreuzlingen on the Swiss–German frontier in 1932. Old Will Cuff, the chairman, was nervous about us playing under lights and asked me: 'Do you think it will affect the lads, Bill?' I replied: 'It's bound to affect us. But it will affect them, too. I tell you what, if we beat them by seven goals or more how about half a quid to the lads?' He thought for a minute then said: 'You're on'. Well, I was just getting the bloody 10th one in before the final whistle went. We travelled all over Germany and on the last night of the tour, in Cologne, I went out to buy a present for the missus. On my way back I stood outside our hotel facing Cologne Cathedral. It was said to be one of the oldest cathedrals in the world and it was a beautiful building . . . I was looking at the cathedral, just admiring it, when two kids came along, I'd say aged between 12 and 14. I heard one of them say 'zwei fussball spieler, polizei'. I knew that meant that some of our lads were in trouble. I asked the two kids to take me to the police station. When I went in there I found two of our lads, little Jimmy Dunn and Phil Griffiths. They had already jimmy riddled on the floor, frightened to death of these bloody big Jerries. I tried to square it up with the old gendarme feller sitting on his desk. I said: 'Here you are . . . here's a couple of quid. Put it in the police fund.' The next thing I know he presses a button and it was almost the last thing I remember. I waded into one of the Jerries and shouted to little Jimmy to run for it, which he did and got away. But four or five of them came in to me with those leather sausages. You've seen egg boxes. When I wakened up my bloody head was like an egg box, lumps sticking up everywhere, and I had two broken fingers. I turned round on this here bed affair and saw these big jack boots. This bloody big German had brought me coffee. I said I'd sooner have tea. Good enough. Off he went and brought me the tea . . . The next thing I know I'm in court. They said I was fined 'Einuddreissig Mark'. 'Jesus Christ,' I said 'that's over a tenner!' Then a German feller said: 'It's £13 10 shillings'. I said: 'By Christ, I'm not paying that. You can stick me back in that bleedin' nick.' Any rate, our chairman Will Cuff and the directors got to know and sorted everything out. Apparently little Jimmy had been robbed in a bar and had chased after the thief. But the Jerries then pulled Jimmy in for disturbing the peace, although he was never charged.

After winning promotion as Second Division champions and then annexing the League title in the two previous years the 1932–33 season completed an unprecedented hat trick and brought new glory to Everton and William Ralph Dean in the shape of the FA Cup. This was the season when new faces began to make their mark in Everton colours. Cliff Britton, later to play for England and, later still, to manage Everton after the War, established himself as first choice right half after being signed from Bristol Rovers in June 1930 and developing in the reserves playing in the Central League. It was also the year which saw the arrival of right winger Albert Geldard who was also destined to appear for England. He was signed in November 1932 from Bradford Park Avenue for whom he had become the youngest player to appear in a peacetime League game in September 1929 at the age of 15 years 158 days, a record equalled by Wrexham's Ken Roberts in September 1951. Geldard's £4,000 transfer fee was an English record for a teenager. Early in the season Goodison welcomed another new recruit, signed as a junior from his hometown club Ellesmere Port, who would prove one of the most respected figures in the history of English football. His name was Joe Mercer, a sublime left half who became an Everton regular in the 1935–36 season.

But in the 1932–33 campaign Everton finished in First Division limbo, in 11th place of 22 clubs. Dixie and his team-mates weaved their magic that season in the FA Cup, although there were other significant successes. At the start of October, Liverpool were leading at Goodison until deep into the second half through Gordon Gunson's

23rd minute goal. Then Dean struck. First, he laid on a chance for Ted Critchley to hit a 62nd minute equaliser. Dixie followed that with a header to put Everton into the lead for the first time in the match. He then had the Everton fans in the 44,000-plus crowd in ecstasy by firing another goal to give them a 3–1 win in the 63rd League meeting of the Merseyside clubs, which generated gate receipts of around £3,000.

Victory was even sweeter for Dixie because he scored his brace of goals against his celebrated adversary Elisha Scott on the Liverpool goalkeeper's 400th League appearance. To complete Everton's joy their reserve side, including young Joe Mercer, won the Central League derby 3–1 at Anfield the same day. Goodison fans could not have been happier if someone had given them a free sunshine cruise which was being advertised by a local travel agent from just £11. Everton and Dixie had a cruise of their own in the FA Charity Shield some 10 days later when they went to St James' Park and walloped FA Cup holders Newcastle 5–3, after losing the toss for choice of venue. Dixie ran riot with four goals, watched by a youngster called Gordon Watson who was destined to become his team-mate and spend a lifetime at Goodison. After Newcastle had taken an early lead through McMenemy, Dean headed Everton level. 'His positioning and mechanical methods of nodding a ball make goalkeepers look awkward and slow,' wrote one reporter. A Tommy Johnson shot put Everton ahead and, after Ted Sagar saved a Sammy Weaver penalty, Dixie extended the lead by half time to 3–1 with another header. Soon after the interval a Cliff Britton pass gave Dixie the chance to complete his hat trick and although Boyd cut the deficit Dean scored his fourth of the game to make it 5–2, before a late strike from McMenemy for Newcastle's third goal. The power and the glory of Dean made a lasting impression on young Gordon Watson. 'I lived near Newcastle and I particularly wanted to see the Charity Shield match to get a first hand look at Dixie,' he recalled. 'He seemed to be in the papers every day for his scoring achievements. If it wasn't three it was two and if it wasn't two it was one! And that day I saw him he got four! He was terrific. Although I was a Newcastle fan as a boy there was no denying that Dixie was the star of the show and I think all the other Geordie supporters thought the same. From that day on, there was nobody quite like him for me and I was a confirmed fan. Right through my life I have still been able to picture him running round St James' Park knocking goals in.'

The teams that day were: – Newcastle: Burns; Nelson, Fairhurst; Bell, J. Higson, Weaver; Boyd, Richardson, Allen, McMenemy, Lang. Everton: Sagar; Williams, Cresswell; Britton, White, Thomson; Critchley, McGourty, Dean, Johnson, Stein. Three months later left half Watson, who cut his football teeth with Blyth Spartans, signed for Everton as a junior and went on, astonishingly, to complete 64 years service to the club as a player (until hanging up his boots in 1949), trainer, coach, promotions officer, barman, steward, and stadium tour guide before his retirement in 1997. His funeral, in May 2001, took place on the very day that Everton unveiled a bronze statue of his hero figure Dean, adjacent to Goodison Park.

Everton's League fortunes in 1932–33 were patchy and on the day a Dean goal salvaged a point for Everton in a wind-tossed 1–1 home draw with Portsmouth on October 29 the severe gales that hit Lancashire left Chelsea with only eight players on the field at Blackpool. Three of them had to leave the Bloomfield Road pitch through exhaustion and Blackpool won 4–0. But in the FA Cup Everton seemed to have the wind at their backs. Dean was on the mark when they launched their Cup mission with a 3–2 third round win at Leicester, Jimmy Dunn and Jimmy Stein the other scorers, and followed up with a 3–1 home knock-out of Bury, secured by two goals from Tommy Johnson and a Dixie single. That was the prelude, though, for one of the most remarkable games in Everton history, staged a week later on February 11, 1933. Dean scored twice and Johnson and Stein also netted . . . yet Everton lost 7–4 to their arch rivals Liverpool at Anfield. It still stands as the record score in more than a century of Mersey derby combat and for Liverpool it could not have been more welcome. They had not beaten Everton in nine League meetings stretching back to 1927 and manager George Patterson gambled by parading a young side against the Goodison visitors.

The teams lined up liked this: – Liverpool: Scott; Steel, Jackson; Morrison, Bradshaw, Taylor; Barton, Roberts, Wright, McPherson, Hanson. Everton: Sagar; Cook, Cresswell; Britton, White, Thomson;

Geldard, Dunn, Dean, Johnson, Stein. It all started so well for Dixie and Everton as he put them ahead with only eight minutes on the clock by capitalising on a mistake by Liverpool centre half Tom Bradshaw. However, former butcher's boy Harold Barton cut through the Everton defence to glide an equaliser over Ted Sagar's head after a quarter of an hour. A pass from Syd Roberts allowed Alf Hanson to put Liverpool in front after 22 minutes with Everton appealing in vain for offside. Nine minutes before the interval Tom Morrison made it 3–1 from a free kick deflected off Warney Cresswell who, with his full back partner Billy Cook, had their work cut out dealing with the pace of Liverpool's attacks. Just before the break Everton reduced the deficit when Albert Geldard dashed down the right flank, beat Jimmy Jackson and picked out Tommy Johnson who coolly accepted the scoring opportunity. The drama was even more intense in the second half with Harold Taylor making it 4–2 to Liverpool and Barton scoring his second of the match. With 15 minutes left Dixie met a Jimmy Stein corner and headed past Elisha Scott for his 16th derby goal. But within a minute Roberts made it 6–3 before Barton clinched his hat trick in the 85th minute by putting Liverpool into a seventh heaven. Stein completed the scoring with Everton's fourth in the last minute.

Manager Patterson's gamble had paid off handsomely. Nine of the Liverpool side had appeared in the reserve team that season and it was the club's highest score since they beat Tottenham 7–2 in October 1914. While they were recording their big win England's cricketers reached 99 without loss in Brisbane, after dismissing the Aussies for 340, and went on to win the Ashes in the controversial body-line series. For Everton it had been a huge body blow to their pride and a few hours after the game the rival players met at a pre-arranged evening social event. As Liverpool skipper Bradshaw walked into the room the whimsical pianist struck up 'Conquering Hero'. When Dean, the Everton captain arrived, he promptly played the 'Funeral March'!

Liverpool were to finish three places behind Everton in 14th place in the First Division and Dixie had his own explanation for his side's unprecedented derby defeat – the fact that they had Wembley in their sights.

We were playing Leeds United in the fifth round of the Cup the following Saturday. Nobody was to get injured. And you were at the right place to get injured if you went looking for it! So none of us got injured. It was common sense on our part . . . Liverpool were hard but they were even harder when I first joined Everton with fellers like the Wadsworth brothers, Harold and Walter and big Jock McNab. Jock would play the mouth organ but he'd kick you to death the next time he saw you . . . They also had Tom Bromilow. He was supposed to be the gentleman of football. Well, he put me in the Robert Davies Nursing Home for about three weeks with a chipped bone. He came from behind and kicked me up the doins! Don McKinlay was another one who'd kick his mother. He was one of the full backs with Tommy Lucas . . . There was Elisha in goal, Lucas and McKinlay the full backs, McNab, Walter Wadsworth and Bromilow as half backs and their forward line included Dick Edmed, Dick Forshaw – who later joined Everton – Harry Chambers, Gordon Hodgson and Fred Hopkin. Fred didn't get many goals. But once when he did score one of the Anfield stands caught fire. If I'd have seen it I wouldn't have piddled on it! Chambers was nicknamed 'Smiler' and played for England. But there's a funny story concerning him and Everton. We had a director at Goodison who was a builder by trade. He came back one day from Wellington in Shropshire and said he'd found a really good player who Everton must sign. So one of our backroom lads went with this director the following week to have a look at this great player. At half time they asked to have a word with him after the match. When the game was over they met him and said: 'How would you like to come to Everton? We've got a form here for you to sign and we'll give your club a few quid.' 'Look,' this feller replied 'I've already been down this road a bit.' 'How do you mean?' asked the Everton people. 'Well,' he said 'I was with Liverpool for 15 seasons!' 'They'd only tried to sign Chambers who was then about 44 or 45. If they'd have come back with him, well . . . ! The Liverpool team, generally, were real hard men. I remember Liverpool playing Newcastle at Anfield when there were three sent off, Wadsworth and McNab of Liverpool and Urwin of Newcastle. I was injured at the time and watched the match. The Newcastle feller had made contact with one or two Liverpool players and they started sliding and hitting each other with mud while they were on the ground. As the two Liverpool players marched off about five yards apart they both stopped and waited for the Newcastle lad. In the end the police went on to the pitch and escorted the Newcastle player to the dressing room. But if Everton players misbehaved in those days old W. C. (Will) Cuff just wouldn't have you. Everton went on the field purely and simply to play football. They never went out to put the boot in or anything like that. That's why Everton were called the School of Science and the feller who first called them that was none other than that great goalscorer Steve Bloomer.

Talking of Will Cuff, he was a real clever man, that. He masterminded a great stroke of business in buying the land that became Everton's training ground, Bellefield, in West Derby. We had a training ground at the corner of Stopgate Lane which the Bents Brewery boss Sir Thomas White wanted to buy. In the end Mr Cuff sold it to him for £60,000. But he'd already lined up this big piece of land in West Derby, which he bought off the Co-op for £30,000.

Everton responded to their substantial derby reverse with a 2–0 home defeat of Leeds United with Dixie and Stein scoring the goals. That booked them a sixth round home duel with Luton Town. Goodison's Third division visitors were hit for six without reply, Dixie again on the scoresheet together with Stein and Johnson, who scored two apiece, and Dunn. They were now in the last four. Everton hit another six five days later in the League, when Dean scored a hat trick in a 6–3 home win over Leicester. That was followed by a 2–2 draw at Portsmouth before they resumed Cup duty against West Ham in the semi final at Molineux. Albert Geldard, said by one observer to be 'so fast he could catch pigeons', missed the Luton tie because of an injury to his left ankle and began a race against the clock to be fit. Harry Cooke even gave the damaged joint a special massage in the mineral baths at Buxton where Everton encamped prior to the semi final. Dixie recalled:

We had a really good solid team and we really trained hard. There was no such thing as saying they'd stay off pints of beer and not smoke and then break their word. I can say that team really stuck to their word.

Mr Tom McIntosh, the secretary-manager, used to have a chat with me and he said: 'Listen, William, it's like this. If we win the League or Cup I'll get a pay rise and it's about time I had one, isn't it?' I said to him: 'Don't worry, you'll be alright.' . . . Two seasons earlier we'd got to the semi final of the Cup but lost 1–0 to West Brom at Old Trafford. They beat us with one of the lousiest goals you've ever seen. It cost us the chance of doing the double of Second Division championship and FA Cup . . . In 1933 we reached the semi again, this time against West Ham at Molineux. The club knew we had a really good chance of doing something that year so the directors gave the go-ahead for us to go off on special training in Buxton. We used to train in all the snow, slush and everything else that was up there but, by jove, we had a fit team. Good enough, the lads who did used to have a drink now and again knocked it off and the lads who used to smoke knocked that off, too.

Geldard lost his fitness race and was ruled out of the semi final. Yet the man who continued in his right wing role, Ted Critchley, emerged as Everton's hero. West Ham were languishing near the bottom of the old Second Division and Everton were hot favourites to flatten the Hammers. But they made heavy weather of it. It was 1–1 at half time, Jimmy Dunn scoring Everton's goal, and the nerves of their supporters were jangling until Critchley scored a scrambled goal after a defensive error to snatch a 2–1 win. Dixie's run of scoring in every round had come to an end. But it mattered not. Everton's win at Molineux meant he would lead out his beloved side to face Manchester City, 3–2 conquerors of Derby County in the other semi, in the Final at Wembley on April 29. Dixie's joy bubbled through in an aftermatch interview within minutes of walking off the Molineux pitch. 'We're there – and now we must land that Cup. The whole of the city of Liverpool is behind us. This is a great day for my old man. In fact, it's a day he's been living for. He retires shortly from Wirral Railways after 40 years service and this will give him something to talk about! I want to have a word with my kiddie about this, too. He's only nine months old but I must tell him all about today's big occasion. It's not just a personal matter, though. This is a team win.'

The looming all-Lancashire contest at Wembley was a prospect to whet the appetite in the six weeks before the big contest in front of the Twin Towers . . . Everton's menacing forward line pitted against a City side boasting a superb half back trio of Mat Busby, Sam Cowan and Jackie Bray.

But the first clash was one of colours. Both clubs wore blue, albeit differing shades, and the Football Association decided one team would wear white shirts and the other red. City staked first claim, saying they wanted to play in red. Dixie was delighted. There was no way he wanted to wear the colours of Mersey rivals Liverpool and he advised Everton directors to agree to City's request. This they duly did and Everton wore what the match programme described as 'white jerseys and black knickers.'

That Cup Final entered the record books as the first one in which the players wore numbers, an experiment that pre-dated the official introduction of numbering by seven years. Everton, presumably on alphabetical sequence, were chosen to wear 1 to 11 and City 12 to 22.

This decision was conveyed to Everton's secretary-manager Tom McIntosh in a letter from FA secretary Sir Frederick Wall which stated: 'I have been instructed to write requesting that the players taking part in this match at Wembley be numbered:- Your club No's. 1–11 (black numbers), Manchester City No's. 12–22 (white numbers). The numbers have been ordered by us and will be sent to you as soon as possible that they may be sewn on the backs of the players' jerseys.' So, fittingly, Dixie Dean, who had made his 16th and last England appearance – a 1–0 win over Ireland – earlier that season, would become the first player in Cup Final history to walk out at Wembley wearing No 9 on his back.

It would be the first time a Merseyside club had appeared at

Wembley, although nine years earlier, in September 1924, the city featured in a 'Liverpool Week' at the newly built stadium as the Second City of the Empire in the British Empire Exhibition.

At that time, Liverpool FC had never won the Cup and Everton's only previous success had been in 1906 when they beat Newcastle 1–0 at Crystal Palace. A member of that winning side, right winger Jack Sharp, an England international at both football and cricket and by then an Everton director, spurred on Dixie and his team-mates by showing them his Cup medal gained 27 years earlier. Everton kept faith with their usual big-match routine by travelling to Buxton to prepare for the Final and three weeks before the game all smoking and drinking was banned. Several of the players, including Dixie, liked the odd cigarette or puff of a pipe, not to mention a few pints in their off duty moments. But, just as they had done prior to the semi final, Tom McIntosh's edict was observed.

If you feel the pre big match fashion for clubs to cocoon and pamper their players at a hotel training camp, escaping the media in the process, is a recent phenomenon this *Daily Express* article during the build-up to the 1933 Cup Final might convince you otherwise. Under the headline 'You Must Not Talk To Them' and written by a 'Special Correspondent' it reads:

'This is the story of the man who moves about Buxton with a bodyguard – and the shyest man in town. They are both members of the Everton Football Club, who are having special training here for the Cup Final with Manchester City. Their names are Dixie Dean and Albert Geldard. If you go to Buxton in search of either of them you will, with good luck, see them – but it is extremely doubtful if you speak to them . . . You will not get near Geldard because if he thinks you want to speak to him he vanishes. And you will certainly not get a word with Dean because you will never penetrate the bodyguard of trainers, managers, directors and so on . . . I went to Buxton today in search of both. Geldard, who came from Bradford this season, is only 19 years of age and it is more than probable that he will get his Cup Final medal. He is the youngest member of the team and

for that reason I wanted his views on Everton's prospects . . .
Fourteen of the players are staying here together with a large
number of club officials including Mr T. McIntosh, the manager,
and Mr Harry Cooke, the trainer. They are resting and keeping
fit after a strenuous holiday programme.

In the morning they go to the baths for water massage
treatment. Mr Cooke sees to that. In the case of Dean he is
accompanied by his bodyguard. The players have their own
private dining room . . . I discovered that Dean (and bodyguard)
had gone to play golf. It was bitterly cold on the links. Snow
threatened but Dean and Thomson appeared quite warm in
flannel trousers and thin sweaters. I nearly spoke to Dean but
every time I thought he was unguarded the bodyguard closed in
. . . Late tonight, four small boys were outside the hotel. They
have been trying since Tuesday to get the autographs of Dean
and Geldard. Those boys will wait an extremely long time.'

Given Dixie's obliging willingness to sign autographs, to which
many people of all ages have paid testimony, the reporter's closing
remarks were born probably more of bile than accuracy. There was no
doubt, either, that in their Derbyshire retreat the spirit in the Everton
camp was bubbling.

Goalkeeper Ted Sagar recalled: 'After we'd beaten West Ham in
the semi final I just can't describe the feeling in our dressing room. I
just couldn't keep still. It got to you alright knowing you were going
to play in the Cup Final. We tried to talk to each other but we just
couldn't keep calm. I do remember, though, that there were no
problems about Cup Final tickets. There were plenty available in
those days. We went to Buxton for our training. We used to call that
"headquarters". At times we'd also go to Harrogate. But Buxton was
the place for us and Harry Cooke, our trainer, used to supervise things.
He was very good.

'The laps and sprints we did were very similar to what we used to
do at Goodison. But going away gave us the benefit of a break in
routine and with Buxton being a spa town Harry also gave some of the
lads a rub down in the special waters in the baths there . . . We were

offered a bonus of £25 to win the Cup . . . I don't know what it was for losing! Anyway, we travelled south by train from Buxton on the Friday, the day before the game, and stayed in a hotel outside London. Next day we travelled by bus to Wembley, which I'd never seen before. I could see the Twin Towers and I couldn't work out what they were. It was very impressive . . . It was a nice, sunny day and, as always, I was nervous until I got onto the pitch. Dixie, our captain, said to us just before we walked out: "OK, lads, all the best and get stuck in." Under the new numbering system I wore No 1 and my opposite number, Len Langford in the City goal, was carrying top weight with No 22 on his back!'

Sagar's right back colleague Billy Cook, who had cost £3,000 four months earlier from Celtic with whom he had won a Scottish Cup winners medal, recounted a pre-match incident concerning his direct opponent, Manchester City's renowned England winger Eric Brook. 'Before the match one of our directors came up to me and said: "Billy, you'll have to keep a close watch on Brook." But Bill Dean said to him: "Leave Cooky alone. He knows what to do." And I did. Brook went past me just once. But I got him good and hard soon after that and he was never the same again.

'I was a good friend of Bill Dean, except when we played each other at snooker. I won the Everton championship every time I entered. That really irritated him because he fancied his chances.'

He also fancied Everton's chances of winning the FA Cup:

With the team we had we had to be confident, although City had a very good side in those days. They had about seven inter- nationals, similar to us . . . When we knew we were playing them it reminded me of a funny story in a game against City at Maine Road a few years earlier. One lad playing for them had just got married. I won't mention his name except to say he was a forward. We scored four before half time and this woman he'd married kept shouting to this lad during the second half: 'There's nothing doing for you tonight if you don't get some goals in there!' The lad did score eventually so I think he was alright for a bit! . . . When we met them in the Final it was one of those very unusual occasions where one of our players was tipped off about one of the other team. Our right back Billy Cook was told to go out and play a good, hard game against Eric Brook. He was a great player, that. But against Cooky he went about eight feet in the air! We'd had a great run to Wembley and had that bit of luck every team needs. That had come in the semi final when we might have come unstuck against West Ham. Their centre forward Dick Watson could have beaten us. He tried to draw Ted Sagar out of his goal but Ted came out and, although he slipped, he still managed to grab the ball. Watson might have scored if he'd shot first time.

The numbers on our backs were something new. Match programmes just listed the names of the players with their position. There were no numbers. The players stayed in their position much more than they do now . . . We had a change in our side from the semi final because right winger Teddy Critchley, who scored the goal that got us to Wembley, made way for Albert Geldard, who was fit again. Critch was a good player and to be left out was a big disappointment for him. But this lad Geldard was faster. He was just the lad you wanted at Wembley. He could do almost even time. He had a good player behind him, to supply him with the ball, and that was Cliff Britton at right half. Cliff was very good.

A psychological factor also aided the Everton cause. City arrived at Wembley hours before kick off and the long wait shredded their nerves. It was something Dixie noticed when he first came face to face with the opposition:

A commissionaire came to our dressing room door and told us to get ready to come out because City were just going down the tunnel. I said: 'It's alright. Don't worry. We'll catch them up later. Shut the door.' Then I lit a cigarette and told the lads: 'There's plenty of time. Let them wait.'

When I went out and got alongside Sam Cowan, the City skipper, he was holding the ball and you could see how nervous he was. 'That ball's shaking in your hand,' I said. 'Put your other hand on top of it to stop it shaking.' You should have seen his face!

The Old London Midland and Scottish Railway ran 40 special trains to ferry both sets of supporters from economically depressed Lancashire to London, with all 700 people on each train having a reserved seat. On arrival in the capital the rival fans happily mingled and even sang together, temporarily putting the harshness of everyday life behind them. Just reaching Wembley had generated a profit of £17,164 for Everton, with City netting slightly more because their third round meeting with Gateshead had gone to a replay, from which City received £479. The coffers of both clubs were further swollen by receipts of almost £25,000 from a Wembley attendance of 92,950.

The share of the Wembley takings for Everton and City came to the grand total of £5,177 each in a season when the Goodison club paid out £20,000 in wages and transfer fees from League match receipts of £50,000.

As well as Matt (later Sir Matt) Busby, Brook and Cowan the City side also included inside forward Jimmy McMullan – who had captained Scotland's 'Wembley Wizards' of 1928 and was making his farewell appearance before hanging up his boots – and centre forward Alec Herd, father of future Manchester United star David Herd.

If City's nerves had been exposed Everton were not without their own jitters. Former captain Warney Cresswell and Jimmy Dunn were two victims of Cup Final nerves as chairman Will Cuff so revealingly disclosed. 'It is impossible to lose the original sense of fear that comes on you as you see Wembley,' he said. 'In that connection I will go further and state from my own knowledge that Cresswell, ice-cool in a thousand games in his lifetime, found the inside rooms of Wembley a trouble to his stomach muscles. He asked a policeman if there was a private room nearby the dressing room where he could have a smoke "to settle my nerves, d'ye know man!" The constable obliged and Cresswell, breaking all known rules about smoking before a match let alone a Cup Final, took out his pipe of intensely strong tobacco, lit up and after a smoke went off to rejoin the Wembley heroes and played like the rest of the side, just ideally . . . Jimmy Dunn was jittery overnight and the director in charge had serious misgivings about not making an eleventh hour change in the team. However, the little man went out and gave a wonderful scoring performance.'

Creswell's rule-breaking pre-match smoke was, perhaps, not so startling. A national newspaper on the morning of the game ran a half page advertisement showing pictures of rival skippers Dean and Cowan, a packet of cigarettes and a banner proclaiming: 'Two Captains and Twenty Players.'

The teams were: – Everton: Sagar; Cook, Cresswell; Britton, White, Thomson; Geldard, Dunn, Dean (captain), Johnson, Stein. Manchester City: Langford; Cann, Dale; Busby, Cowan (captain), Bray; Toseland, Marshall, Herd, McMullan, Brook. The referee was Ernest Wood of Sheffield and he and Everton's Albert Geldard would have reason to remember the occasion until their dying day for reasons connected with the object of both team's attention – the match ball. But that came later. First the teams had to do battle and Dixie was in combative mood:

City were favourites to win with the bookies who had them at 7–4. As far as I was concerned that was a ridiculous price. We knew we could win. We weren't big headed or anything like that. We were just confident.

Mind you, we'd had a bit of a situation the night before the game when Billy Cook was caught drinking and threatened by the directors with being left out of the team. The players turned round and said if Cooky was left out they'd all go home! In the end he was allowed to play and everything was sorted out, although we didn't get to bed until around midnight.

We knew Cooky had been on the batter. But he was a really fit feller, as hard as nails and, of course, he went out and did a great job against Eric Brook. We had tripe and onions for our pre-match meal and we felt good going to Wembley. We had a good, solid, fit, tidy team and we just seemed to take City for a ride. Our lads played well and one of the sharpest in our forward line was Jimmy Stein, the outside left. There was no getting away from it, he was a good player that lad. He was there to put the ball away when the City keeper Langford dropped a cross from Cliff Britton late in the first half.

The goal came five minutes before the interval and seven minutes after the break Everton doubled their lead when the nerve-wracked, tormented Langford again failed to hold another Britton delivery. Said Dixie:

I told the lads in the dressing room at half time: 'Whatever else you do, get the ball into that goal area. Don't be trying to beat another man. Just get that ball over.'

Well, it wasn't long into the second half when Cliff Britton sent another one over. It was a beautiful thing! From about eight yards out I met it and headed it into the back of the net with the goalkeeper Langford lying on top of it. He'd made a last effort to try and grab it but it was right at the back of the net.

Dean's strike was the cue for a brief Royal Box dialogue between the Lord Mayor of Liverpool and the Duchess of York, who attended the game with the Duke as guests of honour in the absence through illness of King George V. His Worship, sitting next to the future Queen Mother and helping her identify the players, said: 'Ma'am, the No 9 is Dixie Dean.' To which the Duchess replied: 'Even I know Dean!'

With 10 minutes left, Everton made it 3–0 through Jimmy Dunn, who had won a fitness race to play in the Final. Dixie recalled:

Our third goal came from a corner by Albert Geldard. He sent a great ball over, little Jimmy ran in and headed it into the net. It was something similar to the one I'd got myself. Little Dunny was so happy he'd scored he started running round the greyhound track. There was nothing wrong with his fitness then! It took us all our time to catch him. But we knew that was it. We'd won the Cup. One man I felt sorry for, though, was Jimmy McMullan. It was his last game in football and the last chance he'd ever have of getting a Cup winners medal.

Goalkeeper Sagar recounted: 'We won quite easily in the finish. I had some work to do very early in the game when City put a cross in. The ball came over, I went out and caught it and kicked it down the field. That gave me all the confidence I needed. Goalkeepers didn't throw the ball much then. We kicked it with the idea of getting it as far as possible from your own goalmouth. After getting that early lead we always had the edge on City and it was really thrilling to win the Cup in that packed stadium . . . A lot of the lads had a drink in the dressing room afterwards. I didn't because I was a teetotaller in those days. But I felt very excited. Then it was on to the banquet with our wives. It was a smashing day and a smashing evening.' Sportswriter Ernest Edwards, writing under his pseudonym 'Bee' in the *Liverpool Post and Mercury*, said: 'Everton won by convincing methods, by their superior craftsmanship, by all-round merit, with hardly a weakness and with a lot of solid work interspersed with the daintier touches of Johnson and Dunn.'

The Everton fans, who had paid two shillings and sixpence (12½ pence) to stand at Wembley, were ecstatic at their team's triumph and the three players – Stein, Dean and Dunn – whose names had been on the scoresheet at the start of Everton's Cup run were on it again at its glorious climax. The 3–0 success was Wembley's biggest margin of victory in an FA Cup Final up to that stage.

The *Daily Sketch* reported: 'The Cup Final success completed a remarkable treble for Everton following their Second Division championship in 1931 and their League championship in 1932 . . . At the core of their triumphs remained the marvellous goal-getting capabilities of William Ralph 'Dixie' Dean, who scored at Wembley and uncomplainingly shrugged off all Manchester City's physical attempts to unsettle him. But Everton were no one-man team. Indeed, Dean was the striking force at the front end of a very sophisticated machine.'

Dean's display, though, was singled out by Matt Busby, later to join and captain Liverpool before taking charge of Manchester United and becoming, like Dixie, a football immortal. 'Dixie took a terrific buffeting,' said Busby. 'We were all at it, trying to cut him down. Yet he was never nasty. To play against him was both a delight and a nightmare. He is the perfect specimen of an athlete, beautifully proportioned with immense strength, adept on the ground but with extraordinary skill in the air . . . Apparently, he can leap from a standing position on to a billiard table and has demonstrated it many times. He can certainly out-jump, out-time and out-head any defender. He must be the finest header of the ball ever.'

In his book *Football on Merseyside* the respected writer Percy M. Young extolled Dixie's virtues:

'Dixie Dean was a player of affecting loyalty, practising his skill with the same determination whether for a winning or losing side. He had, as centre-forwards must have, courage. As a player Dean combined power with grace, intuition, and intellect. His shots were both vicious and accurate but he was a brilliant header of the ball. Dean was a shrewd tactician and master of positional play, which meant that like all great stylists he was in the right place at the right time. The tumults of the years of depression stood still while Everton won the championship, the championship of Division Two, and the English Cup.'

Dixie enthused:

I'll never forget going up to receive the Cup from the Duchess. She congratulated me and said it had been a good game and one she'd enjoyed. We'd stuck by Tom McIntosh and we'd done what he'd asked us to do. He had tears in his eyes at the end and he thanked us all. He got his rise alright! In fact, he took us for a night out later. We could drink what we liked then! Lord Derby was one of the guests at our after-match banquet and during the meal I said to his Lordship: 'I believe you've got a horse running in the Derby.'

'Yes, Dean,' he said 'it's called Hyperion'.

'I know all about it my Lord and I think it'll win it.' I said.

Lord Derby replied: 'George Lambton, the old trainer, tells me he thinks it will win it.'

'Thank you very much, sir, it's very kind of you,' I said.

'I backed the horse but I was away on tour with Everton in Copenhagen on the day of the race. We were sitting in a beer garden outside the hotel watching the race result come through on one of those neon signs.

The two letters H and Y came up and I shouted: 'There's only one H and Y in that bloody race . . . and up went the table!' There was an old gentleman sitting only a couple of seats away and I'm afraid the beer went all over him. Naturally, he jumped up and I said: 'Oh, I'm awfully sorry, sir.' I offered to get his suit cleaned and anything else I could do. And he said: 'It's quite alright, quite alright. I've enjoyed every moment of it. Here, have one of my cards.' It was Jean Hersholt, the old film actor who'd come home from Hollywood to Denmark for a holiday. So we had him out for the night and he had a lot more over his suit by the time we'd finished with him! It went well.

When we brought the Cup back home from Wembley we set the pattern which has been followed by other Everton teams – and Liverpool copied us, too. We went on a tour of the city. But instead of a charabanc we went on the same horse-drawn coach and four which had been used by the Everton team that had won the Cup in 1906. I remember coming up Scotland Road and we had to ease up our speed on account of the crowds. This kiddie was screaming and crying and as I bent down to shake hands with the mother she said to the youngster. 'If you don't stop this noise I won't bring you next year!' Any rate, the kid stopped crying.

When the team arrived in Liverpool's Lime Street Station on the Monday afternoon some 50,000 people were there to greet them. The route to the town hall via Church Street and Castle Street was so crowded that hundreds needed treatment from the St John Ambulance Brigade. 'Even Armistice Night was mild compared with this,' wrote one reporter. Dixie, elegantly attired in suit and waistcoat, delivered a victory speech from the town hall balcony in which he thanked the baying masses and said to huge cheers: 'If we keep on winning like this we'll be entering the Grand National and the Derby!' The Everton

party then re-boarded the coach and four and travelled along Byrom
Street, Scotland Road, Kirkdale Road, Walton Road and County Road,
passing an estimated half a million people, to arrive at Goodison Park
which was packed to the rafters with 60,000 in the ground.

Dixie and the triumphant Everton party had left London on the
4.00 p.m. train from Euston with no idea of the massive crowd and
mass hysteria that would mark their homecoming. The horse drawn
coach – or 'four-in-hand' as it was known – was again driven by Jack
Pagendam who had carried out the same task for the Everton Cup
winners of 1906. 'The coach is the only one left of its kind in
Liverpool and is at present owned by Lewis's store, who have kindly
lent it for the occasion,' said proud Jack. 'It's been kept in fine
condition and in the days before motor cars it was engaged on the
Chester to Shrewsbury route.' Never, though, had it featured in scenes
like the ones sparked by that evening's victory procession from city
centre to Goodison. 'The six mounted police horses heading the
procession reared high upon their haunches but the horses leading
the coach were firmly held down by many willing hands, glad of the
excuse to lead the victors home,' reported the *Liverpool Daily Post*.
'At the first sight of Dean, the captain, holding aloft the Cup – a
bauble only valued in cash at £25 – the crowd went wild with
excitement. The whole victorious eleven perched on the coach waved
back to the crowd, which cheered and cheered again. As the coach
passed the Press Club, Dean turned the cup in the direction of a
balcony on which was Mr George Dobson, who was captain of the
Everton team of 1885–86. Mr Dobson is now 70 years of age. "Good
old Dixie," shouted the crowd. "Three cheers for the Blues."

'Cheering became inarticulate yells when Dean, hatless but wearing
his Everton scarf, stood up on his seat in the driver's box, held up the
Cup with one hand and waved cheerily with the other. When he
pretended to drink out of the hard-won trophy the crowd roared in
delighted appreciation. All the footballers appeared to be dazed. Poor
Dean was perspiring as, perhaps, he had never done on the football
field and, yes, tears were trickling down his cheeks. Certainly the
experience was one to move any man who was the central figure . . .
He smiled again when "Auntie Muriel" presented him with a

monstrous black cat "Wafer", which appears every week in "Auntie Muriel's Treasure Chest" in the *Echo*. Thereafter, wherever he went, Dean dragged both Cup and cat. At the Town Hall the police band played "He's a jolly good fellow" before Dean thanked the crowd and the Lord Mayor, saying: "It's wonderful, marvellous. We never expected anything like this." It was now noticed that a small boy wearing the red jersey and white shorts of the Liverpool club and acting as its mascot was among the company. He had represented the Liverpool club at Lime Street Station and had been squeezed into one of the official charabancs. He came in for much friendly petting. At Goodison Park it was quite dark but through the gloom one could see a mighty throng. They had invaded the pitch and were packed in the enclosure in front of the stand. Three electric lights dimly illuminated the directors' box but it was enough to show the crowd the English Cup once again and they heralded its appearance in no uncertain fashion when Dean brought it to the front.

'When he stepped back the crowd set up a "We want Dixie" chant and cheered him to the echo when he stepped forward to face the microphone. His few words were lost in the cheers and counter-cheers and after a few minutes of vainly trying to make himself heard he retired, hoarse-voiced, weary, but still triumphant.'

Such was the unbounded joy of the supporters that a group of them, prompted by the 27-year gap between skipper Jack Taylor's 1906 Cup winning Everton side and Dixie's team, carried a dummy coffin draped with a banner stating: 'Here lies Everton's bogy – laid for ever more. R.I.P.' They were not to know that this would be the FA Cup's only victory parade on Merseyside in 59 years. The next time the trophy would be back would be in 1965, draped for the first time in the red and white of arch foes Liverpool, with Everton's next success coming 12 months later in England's World Cup winning year of 1966.

Goalkeeper Ted Sagar also had fond memories of the amazing 1933 homecoming: 'Four horses pulled the coach for our tour of the city and I knew the driver. He worked for Thompsons, the funeral directors. It was marvellous seeing the crowds as we were going up Scotland Road with the Cup. They were all out there with their pints in their hands cheering us on as we went past.

'It was an unforgettable trip from the Town Hall to Goodison. When we got to the ground we went up to the boardroom and had another little bit of a celebration there before my wife and I got a taxi home to Chirkdale Street, off Spellow Lane. The taxi cost us 1s 6d.'

But for one member of Dixie's family, the Cup Final cost him his job at a time of high unemployment. Dean's brother-in-law bought a Wembley ticket and went to the match despite his company refusing to waive their demand that he must work, as usual, on Saturday morning. His half day's absence meant the sack when he reported for work on the Monday morning.

The Final also led to the end of Arthur Kingscott's term of office as Football Association treasurer . . . and all because of the choice of the Wembley match ball. Concern over that spherical object also linked referee Ernest Wood and Everton winger Albert Geldard. Up to that time it had always been the accepted referee's prerogative to choose the match ball for the Final. But before the 1933 game Kingscott went into the referee's dressing room and handed furious Wood a pre-selected ball. Geldard, meanwhile, had hatched a plan to claim the ball as a souvenir if he was close to it when Wood blew the final whistle. This is how BBC radio commentator George Allison described the scenes when the whistle sounded:

'The whistle's gone . . . Geldard's got the ball as a souvenir. The referee is going up to Geldard to ask him, as a personal favour I imagine, if he can have the ball. Geldard's not a bit happy about it. Neither is Britton. There seems to be some argument. What's the referee doing? He's talking to . . . (tails off) . . . It has been the custom, of course, I believe, sometimes, for the player who gets this remarkable souvenir to keep it. Mr Wood . . . the crowd are yelling to the referee to give him the ball. They're not a bit pleased about what the referee has done.'

(Unnamed co-commentator): 'What is the etiquette of that?'

Commentator resumes: 'As a rule the players, I suppose, claim the ball. Here's No 9, Dean, who seems to be heading the referee's way.'

Then the commentator drops the subject of who is claiming the ball to concentrate on Everton's walk up the steps to receive the Cup.

Geldard explained the sequence of events thus: 'As Mr Wood blew the final whistle the ball was passed true as a bullet directly to my feet as I stood on the halfway line close to the touchline. In a split second I controlled the ball with my right foot, bent down and picked it up. On two occasions in previous years I had listened to the radio Cup Final broadcast so I was mentally prepared to act as I did if the ball should come my way at the end of the game. Elated by our victory and somewhat excited because I had collected the ball I took a step towards the nearest City player to shake his hand. But Mr Wood came running over and said: "Sorry Albert, I must take the ball to prevent the unsightly scuffle there's been this last year or two." With that, he took the ball from my hands. I thought to myself: "Albert, you've had it." But about an hour later Mr Wood came into our dressing room and said: "Here's the ball, Albert. Nobody seems to want it so as far as I'm concerned it's yours."

'That's how I came to re-possess the ball. It's also where I made an awfully big mistake. I knew that even if I let it down I'd be unable to get it in my weekend bag. I also knew my mother had recently bought a glass cabinet to display my football trophies. "It can go in there, just as it is, wind and all", I thought. So I carried the ball back to Liverpool precisely as it had come off the pitch, still blown up to full size with the original "wind". Just before going onto the Town Hall balcony for Billy Dean to show the Cup to the thousands of supporters one of our directors, Jack Sharp, who had a flourishing sports outfitters in the city, approached me. "Have you got the ball, Albert?" he asked. "If so, can I see it?"

'I took him to where it was. The ball was completely free of any lettering but he picked it up and said: "I know it is one of our balls because of this." He pointed to an "X" written in ink, positioned an inch or two from the lace holes. Mr Sharp was jubilant because we had played the match with the very ball he had submitted. Mr Sharp added: "Four of us were asked to submit a ball. I wonder why mine was selected? Do you mind letting me have it for a week or so, Albert? I'd like to put it in my shop window. It will be a terrific advert for me."

I said "certainly" to Mr Sharp's request . . . and said goodbye to my ball.

'Two or three days later I had cause to visit the club and was told by our trainer Harry Cooke that Tom McIntosh wanted to see me. I went up in the lift to his office. "Albert", he said "We have a letter from the FA saying our chairman, Mr Will Cuff, has to decide what has to become of the match ball. Mr Cuff has decided to get it cleaned up and put on permanent display in the boardroom. You have to go down town to collect a brand new ball from Mr Sharp." That is how I came to lose what I call my "missing link". I collected a new ball from Mr Sharp and the next time I saw "my ball" was in the Everton boardroom some four or five years later, perched on a stand encased in a spherical glass cover. A friend assures me that the "X" is still clearly visible.

'The thought of collecting that ball at the end of the Final then losing possession some two days later will forever remain one of my sporting memories, unhappy though it may be.'

But the repercussions of the Kingscott affair lasted eight months. Wembley referee Wood claimed that his integrity had been impugned by the FA treasurer who had twice been a Final referee himself. Wood told an FA inquiry: 'Mr Kingscott told me "that as the Council had heard you referees are making money in choosing balls for Final ties" they had decided to appoint him to choose it. I resented this remark very much.'

Kingscott denied saying the words and as the FA probe dragged on he refused to resign. Eventually, on December 11, 1933, the FA Council found he had broken rules and dismissed him, thus ending his 40 years of service to the Association. To avoid any further whiffs of corruption the FA decided that from the following year's Final – when Manchester City went back to Wembley and beat Portsmouth – all balls to be considered for the match by the referee had to be unmarked and free of any manufacturer's identity.

An intriguing postscript to the affair was provided by Everton chairman Will Cuff, who said: 'Players in Cup Finals thought that if they could gather the ball the moment the referee signalled the end of the game it was their property. This was quite erroneous but it became

a habit and the mad scrummaging that went on to collar the ball
became a scandal. After our Final against Manchester City, Geldard
was near enough to dash in and collar the ball. He was leaving the Cup
Final scene with the memento only to find an official challenging him
for possession. Such a finale to a Final was quite undignified and the
authorities thereafter stopped this nonsense by instituting a rule
stating that the ball must be handed to the referee at the conclusion of
the game and it was later handed to the captain of the winning club.
When Everton were on the losing end against Aston Villa at Crystal
Palace in 1897 the whole Villa team went into the Everton dressing
room after the game demanding the ball should be handed back to
them. They had seen an Everton player gather the ball and rush off.
Everton players declared they did not know where the ball was. Villa
players searched boots, the skip, every nook and cranny. Their search,
however, was useless for an Everton player, realising the difficulty of
hiding his treasure, had taken out his penknife the moment he got back
to the dressing room, had slit the ball and was proudly going round
saying to the Villa players: "Find the ball and you can have it." He was
wearing it under his football jersey. He kept it there, using it as a chest
protector! Years after, he mellowed and handed his "trophy" to Fred
Geary, the famous little centre forward of Everton, who proceeded to
hand it over to the Aston Villa management committee when they
came our way to play a League game. So ended the chest protector in
its many miles of travel – in the board room at Aston.'

The match ball from the 1933 Final is still on display at Goodison
Park, along with many more items of memorabilia, and is seen
regularly by visitors on the club's guided stadium tours.

Despite the Kingscott scandal commercial spin-offs for Cup
Finalists in the 1930s were low-key and small scale compared to
today's ultra mega-buck hype, although one promotion after
Everton's Wembley triumph produced a memorable photograph of
Dixie and his team-mates dressed in Chicago gangster-type garb.
Gordon Watson, then a starry-eyed junior arrival at the Goodison
club, explained: 'Dixie was the last word for me. He was the greatest.
But he was still one of the lads. That really came home to me after the
team had won the Cup and a gents outfitters offered Dixie a suit if he'd

do some pictures wearing their clothes. He said to them: "I'll do it if you ask the whole team." They agreed and they did a great picture of the first team players in gangster hats and long overcoats. The same happened with Fusco's, an ice cream parlour near to Goodison. They invited Dixie for some ice cream but he said he'd go only if they invited all the players. So we all went.'

For Dixie Dean, the Cup triumph crowned a wonderful three years of success, the latter two of them under his captaincy:

> It was a great team and we were a most happy set of fellers. We had everything covered and, of course, we had the joker in the pack in Jimmy Dunn. Little Dunny got up to all sorts of tricks, including sticking a pair of kippers underneath a table in a hotel restaurant. You can imagine the stink! And when we were making arrangements for the photograph in the gangster outfits Dunny mixed up all the sizes. We looked like something out of a comedy show when we started trying them on! We had a good laugh together off the pitch and we enjoyed ourselves on it. We were all in tune with each other. I used to think we were like an orchestra. We didn't need to practice moves. We knew what the other feller was going to do.

One of Dixie's first acts after bringing home the Cup was to take the prized trophy to his former club Tranmere Rovers the following Thursday, thereby squashing at source the prevailing myth that he was so upset over the terms of his transfer that he boycotted Prenton Park.

Tranmere historian and author Gilbert Upton explained: 'People have put it about that Dixie fell out with Tranmere over his move to Everton and that he didn't go back to Prenton Park until the 1970s. But it's just not true. He actually took the FA Cup there only a matter of days after the 1933 Final. At the end of the season Tranmere traditionally played a game against Everton or Liverpool for what was called the Birkenhead Hospitals Cup. As the name suggests the match was to raise money for local hospitals, which Dixie perhaps had good reason to remember! On this occasion Tranmere were playing Liverpool and Dixie went along to Prenton Park on this own with the newly won FA Cup. He put the Cup on display in the stand and the presence of Dixie and the trophy swelled the crowd to 4,000 and brought in receipts of more than £250 for the hospitals, a lot of money in those days . . . That's not the only occasion Dixie turned up at Prenton. He also played for Everton against Tranmere in a Hospitals Cup match. Then in 1952 he refereed a match at Prenton between Tranmere Supporters Club and New Brighton Supporters Club . . . So to say that he didn't re-visit Tranmere until the 1970's was another of the many myths that have surrounded Dixie's life and career. He was obviously a very generous man who was always very fond of his hometown and he spoke with a perfect Birkonian accent. There is a clear difference between that and the Liverpool voice across the Mersey. It is a slightly softer accent than Scouse. It doesn't have quite the hard edge. Dixie was always proud of being a Wacker.'

# CHAPTER NINE

# *Taking His Name In Fame*

Everton's completion of their unique hat trick of trophies gave a warm glow to their supporters in a chill world that had just witnessed Franklin Delano Roosevelt sworn in as President of the United States, amidst a financial crisis with 13 million unemployed, and power-crazed Adolf Hitler marching along a brutal Germanic path that would lead to war. In Britain, though, there was a big drop in the jobless figures and the very symbol of Evertonian joy was the heroic figure of Dixie Dean, a peerless centre forward who had scored a phenomenal 127 League and Cup goals in 127 games in those three prize-winning campaigns alone. His overall figures since joining Everton eight years earlier were equally incredible . . 302 goals in 304 senior appearances.

One young man enraptured by this dashing, handsome sporting legend was called Patrick Connolly. As a small boy he had been taken to Goodison by his father to see Dixie dramatically set his 60 goal League record in May 1928. In 1933 he went to Wembley to see the Everton captain lift the FA Cup. Dixie made such an indelible impression on Patrick that he decided, when show business beckoned later in life and after he had become friendly with the football icon, to take his boyhood idol's name onto the stage. Thus, Bill Dean, comedian, actor and soap star of *Brookside*, playing the character Harry Cross, was born.

Bill, who once said his face was 'not only lived in but had squatters!' also appeared in the ground-breaking 1968 television play *The Golden Vision*, a title inspired by the nickname of another illustrious Everton No 9, Alex Young. Bill's funeral in May 2000 was attended by Everton representatives amongst a host of mourners and shortly before his death, at the age of 78, he talked to me about his hero figure:

Dixie just didn't know how famous he was. The very fact that he queued for the tram car in Water Street and then strolled into Goodison as if he was going for a kickabout in the park under-lines that. The day he scored his 60th he did exactly that . . . I was about six or seven when I first went to Goodison and I have thousands of memories of Dixie. I know comparisons are odious but to me he was the greatest. I idolised him. They talk about football today and they have fancy names and fancy positions. But nobody could strike like Dixie . . . And they talk now about man marking. I read in the press, for example, if you put a man on Steve McManaman he can't play. This man Dean used to have three round him . . . What's little known is that as well as his 60 goals in 1927–28 he played in a forward line that scored 121 goals in winning the Second Division championship in 1931. He got 39 of them and five other players got into double figures because of Dixie nodding them down. His team-mates had nobody round them because there were three men marking Dixie . . . I was on my father's shoulders at Goodison when Dixie set his 60-goal record in May 1928. I only have vague memories of it. But I was there and I do recall the atmosphere and I remember the crowd singing. Dixie was an icon in my book. He was great in the air but he was equally devastating with his feet and was powerful with both right and left . . . In those days it was legitimate to charge the goalkeeper. Often the keeper would be bundled into the net with the ball. If that happened with Bill the crowd would start singing: 'Are you from Dixie? Well, I'm from Dixie, too.' Dixie's great adversary, of course, was that great Liverpool goalkeeper Elisha Scott. Scott commanded the whole goal and penalty area. But how his team mate 'Parson' Jackson stood Elisha's language I'll never know! Playing in front of Elisha would make you want to give up thoughts of the cloth! . . . When you think that Dixie got only 16 caps yet scored 18 goals

it makes you think! Players come on today as England
substitutes for just a few minutes and are hailed as international
stars. It's just ludicrous. In the last 30 years they've handed out
caps like confetti . . . In Dixie's era there were no 'mickey
mouse' internationals but they did have England trial games
between the Probables and Possibles, which we used to call 'the
Impossibles'! The FA would pick the England team on the outcome of those matches . . . Dixie told me that before one England
match he refused the soup of the day, which was consomme, at
the pre-match lunch. He said: 'I'm not drinking that dishwater.'
And they dropped him for the next game. That's how the FA
worked in those days.

After Dixie had played and scored in that seven goal hiding of
Spain, that great *Liverpool Echo* cartoonist George Green did a
sketch of Dixie turning round to the Spanish keeper and saying:
'What's Za-mora with you?' Dixie probably gave George the
idea because he was a great comedian and raconteur . . . He got
a battering from defenders but he was a fairly hard man. Yet he
never got cautioned, let alone sent off. He told me once that
when they were playing a game against Wolves, a centre came
over, he nodded the ball in and just turned round expecting his
colleagues to come and shake hands with him.

But there was nothing happening because the referee had
disallowed it for offside. Dixie said he went over and said: 'What
sort of so and so referee are you?' The referee said: 'Aye, aye,
William . . . cut that out.' About 20 minutes later Dixie said he
was a yard away from an open goal but ballooned the ball over
the bar. The referee turned to Dixie and said: 'What sort of a so
and so centre foward are you?'

They talk about man-marking today but it was common for
Dixie to have three men around him. He told one centre half,
Herbie Roberts of Arsenal, that he was going to the toilet at half
time and that no doubt he'd be following him there as he'd
followed him everywhere else!

The fact that he could use that type of humour showed that he
had the right temperament to handle all the physical buffeting he

got. And to say that Tommy Lawton could head a ball better than Dixie is just ridiculous.

Dixie could score with his head from 20 and 25 yards out. And he wasn't a tall man. He stood a stocky 5ft 10ins.

The 1933 Everton team was a freescoring side and in his cartoons George Green used to portray the Everton forward line in a tank shooting balls into the net. I went to Wembley for the Cup Final that year on a charabanc. I was amazed at my first sight of Wembley. It was like seeing the American prairie for the first time, it was so huge to me. It was another world. Another planet. Don't forget in those days Goodison didn't have the Gwladys Street stand. It was like a cowshed at the back of that goal with a scoreboard on top. It was strange at Wembley because although all the Evertonians sported their blue and white colours the team played in white shirts and black shorts because the FA had decreed that both teams had to change from their normal blue. I remember being bitterly disappointed Everton were not in their famous royal blue . . . It was a great atmosphere and Everton played extremely well. It was a fine team and they were heady days. It was a great sight to see Dixie get the Cup from the Duchess of York, now the Queen Mother . . . I was only 11 and I was the only person sober on the charabanc coming back to Liverpool. It was a riotous journey home! Everton returned by train on the Monday and at the Town Hall they got on the coach and four that the club had used after winning the Cup back in 1906 . . . I was standing at the corner of Whitechapel, outside a store called Bunny's, to see the team go past with the Cup. Then I jumped on a tram up to Goodison because the ground had been opened. It was packed, just like all the streets were. There were terrific crowds. Dixie and the players showed off the Cup from the stands . . . Dixie was idolised. And Liverpool fans admired him greatly, too, just as in later years Evertonians used to greatly respect Billy Liddell of Liverpool. Yet despite all the adulation Dixie was never bigger than the club.

In those days goalkeepers weren't wrapped in cotton wool as

they are today and if they caught a ball they could be shoulder charged into the net. If Dean couldn't get high enough to head the ball or connect with his foot then he'd take the keeper, the ball, the lot! He was fearless. One of his goals in the 1933 Final was in that mould.

Dixie told me a lovely story about the day he played against Wolves when Stan Cullis was just starting his career. In those days when they kicked off the centre forward sauntered down and the centre half took his position behind him. Stan apparently went up to Bill and said: 'So you're the famous Dixie Dean are you?'

'Yes,' said Bill. 'Who are you?'

'I'm Cullis . . . Stan Cullis,' came the reply. 'That's a co-incidence,' Bill replied. 'That's the name of our coal man.'

'Bill told me that if a centre half started getting a bit heavy in the tackle he'd turn to them and say: 'Are we playing with the ball or without it. It's your choice.'

Everton had a good scouting system in the 1930s and it was a club that players wanted to join. When they signed Tommy Lawton it was clear he had been bought to replace Dixie and there was a certain amount of sadness about that. But in the period they overlapped at Everton Dixie helped Tommy develop his game, particularly his heading.

I'd say that Lawton was faster than Dixie and probably more polished. He was a great centre forward. But given a choice of both at their peak I would go for Dixie every time. In horse racing terms there was a short-head between them. One of the things I noticed about Dixie is that he always kept his eyes open when he was heading a ball. In later years I talked to him about it and he said to me: 'Ninety nine percent of players blink as they're about to head the ball but I always kept my eyes open.' That's amazing, really, because it's almost instinctive to blink before you meet the ball. When I played I think I used to close my eyes even before the ball was crossed!

Dixie could head a ball harder than some people could kick it. He could – and did – score from well outside the area with bullet headers. But his goals didn't just come with his head. He scored as many with his feet. He was powerful with either foot and he wasn't a bad dribbler, either. There were never less than three men round him but he was also very unselfish and set up a stack of goals for his team-mates, especially nodding the ball down.

One of my outstanding memories of Dixie is of him scoring his 200th League goal. It was a bullet header against Bradford. It was memorable because that afternoon Bradford played in rugby-style multi-coloured hooped shirts, which looked very strange to supporters in those days.

When Dixie parted company with Everton he went very unceremoniously. One day he joined Notts County and that was him, gone, like a click of your fingers. I happen to think that, given the opportunity, Bill would have made a fine manager because of his leadership qualities.

The last time I saw him play was during the war when I was stationed in Cambridge and went to watch a match between Northern Command and South West Command at Norwich City's ground. On the team sheet I saw the name 'Lance Corporal Dean' and it turned out to be Dixie. He'd put on about a stone and a half and had a belly like a rag man's bag! But he scored both goals in a 2–1 win for the northern side – and I think he touched the ball only three times! . . . Being in the services myself I made my way through after the game and a few of us had a pint with him. That was the first time I met Dixie. The next time was in 1948 when he had the 'Dublin Packet' pub in Chester. I've known his daughter Barbara since she was a tot.

Over the years I've met Dixie on many, many occasions and, after he'd lost his leg, we went to a lot of functions together. I'm an Evertonian so I chose my showbiz name Bill Dean because I was inspired by Dixie, the greatest Everton player of all time, the greatest centre forward I've ever seen. I'm privileged to have seen him play and to get to know him . . . As a standing gag when we were together he'd say to me: 'What do you think you're so and so doing signing my bloody autograph!' Seriously, though, what irked me was that he wasn't even honoured by the FA.

I've had a good career in show business. I finished up doing what I wanted to do and I've had the great honour and enjoyment of acting with great stars like Elizabeth Taylor, Laurence Harvey, Albert Finney and many more. I enjoyed it so much I'd have done it for nothing. But I freely admit I'd have swapped it all just to have proudly pulled on that royal blue jersey and run out at Goodison to play for Everton. And if I could have played just once in the same team as Dixie that would have been a priceless bonus.

If William Ralph Dean was playing today he'd be worth all the riches of Buckingham Palace and the Vatican combined. Alan Shearer cost £15 million. They'd want that today for one of Dixie's bootlaces.

The aftermath of the 1933 FA Cup triumph, however, was one of gloomy anti-climax for Dixie and Everton even though the following season began on an upbeat note when he scored the only goal of the game in the curtain-raiser against West Brom to give Everton a 1–0 home win and reach another memorable milestone, still aged only 26. It was his 300th League goal of his two-club career, achieved in 310 appearances, another all-time record. Clearly, though, it had not dulled his appetite. Dixie scored in every one of Everton's first half dozen games – collecting a brace of goals at Birmingham and overcoming agonising toothache to score against Sheffield Wednesday – before injuring himself in the sixth game, a 3–1 Goodison win over champions Arsenal.

Damage to his left ankle required surgery for the removal of two pieces of bone that kept him out of action until November. During his absence, Arsenal avenged their League defeat by returning to Goodison in the Charity Shield and defeating the Cup holders 3–0 in what would be Everton's last appearance in the fixture for 30 years.

Dean's return at Huddersfield was short-lived and disappointing. Everton lost 1–0 and he sustained a knee injury which meant a cartilage operation, long before laser or keyhole surgery could have a player swiftly back in action. Dixie was out until late February during which Everton, who had plunged to fifth from bottom of the table, tried and failed to sign the celebrated Hughie Gallacher from Chelsea. So the marvellously versatile Tommy White, switched from centre half to centre forward, continued to deputise and creditably ended the campaign as Everton's 14-goal top scorer, a haul which included a hat trick in an untypical 7–1 home win over Blackburn. Dixie returned at Blackburn on February 24 and also played in the next match, a 3–0 defeat at Tottenham which repeated Everton's third round FA Cup reverse. It was clear, however, he was far short of peak fitness and he made only another three appearances that season yet still managing to score nine times in his dozen outings as Everton finished a mediocre 14th.

In the year the driving test was introduced in Britain, Everton had found their powerful scoring machine mainly locked in the garage undergoing repairs. Dixie's injury problems meant it was the first time in nine seasons that he had failed to score more than 20 goals. Everton's League total of 62 was only two more than his own individual record set in 1928 and it was a goal drought the likes of which the club would not suffer again until 1947, when they achieved a similar meagre total.

Although Dixie had spent most of the season unable to play football he helped to pass the time by running a greyhound he had bought to pursue his interest in gambling, something that still flourished despite the anti-betting climate Britain's National Government was keen to foster. Dixie also kept frequent dates at Walton Prison, his celebrity visits no doubt eagerly welcomed by the inmates. Underlining that a sense of community is not something dreamed up in the latter part of the 20th century, he recalled: 'All the players used to go to the prison every Monday night for the warders' whist drives. But we also met the prisoners. In fact, the good conduct ones got the job of waiters. We played the prison team at football and also at golf and cricket.'

By the end of the 1933–34 season Dixie had fully recovered from the injuries that had blighted his campaign and, as captain, led the team on what was planned to be an end-of-season working holiday to Tenerife, a destination then available in Britain only to a select, rich few. The Everton party arrived after a five-day sea voyage from Tilbury on board the 'Dunbar Castle' and stayed at the Hotel Pino de

Oro in Santa Cruz. They played three games against Canary Islands teams, winning one, drawing one and losing one. The mixed bag of results was not surprising considering that it was not quite the relaxing sunshine break the club had intended it to be, as Dean revealed:

> They were hard games those. And I mean what I said. The ground we played on had no grass and was so hard you couldn't possibly play in studs.
>
> Luckily, the club had got wind of what the pitches were like and one of our directors, Jack Sharp, who had a sports shop, had a set of galoshes made for us before we left. So we played in those instead of boots.
>
> It was good for me to have a few run outs after being in and out of hospital during the season but it was boiling hot in Tenerife, even at night, and there were flies and mosquitoes everywhere. Then one night Dunny (Jimmy Dunn) and I were out when we heard shots. God blimey, we didn't hang around. We were off! We climbed over walls, ran along roof tops, you name it, to get back to the hotel. That was it for us. Dunny and I had a word with the directors and we got the next boat home.

Dean and Dunn had been caught up in the early rumblings of the Spanish Civil War with disputes between rival factions in the Canaries often ending in street confrontations and gunfights. The rest of the Everton squad were far from overjoyed at being there, either, and Albert Geldard recalled: 'With some difficulty the chairman, Mr Will Cuff, was able to transfer our tickets from the 'Grantully Castle' to the 'Avecata' which had been cruising in the Mediterranean, and the team were delighted to leave Tenerife three days earlier than planned.'

In total contrast to the previous season, Dixie was an ever present in Everton's first 36 League and Cup games of 1934–35, the start of which was preceded in July by the opening of the Mersey Tunnel by King George V, linking Liverpool by road with Dean's native Birkenhead. Connected they may have been but in the heart of Dixie he was never anything other than a proud Birkonian, as he was to emphasise many years later in his own irreverent, inimitable manner:

I'm a Wacker because I was born across the water in Birkenhead. Don't go round Argyle Street in Birkenhead and start calling a Wacker a Scouser or you'll soon be put right! I can assure you!

All the Scouse showbiz stars come to live in Wacker land. There's him and his dreamers – I mean Gerry Marsden and his Pacemakers – there's Paul McCartney, Freddie Starr and others, including the boxer Alan Rudkin. Once Scousers get a few quid they come across the Mersey and take our land off us! They all drift over.

During the 1934–35 season Dixie became a father for the second time, his wife Ethel giving birth to Geoff the day after Everton's 5–2 home conquest of Tottenham in December when Dixie celebrated the looming addition to the family by scoring a hat trick. The Deans, who lived in a club house at 12 Goodison Avenue opposite the Everton ground, already had one boy, William Joseph, who was born nine months before the 1933 FA Cup win. Two more children, Ralph and Barbara, would arrive later.

'I was born in Aintree but we moved to the club house by Goodison when I was very young,' recalled Dixie's son William. 'I still have a vivid memory of him when I was aged about two and my dad was a big star. Somebody knocked at the door to see him. My dad was shaving at the time and I remember him coming to the top of the stairs in his vest and with shaving soap on his face to see who it was. I've never forgotten that.

'From Goodison Avenue we moved to Stopgate Lane, where Everton trained at that time. When I was four my youngest brother Ralph was born. My mum had a difficult pregnancy with Ralph so I went to live with my dad's sister, my Auntie Lil, in Claughton Village, Birkenhead and I was there until the War began.'

Everton's FA Cup involvement in 1935 included the famous 6–4 replay thriller against Sunderland. The clubs had drawn 1–1 at Roker Park and a crowd of almost 60,000 crammed into Goodison for the second meeting on a Wednesday afternoon. Left winger Jackie Coulter, signed from Belfast Celtic the previous February, scored twice for Everton to signal what seemed a smooth path to victory.

Davis cut the deficit before Alex Stevenson, a Dubliner signed from Rangers a year earlier, restored Everton's two-goal advantage with only 15 minutes left when he applied the finish to Dean's header down. Sunderland, though, roared back and goals from Connor and Gurney sent the tie into extra time deadlocked at 3–3. Early in the additional period Coulter completed his hat trick only for his goal to be cancelled out by Connor. With only nine minutes of extra time remaining and a third meeting looking likely, Albert Geldard raced through to fire a majestic goal. With a minute left he scored again to secure a 6–4 victory and set the seal on an extraordinary contest, one described as 'the match of a hundred thrills'. Eight of the goals had come from wingers, a football species that became almost extinct after Sir Alf Ramsey's 1966 World Cup-winning 'wingless wonders.'

Dixie accorded the Sunderland thriller full honours:

It was the greatest game I ever played in. The first game up at Roker had been a real, tough affair and that's when I got my shorts ripped off me and had to cover myself with straw while they got me another pair of pants! So for the replay the FA appointed Ernie Pinkston as referee. They called him the 'Sergeant Major' . . . and that's what he was like. He stood for no nonsense. Just before we tossed up before kick-off he said to me and the Sunderland captain: 'Go and get your teams.' 'What for?' we asked. 'Just do as I tell you to,' he replied.

So, good enough, all 22 players gathered in the middle of the pitch and the referee said: 'If one of you so much as lifts a boot today I'll send the lot of you off!' And I could see he meant it, alright.

It turned out to be a tremendous game. We were leading 3–2 in the last minute when Sunderland centre forward Bobby Gurney got in an overhead kick on the edge of the penalty area and it sailed over Ted Sagar's head into the net.

Even after Jackie Coulter put us ahead again in extra time they came back again to equalise. It was a good job Albert Geldard had the strength left to run down the wing and score the two goals that won it for us.

Journalist Ivan Sharpe was an eye-witness to the drama and, dubbing it 'the most spectacular game of my time', reported: 'Like a bombardment was the thud of leather against goal posts and netting; 1–0, 2–0, 2–1, 3–1, 3–2, 3–3, 4–3, 4–4, 5–4, 6–4! Accompanying it a crescendo of excitement as 60,000 roaring folk were for two hours raised up, cast down and thrilled to the marrow.'

It was an amazing occasion on which Sunderland's manager Johnny Cochrane – who stood only 5ft 4ins – could vouch for the iron discipline of referee Pinkston. Everton chairman Will Cuff revealed: 'At the 90th minute the players awaited their trainers for the sponge, the lemons and the drinks but Pinkston turned them straight round. However, before he could restart the game he found a diminutive man on the field of play. Pinkston eyed this man, who was half his massive height, and demanded: 'What do you mean by coming onto this field of play?' The little man replied: 'I'm the manger.' An angry Pinkston replied: 'I don't care if you're the manager of the best team in the world.' At which point the little man interjected: 'I am, I am!'

Another remarkable fact about the epic staged on the afternoon of Wednesday, January 30, 1935, just a fortnight after the birth of a certain Elvis Presley, was that despite 10 goals on the scoresheet Dixie's name was absent!

Those privileged to be amongst the 59,213 crowd, producing receipts of £4,382 5s 6d, rate it the best match ever staged at Goodison. Some 56 years later another FA Cup tie would vie for that soubriquet, the amazing 4–4 fifth round replay between Everton and Liverpool in February 1991 which led within 48 hours to manager Kenny Dalglish quitting Anfield.

Perhaps the enthralled crowd that day in 1935 expected something special. Only a few weeks earlier the two clubs had been involved in an incredible Christmas bonanza that yielded 15 goals in a 24-hour span. On Christmas Day, Everton beat Sunderland 6–2 at Goodison, Dixie scoring one of the goals, but fortunes were starkly reversed in their Boxing Day visit to Wearside when they crashed 7–0.

A week after the Cup conquest of Sunderland, which sent Everton's Wembley ambitions soaring, came the match that confirmed Dixie's England days were over, even though he had only just passed his 28th birthday. England met Ireland and despite the venue being Goodison the great Everton centre forward was not even considered for the game, Ted Drake of Arsenal getting the job and failing to make the scoresheet. His club-mate Cliff Bastin scored both goals in England's 2–1 win. Dixie was on target in the next round of the FA Cup to help topple Derby County but Everton hopes were ended by Second Division Bolton who produced a shock 2–1 sixth round Goodison win.

In the League that season Dean added another two goals to his derby haul against Liverpool, with singles in Everton's 1–0 home win in September and another in Liverpool's 2–1 Anfield victory in March. He finished the campaign with 26 goals from 38 League outings as Everton finished eighth behind champions Arsenal and one point and one place behind Liverpool. For Dixie, it was the ninth time in 10 seasons that he had scored more than 20 League goals, a remarkable record of consistency.

Arsenal's championship triumph completed a majestic hat trick of titles, despite the death the previous June of the great Highbury manager and mentor Herbert Chapman. George Allison, the journalist and broadcaster, was appointed to succeed Chapman and led the club to their third title in a row with 58 points, four ahead of Sunderland. A fortnight after the end of the season Dixie had unfortunate reason to recall his motorcycle crash and brush with death early in his Everton career. It was prompted by the fate of Colonel T.E. Lawrence, famously known as Lawrence of Arabia, who suffered fatal injuries when he swerved his machine to avoid hitting two young cyclists in Dorset. Lawrence, like Dean, sustained a fractured skull but sadly there was no similar happy ending and he died after being in a coma for five days.

For one member of Everton's playing staff the season provided a brief window of opportunity in a door that otherwise remained firmly padlocked. Alf Dickinson, signed from Chester junior club Saltney, was a tall, freescoring centre forward in Everton reserves when his one and only call to senior duty came in March at Portsmouth.

'Dixie was supposed to be injured and I was told I was playing centre forward,' Alf recalled. 'The next day, to everyone's surprise, Dixie came into the dressing room, went to the peg next to mine and put on the No 10 shirt. It was the first time he had played inside forward. We lost 5–1 and I never played in the first team again. I knew I had no chance of getting in ahead of Dixie. He was just too good, the best centre forward playing.'

Dickinson, though, did have one claim to fame. He was the only player ever to wear No 9 when Dixie was in the team. Eventually, he went out on loan but it was one of his former Everton clubmates Warney Cresswell – who ended his fine 308-game Goodison career in May 1936 by becoming manager of Port Vale and then Northampton – who took Dickinson into League football on a permanent basis in 1938 when he signed him for £2,000. Former England full back Cresswell might well have succeeded Dixie's bete noire Bert Cooke in April 1935 when Tranmere sacked their secretary manager of 26 years following boardroom rows over illegal payments to certain directors and to players as signing inducements, prompting an FA investigation. Cooke's fate left Dean feeling that a certain poetic justice had been done but Cresswell's chance of crossing the Mersey to take charge at Prenton Park, potentially as player manager, evaporated because of Everton's demand of a transfer fee which Tranmere could not afford.

A happy Tranmere connection for Dixie in 1935 was his friend and former Prenton team-mate Ellis Rimmer's towering performance in Sheffield Wednesday's FA Cup triumph, the England left winger scoring in every round including two at Wembley in the Yorkshire club's 4–2 defeat of West Brom. After a tour of Switzerland during the summer, when Dixie's fame was evident in the public clamour wherever he went, the 1935–36 season was one of deep sadness for Everton in general and Dean in particular with the death of Tom McIntosh, the man whom Dixie had excitedly run to meet at the Woodside Hotel to sign for the Goodison club in March 1925.

Thomas Herbert McIntosh, born in Scotland in February 1879 and orphaned at the age of six when he moved to County Durham, died from cancer on October 29, 1935, aged only 56. He had been Everton's secretary manager from December 1919 after a football career that began as a right half with Darlington in 1895, prior to becoming their secretary in 1902. He became Middlesbrough secretary manager in

1911 and during military service in the First World War, including three years in France, he obtained a commission and was mentioned in despatches for 'conspicuous bravery'. Little more than a year after the end of hostilities he was appointed by Everton and presided over the winning of two League championships, the club's first Wembley triumph in the FA Cup, the Second Division title, two FA Charity Shield victories and, in Dean, the signing of the greatest player in Everton history and the finest centre forward football has seen. Dixie reflected:

> He was a great man that and when he passed away I was very upset. He was someone you looked up to and respected. Old Tom made my dream come true when I met him that first time down at The Woodside and he asked me if I wanted to join Everton. If any of the lads had any problems you could go to Tom and he'd sort them out. When I was made captain we used to have many a chat about this and that and you never had any trouble talking to Tom. He'd always listen and he'd try to do what was best for all concerned.

McIntosh achieved the not inconsiderable feat of being admired in both the dressing room and boardroom as club historian Thomas Keates revealed: 'The present system of management seems to approach the ideal. Mr Thomas H. McIntosh, the present secretary, with his assistants, spends his days at Goodison Park,' Keates wrote of the pipe-smoking official, whose duties were also that of a manager apart from sharing responsibilities of team selection with the directors. 'He is the consultant and father confessor of the players, a redressor (if it is possible) of their grievances, consulting engineer of the captain and trainer, and prudent adviser and information bureau of the directors.'

Shortly before McIntosh's death, Everton suffered the indignity of a 6–0 Anfield hiding by Liverpool, the biggest margin of victory by either club in more than a century of Mersey derby combat and an even more humiliating experience for Dixie and his team-mates than their 7–4 drubbing in 1933. The game was a personal triumph for 22-

year-old Freddie Howe, signed by Liverpool only six months earlier from Cheshire League club Hyde United and – painfully ironic for Everton – on the recommendation of former Goodison forward Tommy Johnson who had moved to Anfield 18 months previously. Howe scored four, the first Liverpool player to achieve that feat in a derby to equal Sandy Young's quartet of goals for Everton in 1904. Howe headed the opener followed by a couple of goals from Gordon Hodgson before Howe made it 4–0 just before the interval. For Dean, though, it was an even more painful experience. He had to limp off before half time after Liverpool's Jimmy McDougall stamped on his foot, Dixie claiming it was deliberate. With no substitutes permitted at that time, Dixie resumed in the second half but was later found to have a chipped bone in his toe which had to go into splints and ruled him out of the next seven games. Ben Williams was another derby casualty, with a groin strain, and a nightmare day for Everton ended with Howe scoring twice in the last five minutes. It was to be another 47 years before another player from either club would score four in the Mersey series, Ian Rush performing the demolition act for Liverpool in November 1982. One Liverpool supporter at the 1935 contest, John Redmond, recalled waspishly: 'In those days after a derby match they sold 'memory cards' and the only part I can remember from the ones on sale that day were the last couple of lines which went: 'Dixie said we broke his toe, but I think we broke his heart!'

There was more pain to come for Dixie a few hours after the derby, as Bert Edgar revealed. 'As a lad of 18 I was in Aintree and Fazakerley Social Club when Bill came in after the match. He was sitting with his injured leg crossed over the other when someone came in and slapped him on his ankle. Bill shot off his chair and his face went all colours! But, instead of hitting the chap, as many people would, he asked him what he was drinking, hobbled over to the bar and came back with a pint. Bill was also a great joker and he had a favourite trick which he would pull on his snooker opponents. The chap would be lured away from the table and when he returned he would find a red ball conveniently placed over one pocket and the black over another. He would immediately pot the red and then go for the black – but instead of going into the pocket the black would shoot up towards the ceiling.

It was made of rubber!' The return derby that season ended goalless at Goodison in January, with Dean again sidelined through injury. A week later, with Dixie still absent, they bowed out of the FA Cup after a 3–1 home defeat by Preston. In the League Everton finished 16th, but with the slight comfort of being three places above Liverpool. Dixie's injury in the Anfield derby had another unfortunate repercussion. The FA and the Gaumont Film Company came to Goodison to shoot material for an instructional football film for schools and youth clubs but Dean's broken toe prevented the greatest exponent of the art of heading a ball from giving a master class. Thus, posterity and future generations were robbed of the chance to see a legend at work and film archives contain only brief, flickering images of Dixie in match action.

Yet Dixie still managed the creditable return of 17 goals from 29 League appearances that season despite the blow of being dropped in the middle of a campaign in which Jimmy Cunliffe, a Lancashire lad from Blackrod, top scored with 23. The year also saw inside forward Stan Bentham score twice on his debut at Grimsby, the breakthrough at senior level of left half Joe Mercer and the recruitment of centre half Tommy G. Jones from Wrexham. Mercer and Jones would go on to play for England and Wales respectively as two of football's all-time greats and, with Bentham, help Everton land another championship in 1938–39, the last season before the outbreak of the Second World War. Mercer, who later captained Arsenal, managed Sheffield United, Aston Villa, Manchester City and took charge of England for a seven-match spell in 1974 after Sir Alf Ramsey's sacking, had an unforgettable first meeting with Dixie.

I was 17 at the time I'd reported to Goodison for training after turning professional. Dixie, who was exercising as I was getting changed, couldn't get over how thin my legs were. He just stared at them. Then he shouted: 'Hey, lads, take a look at these. Those legs wouldn't last my postman a morning!' Everyone laughed and it was Dixie's way of making me feel welcome. He was so kind and helpful to me in my early days at Everton – and he was the best in a golden era for centre forwards. He was unique, probably the greatest scoring machine the game has ever known or ever will know . . . He hadn't a negative thought in his head; he never showed any nerves or tension, he always believed his team would win and he never stopped scoring. In the air he could achieve anything and everything – gliding, deflecting, nodding it down or, as he did mostly, scoring. On the ground he had two good feet, never needed a back lift, which meant defenders had no time to get a tackle in, and he would regularly poke in goals with his toe end.

Above all, he was a terrific competitor, perfect for the job in physique and temperament. The man manufactured new legends every week, tales that are told and re-told whenever football is discussed. What is forgotten is that his scoring feats were a potent influence on the game. Every opposing team had to wrestle with the problem of how to stop Dixie, but few succeeded. It's been said that as many as four or five defenders were deputed to check him.

Yet all they succeeded in doing was to watch him win the ball in the air and direct it to a team-mate. But Dixie never believed in team tactics. He hated them. I remember in one of my first games for Everton in 1935 the staff decided to copy Arsenal's ploy by playing a third centre back in a game at Middlesbrough. We lost 6–1. Dixie was right! Another time he threw his hat at a table of model footballers which had been set out for a tactical talk and said: 'Never mind all that . . . I've got a wife and kids to support so just make sure you get that bloody ball on to my head!' Dixie was a flamboyant personality and made every match a big occasion. He was good with the public, marvellous with kids and a great captain. Nobody played it better, on or off parade, than Dixie.'

In the final game of the 1935–36 season, against Preston at Goodison, Dixie needed one goal to equal Steve Bloomer's record of 352 League goals for Derby County and Middlesbrough, scored between 1892 and 1914.

Journalist Ernest Edwards, 'Bee' of the *Liverpool Echo*, arranged for the celebrated Bloomer to attend the match. However, when the former England international arrived at Liverpool's Central Station he was met by Dixie and Edwards to be told that the Everton centre forward had been ruled out of the game through injury. Bloomer, who years earlier had nicknamed Everton as the 'School of Science', expressed regret that he would not be seeing the great man in action and delivered a fulsome tribute to him by declaring: 'I reckon Dean is the best centre forward I have ever seen . . . and I saw all the old-time lads. They were good at heart but Dixie has something none of the others ever had. It is his bonny method of getting away from the centre half and his unequalled skill in heading a ball.'

Dean's injury prevented him travelling on the club's end-of-season tour of Germany but in the opening game of the 1936–37 season his header from a Jackie Coulter free kick in a 3–2 defeat at Arsenal equalled Bloomer's record. Whereas the star of yesteryear, though, had achieved his total over 22 years Dixie needed less than 13 years to match it. It earned Dixie the congratulations of both teams and of referee Lol Harper who, by co-incidence, had also been in charge when he scored his record 60th League goal of 1927–28, also against Arsenal.

Lol was a good ref. He used his loaf. He'd calm down situations when they arose because he could talk to the players. In fact, he was the only referee I can remember speaking to me during a match. Not because I'd done anything wrong but to offer me a sweet! He'd say: 'William, would you like a peppermint?' I'd say: 'Thank you, yes.' He'd do that with other players when they were having a bit of a go at each other. He'd give them a mint and say: 'Now suck that and behave yourself'. Plenty of other referees spoke to me as we were walking off at the end of a game. They'd say things like 'well done' or 'great goal' which they could hardly say during the match!

I had 15 major operations during my career – for cartilages, nine bones out of my ankles, a split kneecap and a broken shoulder – as well as getting damaged ribs and fractured skull in the motorbike crash. But I was proud to say I was never booked or sent off. I made it my business never to retaliate.

Fittingly, it was at Goodison that Dean surpassed Bloomer's record. It was the first home game of the season, against Sheffield Wednesday, and Dixie had the fans roaring in admiration with a goal that was virtually a re-enactment of his record 60th in 1928. A corner kick taken by Jackie Coulter from the same spot as Alec Troup's eight years earlier was met by Dean's celebrated head and the ball flashed into the Sheffield net for his 353rd goal of his League career achieved in just 390 games, a startling, unrivalled scoring ratio which mocks any attempt at denigration by comparisons with conditions in different tactical climates or offside laws.

By another coincidence, the first to congratulate Dixie was Ellis Rimmer, the Sheffield Wednesday winger and his former schoolboy, Tranmere and England team-mate. 'Yes, my old Birkenhead school-boy team mate Ellis was first over to shake my hand,' said Dixie. 'I remember that goal well. There were five Wednesday players on the line. So instead of meeting Jackie's corner and heading the ball down on to the line I thought it would be easier to flight the ball between their legs. So that's what I did. And in it went.'

Dean's feats and Everton's style had inspired Michael Foot, a future leader of the Labour Party but briefly a journalist in Liverpool, to leap into poetry with an *Ode To Everton* which referred to 'Dixie's priceless head' and also 'God's lesser breed of men at Liverpool' which he later admitted 'got me into much trouble with Liverpool supporters.'

Dixie's breaking of Bloomer's record only added to the celebrations in the Dean family that September as they welcomed the birth of a third son, Ralph, to Dixie and Ethel. To add the icing to the christening cake, in the same month the great man scored another goal against Liverpool in a 2–0 home win, Alex Stevenson scoring the other. It was Dixie's 19th Mersey derby goal, a record for either club that stood for more than half a century until Liverpool's Ian Rush overtook it in 1989 and went on to score 25. However, Rush's goals came in five different competitions, including the transient Screen Sport Super Cup.

In the League, the great Welsh striker scored 13 times against Everton, compared to Dean's 18 against Liverpool. Dixie's last appearance against his keenest rivals was the return derby of 1936–37 when two Stevenson goals were not enough to prevent Liverpool winning 3–2 at Anfield.

Everton's game at Leeds in October that season marked the debut of Thomas Gwynfor Jones, the centre half who became known famously as 'T.G.', captained Wales as a teenager and was rated by Dixie as 'the finest all-round player I've ever seen.' Tommy recalled:

Dixie was getting to the end of his great career when I joined Everton as a teenager in March 1936. But as a schoolboy I saw him play when my aunt took me to an Everton match and I was also at Goodison to see him score his record 60th League goal against Arsenal. I wasn't particularly an Everton fan as a boy and I became an apprentice with Wrexham. I was 16 when I first played in their team. Everton then wanted to sign me but I had to wait until I was 17 before I could be transferred. Dixie was a great character. His character was so strong that it helped tremendously on the field of play. He was a dominant personality. We had Albert Geldard on the right wing who used to be faster than the wind and Dixie would say to him: 'I'll give you an early ball and just get it over to me.' So in the first few minutes of the game Dixie always tried to get the ball to Albert, who'd race down the wing, cross it at 100 miles an hour straight into the goalmouth and the goalkeeper and the ball would end up in the back of the net because Dixie was so powerful. It meant that goalkeepers used to watch Dixie more than they watched the ball.

Dixie was very good to me as a young player. He got me into the team. When Dixie was at Goodison he WAS Everton Football Club.

The first League game I played for Everton was at Leeds a few months after I'd arrived. Dixie, of course, was centre forward and captain. And I had the distinction of putting through my own goal and we got hammered 3–0. The outcome was that I went back into the reserves, playing in the Central League.

At the end of October, Dixie made his 400th League appearance –

in which he had scored 359 goals – in a 2–0 defeat at Middlesbrough and a week later scored the final first class hat trick of his career in a 4–2 home win over West Brom. The game was notable for another reason and became known by supporters as 'the day Dixie headed a penalty'. That label was not strictly accurate but the incident was memorable nevertheless. When Everton were awarded a spot kick Dean took it and saw his shot parried by goalkeeper Pearson. The Everton legend reacted instantly by racing in to head the rebound into the net.

That winter saw the Jarrow hunger march to London where guests at The Ritz taking afternoon tea where astonished when marchers invaded the hotel. The entire nation, however, was stunned shortly after by the abdication of King Edward VIII, who relinquished his throne to be free to marry Wallis Simpson, 'the woman I love', as he referred to her in his radio broadcast which plunged Britain into a constitutional crisis. The Duke and Duchess of York, who had presented Dixie with the FA Cup at Wembley three and a half years earlier, acceded to the throne as Everton were welcoming a man who, in a football sense, would succeed the crowned head of William Ralph Dean, the king of goalscorers. The new arrival was Bolton-born Tommy Lawton, a player destined for greatness and worthy of picking up Everton's centre forward torch from his legendary predecessor.

At 4.30 p.m. on the afternoon of December 31, 1936 Everton directors Will Cuff and Tom Percy together with secretary-manager Theo Kelly, the man appointed to succeed the late Tom McIntosh, were shown into the boardroom at Burnley. The reason for their trip to Turf Moor was to sign Tommy Lawton, who was less than three months past his 17th birthday. After seeking advice from his grandfather, who was the Burnley groundsman, the young Lawton agreed to join Everton. Burnley had rejected offers from eight other clubs before accepting Everton's bid of £6,500, then a record fee for a player under 21. Lawton caught the 9.08 train from Burnley the following morning, New Year's Day, arriving in Liverpool at 10.30. Lawton, who died in November 1996, recalled:

I don't know what I expected but when I stepped out of Exchange Station, Liverpool that first day of 1937 there was nobody to meet me. It didn't worry me unduly. But if I had been conceited the next few minutes would have dented my ego. Directed to Dale Street to catch the tram for Goodison I inquired from the conductor whether the vehicle passed the ground. He looked at me silently for a few seconds then said: 'Are you Lawton?' A trifle flattered at being recognised so quickly I said I was.

Another pause then he said: 'You'll never be as good as Dean!' What a welcome! But when I got to Goodison I knocked on the door of the players' entrance and guess who opened it. Yes, Dixie himself. He said to me: 'You must be Lawton. Welcome to Everton, lad. I hope you're happy here. Anything I can do to help you I will.'

It was a lovely welcome because they don't come any better than Dixie. Everton drew 2–2 with Preston that day. It was the first time I'd seen Dixie in action and I was certainly impressed. After the match I was taken into the dressing room by Theo Kelly and introduced to the lads. They were very friendly and we were to have such grand times together.

Before that day's game Mr. Kelly told me to hold myself in readiness for the trip to London for the match with Brentford the following day. But, instead, I was chosen to play for the reserves at Goodison . . . against Burnley reserves! It was a strange situation. The previous week I'd been playing for Burnley's first team. Now I was playing against their reserves. The centre half, Bob Johnson, bet me I wouldn't score against him. He lost his bet. We won 2–0, and I got the second goal.

Dixie recalled Lawton's signing: 'I told him all about Everton and wished him all the very best. I said to him: "It looks as though you're the one who's going to take over from me". So I had him with me for days and days after he arrived, teaching him the old heading trick. We used to play head tennis.'

The nature of those bouts of head tennis, though, were remarkable as Gordon Watson, who made his Everton debut the day after Lawton's arrival, revealed: 'When Tommy arrived at Everton Dixie knew he had come to take his place. But he took him out training and did everything he could to help him. After training was over those two would stay outside and Dixie used to teach Tommy how to head a ball. They used to have an old medicine ball with a leather case and stuff it full of wet paper. Then they would throw it up against a wall and try to head it against a target. That's how Tommy became almost as good as Dixie. You had a job just lifting the medicine ball. But Dixie and Tommy would head it to develop their power in the air and their neck muscles. We could hardly throw it, let alone head it! It was a dead weight. Even the old leather case balls were very heavy in wet weather and they had laces in them. Yet Dixie never had cut eyes. It was another example of his amazing preparation. He and Tommy could head a ball as hard as many could kick it.'

Watson remembered that he, too, was the beneficiary of Dean's consideration for younger players when he made his senior debut at Brentford on January 2, 1937: 'Jock Thomson switched from left half to left back and I came in at No 6. As we were going out onto the pitch Dixie said: 'Come on, Gordon, you get behind me.' So I walked out behind him. When we got out there he gave me the ball and said: 'Here, kick it around and get used to it." I just stroked the ball back to Dixie. But he said: "No, have a real kick at it. That'll settle you down a bit." That was the type of fellow he was. There was a great spirit in the camp and we all looked up to Dixie. I remember during my debut at Brentford being hit by their little Welsh outside right. He knocked me out. When I came round Jock Thomson told me to get on with the game and not to worry. A few minutes later the fellow who hit me was lying on the floor. Somebody had got him. That's the way it was. Everyone looked after everyone else. It was all for Everton FC. This came from Dixie. He was the greatest, he wasn't big headed and he did everything for the team.'

Dixie was still banging in goals, including two in a 7–0 Christmas Day drubbing of Derby County, and collected another brace in a 3–0 home conquest of Sunderland in February to crown a display hailed by punters and pundits alike. One of his goals that day came when he switched from defensive duties in his own penalty area to attack down the right flank, cut in, fox a couple of defenders and unleash a 30-yard shot that flew in a blur past Sunderland's Birkenhead-born keeper

John Mapson. 'This goal will find the highest place in Dean's records long after he has given up football,' wrote one observer.

Everton's decision to rest Dixie for the trip to Wolves a week later saw Lawton called up for his debut in Dean's famous No 9 jersey. It was not an auspicious day. Although the new boy, who had scored 16 times in 25 matches for Second Division Burnley, collected his first senior Everton goal the team were thrashed 7–2. Lawton recalled:

I was schooled and groomed with the reserves for little over a month before I got my chance in the first team. Dixie was rested and I was selected at centre forward for the match at Wolves. It was my first visit to Molineux and my first sight of Stanley 'Flipper' Cullis, later to be many times my colleague in the England and Army sides. Although we lost heavily, I had the satisfaction of scoring my first First Division goal. It was from a penalty, which big Jock Thomson told me to 'have a do at'. Those are the gestures that make a youngster eternally grateful to the experienced player for the chance to get rid of debut nerves.

Lawton was back in the reserves a week later when Dean returned for the home fifth round FA Cup clash with Tottenham, then in the old Second Division. The game, watched by a 57,000-plus crowd, was still goalless with only five minutes left. Then visiting keeper John Hall saved a Dean penalty as well as his follow-up attempt from the rebound. Hall's clearance set up a Tottenham raid which ended with Jimmy McCormick scoring. Only seconds remained when Jackie Coulter scored the equaliser to take the tie into a Monday replay for which Lawton was recalled in the No 10 jersey, the first of nine occasions that he and Dean partnered each other. The combination of master and pupil began in blistering fashion, each scoring in the opening 20 minutes from headers off Albert Geldard crosses. Jack Morrison reduced the deficit shortly before half time and early in the second half the referee pointed for an Everton penalty after Dixie had been fouled. Alas, for Everton the official belatedly noticed a linesman flagging for a foul throw by Joe Mercer and rescinded his spot kick decision. Tottenham had a 'goal' disallowed – for a push on Ted Sagar

– before Dixie scored his second after 63 minutes to put Everton 3–1 in front. 'I shot for goal from about 25 yards, the ball hit Dixie in the middle of his back and, quick as a flash, he turned round and flicked it into the net,' Lawton recalled. 'It was then that Spurs started to roar their team into action and for a club game I don't think I've heard anything like it. It was like a miniature Hampden Roar.'

Morrison revived Tottenham hopes with a second goal for the London club, with Everton claiming offside, and then created an equaliser for Joe Meek with five minutes to go. With the contest in the 88th minute Tottenham struck for a dramatic winner, with Morrison completing his hat trick in his side's 4–3 victory. Lawton remembered the moment like this: 'Les Miller, their left winger, crossed a high ball which bounced off the back of Charlie Gee, our centre half. By a miracle, it went back to Miller who centred straight away. The ball flew into the middle, Teddy Sagar couldn't reach it and Morrison was there to head into an undefended net. What a game and what a finish!'

Such was the thrilling quality of the contest that *The Times* acclaimed it 'as exciting a game as can be imagined' and added: 'If Tottenham deserve congratulation, and indeed they do, so do Everton deserve condolence.'

That match convinced Dixie that, in Lawton, Everton truly had found his successor. 'When I saw Tom score his goal I knew that was it. I knew that he was the one to take over. He was ready made. He went looking for the ball, he wasn't afraid of it and, when he got it, he knew what to do with it!

'I could see right away that he knew how to head a ball which was an art in itself in those days with the old leather balls, especially when they were soaking wet. If you headed it properly there was no problem. But if you caught it on top of your head it would knock you sick.'

The game at Tottenham spawned a story which has been passed into folklore but which Dixie's son Geoff believes is of doubtful veracity. The tale goes that as Dixie was walking off the White Hart Lane pitch a spectator close to the perimeter wall shouted to him: 'We'll get you yet, you black bastard!'

Thereupon, it is said, Dixie told an approaching policeman who had heard the remark: 'Don't worry, I'll handle this myself' and sent the loudmouthed fan sprawling with a punch. Then, it is alleged, the policeman said: 'That was a beauty, Dixie . . . and I never saw a thing, officially or otherwise.'

It has to be said that it was a story Dean himself told, although son Geoff feels that while there might have been some kind of incident he does not believe his father punched a spectator. 'Even though he would have been furious it was just not in my dad's nature to raise his fists and hit anyone, let alone a spectator,' says Geoff. The tale, though, has been told and re-told in publications around the globe and, accurate or not, has become part of the mythology in which the Dixie legend is draped.

Everton's Cup knock-out at Tottenham was followed by a 2–0 defeat at Birmingham and then a massive 7–1 hiding of Leeds at Goodison when Dixie scored twice and Lawton once. Strangely, it was the only game of the nine in which they played together that Everton won. But the extravaganza against Leeds preceded an alarming slump to the end of the season. Everton failed to win any of their final 11 games, losing seven and drawing four, and finished 17th in the table, one place above Liverpool.

Dean was a member of the Everton party that toured Denmark at the end of the season, the club's absence coinciding at home with the coronation of the new King George VI and Queen Elizabeth who, the following year, would open Goodison's new Gwladys Street Stand.

For Dixie Dean, though, the closure of his incredible Everton career was imminent.

# CHAPTER TEN

# *Farewell To Goodison*

The relationship between Dixie Dean and Everton secretary Theo Kelly, never a warm one, had become ice cold by the start of the 1937–38 season and signalled the great centre forward's shock departure from Goodison Park. The admiration and respect that had existed between Dixie and Kelly's predecessor Tom McIntosh had given way to a feeling of suspicion and growing dislike by Dean for the man now responsible for the day-to-day running of the club and whom he branded a despot.

Dean played in the opening three games of the campaign, scoring in the first game against Arsenal, but all three matches were lost. In the last of them Dixie shrugged off a teeth-loosening Bloomfield Road clash with Bob Finan of Blackpool, played on and gave an impressive display. Yet he was promptly demoted to the reserves with Tommy Lawton taking over his celebrated first team No 9 jersey. Dixie, then 30, felt certain that Kelly's ambitions to be Everton's first officially-appointed manager – duties he effectively already carried out – lay behind what he felt was a campaign by the official to sicken him and force him out of Goodison. Yet throughout this period Everton publicly insisted they wanted to keep him and had no intention of selling the greatest player in their history. Dixie felt otherwise.

This chap Kelly had no time for the older lads, especially me. I just couldn't get on with him. He was secretary but I didn't care what he was. I knew what was happening. He wanted to get rid

of me and also one or two other people who looked like being in
with a chance of becoming manager one day.

I didn't want to leave Everton. But Kelly was the reason I did
leave. It wasn't on account of Tommy Lawton arriving. It was
nothing to do with that. This feller Kelly just didn't want me
there long.

It says much for Dixie's character that during this period of
personal animosity between himself and Kelly his commitment to
Everton never wavered. No super star flounces or walk-outs at being
relegated to the reserves but rather a devotion to the younger players
cutting their teeth in the Central League.

Tommy took over from me in the first team and I went into the
reserves as old Mr Cuff, the chairman, had wanted me to. We
were nine points ahead by Christmas and although I left before
the end of the season the lads went on to land the Central League
championship and I got a medal.

Tommy G. Jones, who played in the reserves with Dean before
graduating to the senior side later that season, enthused: 'That reserve
team was very strong and you couldn't help but win the title! I had
Scotland international Jock Thomson at left half alongside me and
Stan Bentham was inside right. Jackie Coulter, an Irish international,
was on the left wing, and as well as the great man Dixie up front, we
also had Bob 'Bunny' Bell, who had been signed from Tranmere after
scoring nine goals in a match against Oldham. I played only 14 times
in the reserves and Dixie told Theo Kelly that I should be put into the
first team, who were not doing very well at the time. He acted on
Dixie's recommendation and into the team I went.'

Jones also succeeded Dean as captain but it was to be another
gloomy season for Everton. Although Lawton finished as 28-goal
First Division top scorer, displaying the marksmanship that would
bring him 23 England caps in a career that also embraced Chelsea and
Notts County, Everton struggled.

Along the way Jackie Coulter inflicted a blow to his former club by scoring the winner for Grimsby in a 2–1 home victory over Everton soon after his transfer to Blundell Park. The visiting team included Dean, recalled for a one-match stint because of injury to Alex Stevenson. At one stage Everton faced relegation but four wins and three draws from their final eight games ensured safety and a finishing position of 14th, three places below mid-table Liverpool, with Arsenal winning the championship by a point from Wolves.

Dean's 399th and final League appearance in Goodison colours was in a 1–1 home draw with Birmingham on December 11, 1937 and his failure to score meant that his goal in the season's opening day defeat by Arsenal – who else, you may ask, could it have been against? – proved to be his 349th and last in the League for Everton, an all-time record for any player with one club.

It would have been a fitting tribute to Dixie and superb public relations to have selected him for one more game to chalk up his 400th League appearance and with it the chance to make it 350 goals. After all, he was an icon to the Everton faithful, a god-like hero who had led them to triumphs and rescued them from the debacle of relegation to a new promised land. The extent of Dean's veneration by Everton supporters was captured perfectly by a letter from lifelong Goodison follower, Gerry O'Neill, published in the club programme more than 60 years later, in 1998. He wrote: 'We couldn't believe our luck when my dad's friend brought Dixie to our home one Sunday morning in 1937 . . . Half an hour before the promised time of arrival we were all waiting in our parlour, as though for royalty. The doorbell rang and my father answered it. After what seemed like an age my father and his friend came into the room and after a short pause, by dad's friend announced: "Dixie Dean" . . . My heart literally stopped. For a moment I felt faint. Then the doorway seemed to be filled with a golden radiance and there stood the great man. The dark shock of wavy hair, the bronze tan, the broad smile were unmistakable. Our dream had come true. The Gods had come down from Olympus.

'Dixie made us feel relaxed immediately. He was especially nice to my mum and dad. Most of the conversation between my dad, my brothers and Dixie were a blur to me in my ecstasy but then he turned to me and chatted about school and whether I played football. Then he bent down and felt my calf muscles. He turned round to my dad and said: "Well, he certainly has footballers' legs." Unfortunately his words never came true. I never made it beyond captain of the third house team at St Edward's College but his words have lived with me ever since.'

A 400th League outing for Everton was sadly to be denied Dixie who, given the increasingly acrimonious situation between himself and Kelly, decided that he must urgently but reluctantly seek pastures new before the March 16 transfer deadline. His last outing in an Everton jersey was in the reserves in the Liverpool Senior Cup semi final against South Liverpool at Holly Park on March 9, 1938, when Joe Mercer played at left half, and once again Dixie showed he was box office.

'I was privileged to play against Dixie for South that day,' recalled Ernie Dodd. 'There was a good gate and how the crowd loved the maestro! Every time he went for the ball there was a cheer. One incident, though, still stands out. Dixie was running at full speed towards our goal but the ball went wide and he couldn't stop himself. So he had to jump over the fence behind the goal, which was only a few yards from the by-line. The spectators grabbed him and wouldn't let him go back on the pitch for quite some time. Oh, how they admired him!'

Two days later Dixie was sold to Notts County in the Third Division South, for £3,000, repaying the fee Everton had paid Tranmere 13 years to the week earlier. The press and the public were stunned by the news with the pundits surmising that the transfer had gone through by amicable mutual agreement between Dean and the club in the best interests of both. 'The best deal in football history,' proclaimed one newspaper. In truth, Dixie felt insulted and deeply resentful of Kelly's behaviour and revealed:

Kelly started telling lies about me and things got worse. He wanted to have that manager's job and definitely wanted to get rid of me. I could see that. So I had it out with him and decided to move on. He'd already rung up Notts County and their manager (Harry Parkes) came through and had a word with me.

Once the papers had been signed Kelly went out without saying a word and nobody from Everton said goodbye to me. I went back with the County manager to Nottingham and became their player. But after my second match for them I broke another bone in my foot and had to go into Nottingham General Hospital to have a piece of bone out.

It was the first time I was able to watch one of my operations. I sat up watching it as they took this piece out of my foot. It was quite cosy! But it was yet another piece out of my body.

The circumstances of Dixie's departure from Goodison only strengthened his belief that the welfare of players was woeful. He was a passionate advocate of the work of the Professional Footballers Association, the players union which had been formed in the year of his birth, 1907. 'The work of the early fellers and the players in my time paved the way for the Kevin Keegans years later,' was Dixie's proud claim. During his career he also took every opportunity to play in cash-raising games to swell the coffers of the benevolent fund for injured players which was then still grossly inadequate. Everton, meanwhile, went on to win the championship in 1938–39 – Lawton again First Division top scorer with 34 goals – after which Kelly was duly appointed as their first official manager. He held the position through the war years until September 1948 when he stepped down and reverted to secretary with Everton struggling in the First Division and following the unpopular sales of unsettled Lawton and Joe Mercer to Chelsea and Arsenal respectively. Lawton, himself one of the finest centre forwards football has seen, always held Dean in glittering esteem. 'People ask me who was the greatest,' Lawton reflected. 'I have no doubt it was Dean.'

Dean's signing by Notts County was the latest in a series of star centre forward arrivals at Meadow Lane. He had been preceded by Jim Smith, the Ayr United player who scored a British record 66 goals in 1927–28 for the Scottish Second Division club while Dixie was tearing up the record books in England. They also signed Hughie Gallacher, once an Everton transfer target. Dixie was appointed County captain for the start of the 1938–39 season which started

Dixie in the striped shirt of his last
Football League club, Notts County
(Copyright *Keystone/Radio Times
Hulton Picture Library*)

brightly for him with three goals in his
first six games. But in that sixth outing
he broke a bone in his instep and, on
medical advice, County decided to
release Dixie although they continued
to pay him under his contract until he
found new employment. The call for
his services came from across the Irish
Sea, as he recalled:

While I was at Notts I was asked
by Sligo Rovers in the west of
Ireland if I could find them a
centre forward. I tried quite a
number of lads and asked them if
they'd like to go over there. But
none of them would have it. Then
Sligo wrote and asked me if I'd
go myself, which I did. I had a
very good time there. I helped
them move up the League and we finished second. We also
finished runners up in the Irish Cup. It was great, marvellous.

When I joined them they were £200 in debt. They paid me £15
a week, all found, even off-the-field clothing and, in all, I scored
27 goals for them. At times it was pretty rough. In our match
against Dundalk five players were sent off and the referee was
carried off. But we did well and I enjoyed myself there. By
reaching the Irish Cup Final the club made £600 clear profit and
they really celebrated, I can tell you!

We had a banquet in Dublin and I came back on the night boat.
At the banquet the Sligo chairman Mr Flattery had handed me an
envelope. I didn't know what was in it. I thought he might have
bought me a couple of ties or something. But when I opened it
on the boat I found eighty quid in it, in English pound notes. In
those days I think the difference used to be a shilling in the
pound. Sligo must have thought as highly of me as I did about

them. They wanted to see goals and, well, they got some.

Dean signed for Sligo on January 25, 1939 and played in 11 games between then and May, helping them reach the FA of Ireland Cup Final for the first time in history – losing 1–0 to Shelbourne in a Dublin replay after a 1–1 draw – and reaching their highest League position as runners-up. Matt McPeake, then a young Ulster footballer and later to wear the colours of Everton, New Brighton, Grimsby Town, Tranmere and Marine before becoming a Goodison scout, recalled the impact of Dixie Dean's arrival on Irish shores:

'I was an amateur playing with Larne in Northern Ireland on ten bob a week. In the middle of the season I got a telegram from Sligo Rovers – nobody could afford a telephone then – offering me a £10 signing-on fee and £4 a week. That was about £100 a week in those days! I told my mother about it and said I'd be able to give her some money. "You're not going down there playing amongst those Republicans on a Sunday, blackening the

---

## ENGLISH FOOTBALL STAR IN SLIGO.

### REMARKABLE WELCOME TO " DIXIE" DEAN.

#### BIG RECEPTION AT STATION.

#### LEADER IN LEAGUE OF IRELAND MATCH AGAINST SHELBOURNE.

#### ADMIRATION FOR ROVERS' COMMITTEE'S AND SUPPORTERS' ENTERPRISE.

#### THE STORY OF HOW HE CAME TO BE SIGNED.

Football history was made in Sligo last week in connection with the signing of " Dixie" Dean, the famous English star centre forward, and the remarkable reception given to him on his arrival at the station on Friday night, and the warm ovation which he received when he turned out against Shelbourne on Sunday last before a record crowd.

It all came about in an unexpected Ewing

---

Irish eyes were smiling at Dixie's signing by Sligo: how the *Sligo Independent* greeted his arrival in 1939.

Sabbath," she replied, quite adamantly. But I said: "Mother, Dixie Dean's there." She replied: "Oh, if Dixie Dean's there you can go. Yes, by all means." Dixie was the number one in those days. There was no television, of course, but everyone knew about him. So, just imagine, there I was going down to Sligo to play in the same team as Dixie! I stayed in digs for about 25 bob a week . . . Sligo came to a halt to welcome Dixie. It just closed down. The shops and the factories were shut. But the bugger didn't turn up! They'd got the wrong day! They all closed again the next day – and he did arrive.

'The greatest memory of him was when we played Waterford and beat them 7–1. I don't think Dixie ran 100 yards in the whole game but he scored five with his head. He was always in the right place at the right time and absolutely brilliant. Yet he was such a modest man and so humble . . . To me he was the next thing to God. I'd read about him in the papers in Ireland but never seen him. I was frightened to death about meeting him. But I couldn't have been more wrong. He was so down to earth with no edge to him. He was a bit of a comedian as well. He went to watch a game and somebody asked him how a certain player had done. "For heaven's sake", said Dixie "he had two kicks of the ball and they were both headers!"

'For me, Dixie was the greatest centre forward who ever breathed. He'd be beyond price today. A wonderful, wonderful fellow.'

With his family continuing to live in Nottingham, Dixie's period in Ireland amidst the delights of Sligo Bay, its mountains and salmon fishing, helped to hone his golf prowess as he pitted his scratch game against Irish professionals as well as playing a challenge match against Irish Walker Cup star Cecil Ewing. Dixie emerged from this enjoyable four-month sojourn with a couple more football medals for his collection thanks to Sligo's two runners-up spots. However, his Cup runners-up medal went missing amidst the post-Final celebrations and was nowhere to be found. He did finally get it back . . . almost seven years later in an anonymous parcel bearing an Irish postmark delivered to his appropriately-named pub 'The Dublin Packet' in Chester! Sligo never forgot Dixie's period with them. When they again appeared in their Cup Final, 31 years later in 1970, they invited him to attend as guest of honour to lead out the team. He even overcame his qualms about flying to accept the invitation and the aircraft pilot gave Dixie a stint at the controls as they flew across the sea.

Dixie's return to England and move with his family back home to Merseyside did not, as was once widely thought, spell the end of his football career. Painstaking research by Tranmere archivist and Dean admirer Gilbert Upton revealed that he had a brief spell with another North West team after signing at Liverpool Press Club to become the country's highest paid player!

'When Dixie came back after playing for Sligo it was the cue for a great coup by a Cheshire County League club called Hurst, in Ashton-under-Lyne, later re-named Ashton United. They were a fairly ordinary team but their chairman Joe Townsley, a local, successful businessman who had taken over the club, obviously felt he needed to do something to turn things round. Townsley told the *Ashton Reporter*: "We are paying more than we have paid any player before but I think our move will be justified. Dean will bring the crowd flocking to Hurst and I expect we will go a long way to meeting our expenses in the first few weeks of the season."

'I suppose you could say he pulled off the Cheshire League's transfer of the century by signing Dixie, who was ready to play for Hurst in the new season. Unfortunately, of course, war was declared on September 3, the football season scrapped and Dixie's contract rendered void. But he did play two games for Hurst, one in the Cheshire League against Stalybridge, which they lost 4–0, and the other in the Cheshire County Challenge Cup against Hyde United which they won 4–1. Dixie scored in that game on Tuesday evening, August 29, 1939. It was to prove his last goal and last appearance in a competitive match. He should have played in the next game but a chipped bone in his

A cartoon from the *Ashton Reporter* from September 1939, depicting Dixie's deeds for his last club Hurst in the Cheshire League. His brief spell with them ended with the outbreak of war.

ankle kept him out and then war broke out. His professional career was over and he was only 32. You couldn't envisage a player of his great quality finished at that age now. It was a big benefit for a player to drop out of the Football League in those days because it meant the League's maximum wage of eight pounds a week and a two pounds win bonus did not apply. So it was an opportunity for Dixie to make some extra money. He was on higher wages with Hurst than he had been at Everton! It was said that when Alex Jackson had joined Ashton National in 1932 he was on £15 a week, almost double the League basic. So one can surmise that Dixie was on a similar sum with Hurst, who themselves announced that his deal with them made him the highest paid footballer anywhere in England . . . But Dixie had pulling power. He was box office. For the match he played against Stalybridge Celtic the attendance at Hurst was 5,600 with gate receipts of £140. I would suspect that their usual crowd figure prior to Dixie's signing was 1,500 to 2,000. So he tripled their attendance. The *Ashton Reporter* at the time published the most magnificent picture that proves it is true what they say about Dixie. It shows a goalkeeper leaping as high as the crossbar . . . and Dixie is above him going for the ball. It captures everything people said about his heading.'

Towards the end of his Everton career Dixie had opened a sports outfitters shop in Grange Road in his native Birkenhead. The business was short-lived but Dixie's kindness and help for youngsters shone through.

'I was just a boy playing for a Sunday school team in Moreton in the 1930s when Dixie had his sports shop,' recalled Arthur Mason of the Wirral. 'Funds those days were very meagre. My father ran the team and we were on our uppers as regards kit. As a last resort my father wrote to Dixie with a plea to help us out. Duly a reply came to say that if someone would call at the shop, gear would be available. I was the lucky lad to present himself at the counter and, sure enough, the great man made me most welcome and presented me with shirts, shorts and a football (leather, by the way).'

At the outbreak of the Second World War, Dixie took a job at a Birkenhead abattoir.

Then one day in 1940 when he got back to the family home in New Ferry on the Wirral a letter awaited him. 'It was from the King. He'd sent me an invitation to work for him! Yes, they were my call-up papers and I reported for duty with the Army at Formby.' He enlisted as a private in the King's Liverpool Regiment and during his primary training on the Lancashire coast he was asked to pick a football team to play a side of former professionals who had joined the physical training section. Dixie was delighted to report that his team beat the ex-pros 8–3! He also guested – and scored – for York City in 1941–42 and when he turned out for Cambridge Town against an RAF side his team won 15–1, Dixie bagging eight of the goals.

On Christmas Day 1942 he was listed in the Tranmere programme to guest for his former club against his favourite adversaries Liverpool at Prenton Park in a wartime Football League Northern Division game. For reasons unknown, though, his potentially exciting appearance never took place.

One of Bill's comrades in uniform, who still preferred to remain anonymous years later, was a bizarre beneficiary of Dixie's fame and reputation. He recounted: 'Just before Christmas 1940 I travelled from Bowerham Barracks in Lancaster to Harringon Barracks in Formby. As I jumped off the Army lorry a sergeant asked me if could play football. I said I could and he told me he was looking for a good centre forward. Just then, the greatest of them all came out of the cookhouse. But Dixie was getting a lift to Birkenhead at 12 o'clock and he said the sergeant had his name down to play for A Company v. B Company. He asked me to cover for him, say my name was Dixie Dean and play centre forward. I waved Dixie off and I made my way to the Blundell Arms. After six pints of bitter I went back and got my kit from the hut. I duly played centre forward and, against what proved very poor opposition, we won 10–0 and I scored the lot! I didn't see the same sergeant until two weeks later, on Christmas Eve at Liverpool's Exchange Station. "Why the hell didn't you tell me you'd played for Everton and England?" he demanded. Before I could make any protest and tell him the truth he dragged me into a bar and gave me five pints!'

Far from British shores, RAF Aircraftsman Patrick Connolly, an armourer in 252 Squadron who spent six years in Egypt and later became actor and comedian Bill Dean, was discovering at first hand the extent of the global impact of Dixie's deeds. 'We'd rounded up a regiment of Italian prisoners in the desert and we were checking them through when one of them scowled and spat into the sand. Then he said in broken English: "F—— a ya Weenston Churchill and f—— a ya Deexie Dean!" Being an Evertonian with Dixie my hero I thought it was a great moment. I'll never forget it. I just smiled. I don't know what the Italian POW thought but he'd made my day.' His son Peter Connolly recalled: 'When we were kids my dad used to regale the family with the story of the Italian prisoner bad mouthing Churchill and Dixie. It was a story he loved telling. In his house my dad had a wall with photographs of some of the many showbiz stars he'd worked with and there, right in the middle of them, was one of my dad with Dixie. He idolised him and, of course, took his stage name from him.'

Dixie volunteered to transfer to the Royal Tank Regiment as a mechanic instructor with the rank of corporal. When the war was over he became manager of the Chester Army Cadets football team where he met up with a player who himself was to become a memorable Everton centre forward. His name was Dave Hickson. The end of hostilities, though, meant that Dixie had to face up for the first time to a new livelihood away from football. After being demobilised from the army he and his wife Ethel decided they would like to run a pub and Dixie successfully applied to take over the 'Dublin Packet' in historic Chester. His son Geoff recalls:

'Just before the outbreak of war our family moved to New Ferry and when the air raids began my elder brother Bill and I were evacuated to North Wales. My dad took over the 'Dublin Packet' shortly after the war. I was 11 at the time and I remember my dad going to the brewery to ask if he could have that particular pub. He ran it for about 16 years and it was the only one he ever had . . . After we'd moved into the pub my dad started playing for the old Northgate Brewery team in Chester and I used to go to watch him. One incident from those days still brings a smile to my face whenever I recall it. During one of the games the ball was crossed, aimed for my dad. He headed it and the ball was going about a foot wide of the post I was standing by. So I just stepped on and kicked it into the net! The ref blew for a goal and the keeper frantically kept shouting to him: 'That young kid kicked it in!' But the goal stood! There must have been something about goals in my blood. It seems so funny looking back on it.

'Our pub was full quite a lot, especially when Chester Races were on. It would be packed out then, with a lot of people from Liverpool. They'd call in to see my dad before making their way to the course. Celebrities of all kind would drop in to see him. We'd also get many Irish people calling in, looking for digs or a job. My dad would fix them up with somewhere to stay or put them in touch with one of the Irish foremen for them to get work on the building sites . . . He liked to meet people and spent a lot of time talking to the customers in front of the bar rather than be behind it. I don't think my mother was too pleased with that because it meant she had to do all the serving! . . . The pub was full of mementoes of his career. There was a showcase in the pub with all his caps, medals and trophies in it. People asked if they could bring their lads in to have their pictures taken with my dad and he'd sign autographs for them. He was really thrilled just to sit round the bar and talk about his life in football and there'd often be 20 people sitting around him. He enjoyed that. I was very proud of the fact that in 1931 he was presented with a medal specially struck by the Lewis's store in Liverpool to commemorate him scoring 200 League goals in 199 appearances. That's averaging a goal a match over four season, not including the FA Cup goals he scored during that time. Everton and England would love to have someone like that today! Another lovely memento of my dad's is the Hall of Fame trophy which he left to me. He was presented with it in 1971 when London's Hall of Fame opened and my dad was one of the first to be included in it along with the likes of George Best and Bobby Charlton. All three of his sons, myself, Bill who went to Australia, and Ralph, all followed him into the licensed trade. My dad wanted us all to be footballers. I wish we could have been . . . it would have been easier than pub life!

'In fact, all three of us love football and we played it a bit. But none of us was anywhere near good enough to follow in dad's footsteps! After all, he was some act to follow!

'My wife Pat and I took over our first pub when I was 21. It was the "King's Head" at Fen Ditton, outside Cambridge. About nine o'clock one Sunday morning we were in bed after a late Saturday night with a few "stay behinds" when there was this loud banging at the front door. We wondered who on earth it was. I got downstairs a bit bleary-eyed, opened the door, and there was my dad on the doorstep. He had the "Dublin Packet" at the time and apparently he'd told my mum on the Saturday night that he was going down to visit us. He caught a train to London and slept on some railway trucks while he was waiting for his connection hours later to Cambridge. One railwayman came up to him and said: "Why are you sleeping on that truck?" To which my dad replied: "If you can find me somewhere better, I'll be delighted!" That was him all over! My Dad wasn't just a legend . . . he was a comedian and a hell of a nice guy.'

Dixie's eldest son William recalled:

'When I came out of the Army in 1952 my Dad persuaded me not to join the police force as I'd planned. Instead, he got me roped into working with him in our pub. The "Dublin Packet" was a wonderful pub and my dad did a great job there.

'He was the sort of man that if the Irish lads came in on a Monday or Tuesday and sat there with just a pint he'd go over and slip them a ten bob note. He was a very kind man. I remember him coaching the factory football team at Foden Motors, which was famous for its brass band. I went with him a couple of times and we had bacon and eggs at a farm house on the way, which was a great treat with food still rationed at the time.

'My dad was also a great tap dancer. He could perform like

Fred Astaire. He said that learning it helped his balance, which is the secret of any sport.

'When I was a boy I saw him play in a charity match at Ellesmere Port with Tom "Pongo" Waring, his former Tranmere and England colleague, and Tom Gardner, a former Liverpool player. From a throw-in, Gardner put the ball on Pongo's bald head and he in turn nodded it to my dad who was surrounded by four defenders.

'But he took a step one way, taking the defenders with him, then turned in the other direction and headed the ball into the net. He could roll the ball around his head and it was a great example of his perfect balance, which his dancing helped develop.

'He used to tap dance in the pub on the wooden lift-up door in the floor that led to the cellar. It was like a little stage and he'd regularly give us a demonstration. He'd have been in his late forties then but his technique was superb.

'Before I was called up for National Service I played football for Claughton Rovers in the Wirral League. I played full back but I was 6 feet 2½ inches and my dad said I was too awkward. So when I came out of the army I went in for ballroom dancing and that made me a better player. I can thoroughly recommend it to athletes and footballers because it does vastly improve your balance.

'I went into it quite seriously and danced at places like the Grafton in Liverpool when it was in its heyday. On leaving the forces I was keen to get a game of football and I started to play for the team at Deva Hospital, a local asylum.

'In one particular match I conceded two own goals. When I got back to the "Dublin Packet" I found out that one of the hospital outpatients had called in and asked my dad for a large brandy. He drank it but my dad didn't get the money! This chap said to him: "It was to celebrate your son scoring two goals today." When I rolled up at the pub later my dad told me the story. I never let on they were own goals. My dad didn't know until the following week's local paper printed "O.G." twice against my name. What my dad said to me isn't printable. I took a long time to live it down because I'd cost him a large brandy as well!

'Gradually, I got more and more involved with the brewery and ended up going into the liquor, pub and hotel business. When I went into the licensed trade my dad gave me some sound advice. He said: "Keep your pipes clean and your bowels open!"

'In 1967 my wife Kathleen and our two boys, Simon and Matthew, had this crazy idea of going to live in Australia and it's something we've never regretted. We now live in Mandurah in Western Australia. It's an aboriginal area with a marvellous community spirit just like we used to know when we were young. I still keep up to date with English football from afar, although I also follow the Aussie Rules game.

'The last time I saw my dad was in 1978 when we made a trip home, during which we saw Everton's game against Chelsea when Bob Latchford scored twice to reach thirty League goals for that season.'

Dixie's daughter Barbara has a special reason to remember the days her family spent in Chester:

'I was born in the 'Dublin Packet' in 1945. Loads and loads of people, the famous and not so famous, would drop in to see my dad.

I remember, for instance, Lester Piggott knocking on our door at seven o'clock one morning. My grandad, my dad's dad who I called 'poppie', was a bit deaf and he answered the door. Lester asked to see my dad and my grandad said: 'Who are you?' When he told him Lester Piggott my grandad shouted to my dad: 'There's a kid here to see you from Leicester!' I remember Lester coming in and drinking a pint of milk. On another occasion, when I was only very young, we had a visit from Prince Monolulu, the racing tipster with the catch phrase 'I've gotta horse'. He was a tall, massive figure adorned with Indian feathers. When I opened the door and saw him standing there I just screamed my head off, ran up the stairs about 20 at a time and hid under the dining room table. For a youngster he was an awesome sight.'

From his own myriad memories of running the pub, Dixie recalled one incident when he had to use brute force – and received an official pat on the back for doing so:

I had the 'Dublin Packet' pub in Chester for 16 years and that was plenty. A feller came in one night and said he was the welterweight champion of Mayo. He started smashing glasses and pushing and barging everybody. So I ducked under the counter and kicked him in the shins. Down he went. And just as he was coming down he went through the bloody window.

Dixie behind the bar of his popular Chester pub 'The Dublin Packet' (copyright unknown)

He was then ex welterweight champion of Mayo. I was the new champion!

They took him off to hospital and just after midnight a police inspector arrived at the pub and said: 'Bill, you'll have to go to court in the morning.' 'Why, is he dead?' I asked. 'No,' said the inspector 'but he's next door to it.'

So I had to appear in court and it turned out that this feller had been wanted in the four countries for indecency against children. When the case had been heard and they're taking this feller off the magistrates' clerk sent a copper over with a shilling to give to me!

One day a coachload of pensioners arrived at Dixie's pub and one elderly chap said to him proudly: 'I remember when you came down Scotland Road with the FA Cup.' Dixie, prompted by the fact that there had been a turn-out of thousands for that 1933 victory parade, quipped in reply: 'Did you see me? Funny, I didn't see you.' After the laughter had died down, Dixie added: 'Anyway, if you're an Evertonian what are you wearing a red tie for?'

'It's the only one I've got,' came the reply. With that, Dixie left the bar and returned with a blue tie for his elderly visitor.

On another occasion, the sports presenter and commentator Raymond Glendenning arrived at the pub to record an episode for the BBC TV series '*The Hall of Fame*'. As he walked into the bar he raised his Homburg and, pointing to Dixie's row of displayed international caps, quipped: 'I'll swap you my hat for one of those.' To which Dixie instantly replied: 'Not bloody likely – yours would be too big for me!' The anecdote, though, does have a sad sequel for all 16 of his England caps went missing and were never recovered after being loaned out for a charity function.

Dean's great former Liverpool rival Elisha Scott, the goalkeeper he rated the best ever, was also a celebrated visitor to his pub and Dixie's youngest son Ralph remembers the moment: 'Elisha walked in with all kinds of presents for us. My dad, who was behind the bar, joked to him: "Don't be coming in here with all that stuff thinking you're going to buy your way into heaven."'

Although Dixie was now an established celebrity publican his playing days were not quite over. One lunchtime the first citizen of the city of Liverpool dropped into the 'Dublin Packet' requesting Dean to put on his boots again.

Dixie recalled:

> I was pulling a pint behind the bar when in came Alderman Joe Cleary, who was Lord Mayor of Liverpool, and the committee of South Liverpool FC. They asked me if I could help them organise and play in a charity game between a team of old Everton players and a team of old Liverpool players. I had a drink with them and I agreed that it would be nice to see a lot of the old players from both clubs back in action. So we arranged a game at South Liverpool's ground, Holly Park, and 16,000 people turned out with the gates locked. Big 'Tiny' Bradshaw was in the Liverpool team and I brought a kid with me from Chester called Dickie Yates, an inside forward who'd already played for Wolves and Wrexham and he went on for me in the second half. But I played the whole of the first half. I scored after 10 minutes and set up another. When I didn't go on for the second half I found all the reporters and photographers chasing me. 'What's up Bill, what's wrong?' they kept asking. I said to them: 'You fellers are never satisfied. I've got you a big crowd in here, I've scored one goal and made another, what more do you bloody well want for two bob!'
>
> Anyway, we went on to win the match 5–1 and after the game we all went to Reeces cafe in Liverpool city centre and had a great night.

In fact, Dixie's agreement to be the star turn at the charity match was done at a personal expense unknown to the public. His eldest son William revealed: 'Late in 1949 my dad was a passenger in a car with some friends on a trip into North Wales. As the vehicle was cornering a bend the driver lost control and the car turned over. My dad was injured, not too seriously but bad enough to hamper his work in the pub, for which he made an insurance claim.

Spotlight on the 'old boys' of Liverpool and Everton: George Green's cartoon from the *Football Echo* in January 1950 (copyright *Liverpool Daily Post & Echo*)

'When he was asked to play in the charity match not long after the accident he knew that if he appeared in the game his insurance claim would be thrown out. But he still went ahead and agreed to take part because that was his nature. He was a kind man and used to say to me: "If you can't do someone a good turn don't do them a bad one." '

The game was staged on Wednesday, January 25, 1950, four months after South Liverpool had become the first club on Merseyside and one of the first in Britain to stage a floodlit match, when a Nigerian touring side provided the opposition.

Sadly, the club that would later include John Aldridge and Jimmy Case on its player roll, folded in 1991 and had to quit Holly Park before being relaunched as members of the Liverpool County Combination playing in Garston. However, the exciting innovation of floodlights clearly inspired the editorial writer in the 6d souvenir programme for the game between former Everton and Liverpool stars to proclaim with some degree of hyperbole:

'Tonight's match throws the floodlights on both sides of the fast-flowing river of soccer. Spectators are privileged to stand on a bridge which connects yesterday with today. While, though, many have followed in his wake there remains only one Dixie Dean, one William Ralph whose skills transcend anything which his successors have been able to produce. Tommy Lawton has been the nearest approach but Dean had that certain something about him which others have envied but never had.'

Although Dixie had left Everton almost 12 years earlier his pulling power was still magnetic. The ground was bulging at the seams and police took youngsters out of the crowd and sat them around the touchline for their own safety. The ex-Everton side won 5–1 and other scorers were Irish international Alex Stevenson, who scored twice, Charlie Leyfield and Yates with Tom Gardner netting for the former Liverpool team. Match reporter Leslie Edwards wrote in the *Liverpool Daily Post*: 'Someone shouted last night as the great W.R. Dean and Matt Busby led out their respective teams "Is it true what they say about Dixie?"

'The answer came within the first 15 minutes when the massive figure shot at goal, hit the post and lofted a pass over to Charlie Leyfield for that player to score with ease. Dean was playing under lights for the first time in this country but his head found the ball unerringly from a goal-kick and steered it with old time accuracy towards the wing. No loss or lack of judgment there. Dean trotted back, stamping his feet in joy as he used to after scoring and, although not often in the game, was always there or thereabouts for the through pass or the centre. He retired gracefully at the interval because a motor accident a few weeks ago had necessitated stitches in his head. It was exhibition stuff of high order on an iron ground. Floodlighting is a good alternative to no football at all but imagine this game played in warm sunshine at Anfield or Goodison Park. Its attraction would be unceasing.

'We were left wondering what an earlier vintage of veterans in Tom Fern, Harry Beadles, Bill Lacey, Jimmy Dunn, Chris Harrington, Cyril Gilhespy, Jack Bamber, Jimmy McDougall and Eph Longworth might have shown us had they been asked to strip instead of merely to make a bow. Good to see them all.' The teams lined up: – Everton: Frank King; Willie Cook, Gordon Watson; Cliff Britton, Charlie Gee, Jock Thomson; Ted Critchley, Albert Geldard, Dixie Dean (Dick Yates), Tom Johnson, Charlie Leyfield. Liverpool: Stan Kane; Ted Savage, Tom Bush; Matt Busby, Tom Bradshaw, Jimmy McInnes; Harold Taylor, Bill Kinghorn, Tom Gardner, Alf Hanson, Lance Carr. Referee: Bill Evans (Liverpool).

Such was the huge success of the 'old timers' contest that a re-match was organised three months later on April 19, 1950 again at Holly Park and again including 43-year-old Dixie. He did not disappoint a 9,500 crowd, scoring with a left foot shot in a 2–2 draw. With him in the Everton ranks was Ted Sagar, the evergreen goalkeeper who was still playing League football and would remain on Everton's books until retiring in May 1953. As well as Dean and Sagar, two other members of Everton's 1933 FA Cup winning side, full back Warney Cresswell and inside forward Jimmy Dunn, also played.

Sagar won praise from one reporter who wrote: 'He brought off a save of distinction from a penalty kick taken by Bradshaw.' Dixie

# Ex-Everton v Ex-Liverpool at Bootle Stadium
## played 4 May 1950

### 2-2

### Bootle Times of 12 May 1950

A cartoon from the *Bootle Times* inspired by a match between former Everton and Liverpool starts in May 1950 (copyright *Liverpool Daily Post & Echo*) scored the opening goal with Alex Stevenson the other Everton marksman. Liverpool's goals came from Tom Gardner and Alf Hanson, who became South Liverpool's player manager after his League career ended.

'Everybody yearned for a Dean goal,' said the *Liverpool Daily Post*. 'That famous head came very near to getting one inside 10 minutes from a Leyfield centre. In the end, Dean drove home the first goal from another Leyfield offering to give Everton the lead. Dean and Bradshaw retired at the interval but the charm of the game remained.'

Everton's line-up was: Ted Sagar; Warney Cresswell, Norman Greenhalgh; Hill, Gordon Watson, Charlie Leyfield; Ted Critchley, Jimmy Dunn, Dixie Dean, Alex Stevenson, Wally Boyes.

Liverpool's team, supplemented by guest players, was: – Stan Kane; Bob Done, J. Kane; Ted Savage, Tom Bradshaw, Les McDowell (former Manchester City); Bill Kinghorn, Albert Malam (former Huddersfield and Doncaster), Tom Gardner, Alf Hanson, Lance Carr.

The programme notes for the game included a paragraph many would feel is pertinent today. Reflecting on the first meeting of the former stars the writer observed: 'The first match was a definite contrast in style to present day football and young people will probably understand after this match why older ones maintain that today's football is not so attractive as it used to be. Greater speed seems to have given less time for accuracy.'

The public appeal of these matches was such that a third game was organised just over a fortnight later this time at Bootle Stadium, then the home of Bootle FC, who once had been brief but proud members of the Football League, spending one season in the Second Division in 1892–93 when they finished eighth of 12 clubs. They had long since drifted into non league circles yet the visit of Dixie Dean and company that Spring day in 1950 drew an astonishing crowd of 17,000 who paid the not inconsiderable sum for that time of one shilling admission. And they were to witness a piece of football history. May 4, 1950 was the date. Some 24 hours earlier, in Dixie's native Birkenhead, the 36,800 ton HMS 'Ark Royal' was launched and the third match in the veterans' series coincided with Sir Malcolm Sargent succeeding Sir Adrian Boult as conductor of the London Symphony Orchestra. It also marked the last public performance in an Everton jersey of the man who composed his own goalscoring concerto . . . the unforgettable, unrivalled William Ralph Dean.

Five days earlier at Wembley, the then current Liverpool side had lost 2–0 to Arsenal in the FA Cup Final. Despite the disappointment amongst the Red half of Merseyside the public were again eager to see the stars of yesteryear, of whom Dixie still shone brightest of all.

Everton's line-up was: Ted Sagar; Warney Cresswell, Norman Greenhalgh; Gordon Watson, Tom Griffiths, Charlie Gee; Albert Geldard, Jimmy Dunn, Dixie Dean, Alex Stevenson, Charlie Leyfield. Reserves: Frank King, Ted Critchley, George Jackson.

Liverpool's team was: Alf Hobson; Bob Done, Tom Bush; Tom Gardner, Tom Bradshaw, Lance Carr; Bill Kinghorn, Albert Malam (former Huddersfield and Doncaster), Fred Howe, Syd Roberts, Alf Hanson. Reserves: Harold Taylor, Norman James.

The bumper crowd, a record for Bootle Stadium, saw a 2–2 draw, Leyfield and Geldard scoring for Everton and Hanson and Malam replying for Liverpool. Fate decreed that it would not be a scoring farewell for Dean, one reporter noting: 'What everyone wanted to see once again was a Dean goal. The head that nodded in so many for Everton failed last night, but there was a number of near misses.' The Bootle club's own archives recorded: 'The game was arranged by the influential Wally Halsall and there was a great local presence involved as Tom Gardiner, 'Tich' Malam, Syd Roberts, Alf Hanson and 'Bunny' James, all had their roots in Bootle. The 2–2 result didn't really matter. The main outcome was that Bootle FC made a much needed profit of £350. Just as important to the players was the entertainment they received at Bootle Town Hall after the match as guests of the Mayor. I am also reliably informed that the players entertained themselves in a few Liverpool city centre pubs before the game. The spin-off from the game, apart from the profit, was the signing by Wally Halsall of Alex Stevenson just a few weeks after the game. Stevenson was an Everton idol at the time, a regular Irish international before and after the war, and was to take over the reins as player-manager with Wally Halsall assuming the secretary's position.'

The game prompted the *Bootle Times* to enthuse: 'Long will the thousands present remember the touches of classic brilliance so evident right to the final whistle. And long will the players remember the tremendous ovation as they left the field. That was Bootle's way of saying "thanks for the memory". Following the match an excellent supper was served at Bootle Town Hall where Dixie Dean thanked everyone for the reception they had given both teams. Coming back to Bootle had enabled him to meet a very old friend, Mr T. Bell, former Chief Constable of Bootle, whom he had been very pleased to see.'

Dixie, though, was to make two more visits to Goodison Park. One of them would be for a belated salute from Everton and the supporters. The second would be bathed in sadness.

# CHAPTER ELEVEN

## *On Stage Again For a Belated Salute*

The legend of Dixie Dean soon became evident to his young daughter Barbara who, as a child, realised that her father's fame not only drew people to the 'Dublin Packet' but meant that whenever he went out in public he was like a Pied Piper.

'I can remember my dad taking me to Liverpool to see a firework display when I was about two and half or three. It caused absolute mayhem because we left home early one morning and didn't get back until four o'clock the next morning! We never saw the fireworks. He got involved with so many people and I can remember falling asleep in different pubs along Scottie (Scotland) Road. That was probably my first memory of him. So even at a young age I realised what a star my dad was and that so many people wanted to talk to him and be in his company . . . To be honest, because football was all we ever heard in a house full of men and being brought up in a pub I switched off from it. I wasn't really interested. It was football all the time but I really don't know a lot about it.

'My dad was quoted as saying I had the determination, strength and courage to play football but that I was the wrong sex for it. There was very little women's football then. But I've always supported Everton. You've got to be loyal, haven't you. One of my brothers, Ralph, is a Liverpool fan and my dad used to joke to him: 'I must have been drunk when you were conceived.'

Back in 1928, on the watershed May afternoon for Dixie and English football when he scored his 60th goal of the season, a talented, ambitious 32-year-old businessman was among the packed, enthralled crowd watching the Everton centre forward make history. From that moment, John Moores was captivated by Dixie Dean . . . by his style, by his aura and by his ability. Five years earlier with two partners Eccles-born Moores had launched his first football pools and, after initial teething problems, the business grew into the world famous Littlewoods Organisation, becoming Europe's largest private company. In 1960 he spawned a revolution in Goodison fortunes and became Everton chairman after offering the club a then massive interest-free loan of £56,000. Star players were signed, a new manager in Harry Catterick was recruited – his predecessor Johnny Carey famously being sacked by Moores in a London taxi – and two League championships and an FA Cup triumph followed during the next decade. The financial clout of Moores earned Everton the label of 'The Mersey Millionaires' but the little man of huge wealth never forgot Dixie Dean nor the fact that the club's greatest ever player had been allowed to leave Everton unheralded.

'I saw my first football when I was seven or eight and that was Manchester United.' Moores recalled. 'That was when they played in Clayton and my father bought me a ticket and used to take me down and let me sit on the grass. The players looked enormous to me. When I came to Liverpool I began to watch Everton and, like most people, once I got a feeling for one team it stuck with me. I was a spectator when Dixie Dean scored his 60th League goal in the match against Arsenal and he made a great impression on me. He had a marvellous scoring technique, one that's never been equalled. He was wonderful, of course, with his head. But when he shot he did it with a very short back swing of his foot. He must have had great leg power. I truly admired Billy Dean because he always played the game. By God, football needs a lot more like him.'

The first act by Moores for Dixie came in 1961, the year Dixie and Ethel gave up the 'Dublin Packet' and returned to Wirral to live at Teehey Lane in Bebington, later moving into a bungalow in Upton.

At the age of 54 Dixie took up an offer from the Everton chairman to become a security officer with the Littlewoods Organisation in Birkenhead, subsequently transferring to the company's Liverpool offices as a porter.

'The brewery were kind to me and looked after me quite nicely. But I couldn't afford to sit back and do nothing. Besides I was only 54. So I contacted Littlewoods and they gave me a job right away.'

'My dad was always a worker,' said daughter Barbara. 'After John Moores had made a job for him at Littlewoods in Liverpool instead of catching the train my dad used to get up very early and get a lift through the Mersey Tunnel in the *Liverpool Echo* van between four and half past four in the morning!

'Even if he'd been to a function or dinner the night before, he'd still get up. You wouldn't get many people who'd had his fame doing that, would you? He also had a great sense of humour. I think all my dad's job entailed was sitting at the Littlewoods front desk to speak and chat to people as they came in. It was something John Moores created for him. He didn't like eating in the canteen – he wasn't keen on the chef – so my mum used to make him sandwiches. "What do you fancy?" she'd ask. "I'd like some sardine butties," he'd reply. Because he said he'd like them my mum used to make them time and time again. Then one day he looked at my mum sideways and said: "Do you know, at work they don't know whether to call me Bill Dean, Dixie Dean or bloomin' sardine."'

Moores, who was knighted in 1980 for charitable services, decided that Everton should stage a public thank you to Dixie, one that would also help him financially. It spurred him to organise a testimonial match at Goodison Park on April 7, 1964 to honour Everton's finest son, as a belated appreciation of his fantastic contribution to the club's tradition, heritage and prestige.

Some 26 years after his departure Dixie stepped back onto the Goodison stage to kick off his testimonial match and was roared emotionally all the way to the centre circle and back after setting the ball rolling. With moist eyes he waved to his adoring gallery. A remarkably large crowd of 36,870 – many of whom had never seen Dixie play – turned out to salute the old master and watch a match between 'Liverton England', a team of English players from Everton

Back on the Goodison stage. Dixie walks out to kick off his testimonial match in 1964 between 'Liverton England' and 'Liverton Scotland', flanked by captains Ron Yeats (left) and Tony Kay (copyright unknown)

and Liverpool managed by Goodison boss Harry Catterick and captained by Tony Kay, and their Scottish counterparts from the two clubs in a Liverton Scotland' side, managed by Bill Shankly and captained by Ron Yeats.

Merseyside's England team lined up liked this: Andy Rankin (Everton); Gerry Byrne (Liverpool), Ronnie Moran (Liverpool, replaced by Chris Lawler Liverpool); Tony Kay (Everton, captain), Brian Laborne (Everton), Brian Harris (Everton); Ian Callaghan (Liverpool), Dennis Stevens (Everton), Fred Pickering (Everton), Derek Temple (Everton), Johnny Morrissey (Everton). The Scotland side, supplemented by Northern Ireland international Jimmy Hill who replaced injured Wales star Roy Vernon and with Bobby Graham coming in for injured Ian St John, was: Tommy Lawrence (Liverpool); Sandy Brown (Everton), George Thomson (Everton); Jimmy Gabriel (Everton), Ron Yeats (Liverpool, captain), Willie Stevenson (Liverpool); Alex Scott (Everton), Bobby Graham (Liverpool), Alex Young (Everton), Jimmy Hill (Everton), Gordon Wallace (Liverpool).

Scotland won 3–1 through goals from Wallace, Gabriel and Stevenson with Pickering replying for England. *Liverpool Echo* match reporter Michael Charters waxed lyrical about the skills on view and the effectiveness of the Scotland half back line of Gabriel, Yeats, and Stevenson. He noted, though, that the presence of Dixie predominated. 'This was his night and his alone,' he wrote.

Gate receipts amounted to around £7,000, money which Moores arranged to be held in trust for the celebrated beneficiary whose pre-eminence among goalscorers led to his appearance on the Eamonn Andrews television show to debate the state of football with another, much later, British icon of the game, George Best. Dixie, perhaps not surprisingly, stole the show with one deathless aside. As the subject turned to comparison of players' earnings he quipped: 'When I was playing I couldn't afford a pair of boots never mind boutiques.'

Decades after he had hung up his boots, Dixie was still a celebrity to young and old alike. Former *Daily Mirror* sportswriter Dave Horridge recalled: 'I used to have a drink with Dixie in Birkenhead during the 1960s when he'd be in his late fifties. We would have a pint or two in the old Conway pub on Conway Street and youngsters were always coming up to him and asking for his autograph. Every time, he'd pull out a piece of paper from his pocket and give it to them. I was curious about this until Dixie explained: 'I stay in on Mondays and sign all these bits of paper so that when the kids ask for my autograph it doesn't interfere with my drinking!'''

In 1971 Dixie's status in the game was recognised when he was one of the founder inclusions in London's 'Football Hall of Fame' and received a handsome, inscribed trophy. The following year he retired from Littlewoods on a pension at the age of 65, by which time his three sons and daughter had all married. Soon after, he overcame serious illness. He was rushed to hospital and placed on the danger list when a duodenal ulcer burst. As always, Dixie's humour shone through adversity. 'They told me I had special blood, Rhesus Negative. They said it was the rarest type. "Never mind that ," I said. "Is it the dearest?" I needed 15 pints of the stuff to bring me round.' His recovery spanned five weeks in an intensive care unit.

Dixie with his beloved grand-daughter Melanie (copyright *Daily Express*)

In 1974, only 18 months after moving into the Upton bungalow, tragedy struck when Ethel suffered a heart attack and died. Daughter Barbara and her husband moved in and looked after grieving Dixie who became devoted to his grand-daughter Melanie. 'My daughter Melanie was the apple of my dad's eye,' Barbara recalled.

'I remember coming home one evening when she was only eight or nine to find her holding a pair of pliers in my dad's mouth after he'd asked her to try and pull out a sore tooth! Another time he'd tied one end of a piece of string to the door, the other end to one of his teeth and asked her to slam it!'

Dixie accepted an invitation from the Football Writers Association in April 1976 to present the Footballer of the Year Award in London to that year's winner, ironically Liverpool's England star Kevin Keegan.

He was also asked to make an after dinner speech and his wit and timing surpassed all others on the night, earning him a standing ovation from the celebrity audience which included politician Michael Foot, who had once committed the Dean magic to poetry.

The Football Writers presented Dixie with a silver salver on which was inscribed: 'To Dixie Dean . . . 60 goals in a season . . . more than most TEAMS score today.' To those who were fortunate to have experienced a Dean 'after dinner' his barnstorming display in London was no surprise.

Dave Russell, a former manager and long-time servant of Dixie's first League club, Tranmere Rovers, recalled: 'Dixie was fantastic on the field but also marvellously entertaining off it. He used to come to speak at Tranmere celebrity dinners and he'd bring the house down with his stories.

'His delivery was perfect and when Dixie was with Joe Mercer you had the best couple of comedians you could imagine. It was marvellous to sit and listen to them. There'd be great banter between them and Dixie would tease Joe by saying: "He used to clean my boots!"'

The banter in which Dixie loved to indulge was also much to the fore in this dialogue with his son Ralph when I interviewed them over lunch in September 1975:

Dixie: Ralph's a Liverpool fan and that all came about through his Uncle Walter taking him to Anfield when he was a boy. He also got him a ticket to see Liverpool play at Wembley in the 1950 FA Cup Final when they lost to Arsenal.

Ralph: I know my Dad was an Everton legend. But I only saw him play on film. Once I saw Billy Liddell in the flesh play for Liverpool I became a Red. My son, Billy, is also a Liverpool fan. Liddell was a true great, a hell of a player.

Dixie: I agree that Liddell was a great player and one of the game's true gentleman. Brilliant.

Ralph: The Anfield atmosphere was another reason I became a Liverpool fan. There's nothing like it.

Dixie: To be honest, I haven't been inside Anfield since the last time I was paid to play there which was in 1937. There's no point in me going. I'd get no gee-up or benefit from going, although I do watch Liverpool on television. Ralph's a Red but he uses my name to get tickets. But I always let him go his own way. If he wanted to be a Liverpool fan that was up to him. I've always said he's crackers.

Ralph: I remember what happened to Liddell in the 1950 Final. Arsenal's red headed Scotsman, Alex Forbes – I could call him something else! – did Billy in the first couple of minutes and we lost the game 2–0.

Dixie: What happened in that Final made no difference to me. You hear people on Merseyside say that if their team can't win a particular trophy they'd like the other team to do so. But I don't look at it that way. Having played against Liverpool so many times something drives you to get stuck into them.

Ralph: You were giving free beer to Evertonians in your pub the night of that 1950 Final.

Dixie: I was, yes. That was because your lot got licked.

Ralph: You said you weren't biased . . . but you must be.

Dixie: I don't want Liverpool to win the Cup or the League, do I? I always thought that we were the better football team. Your lot had to go back into the Second Division in the 1950s to know what football really was. And you were there for eight years trying to find out whereas Everton went down for one season and came straight out again.

I admit that Liverpool have done well since the 1960s and it was down to a stroke of luck that can come into any man's life whether he's in sport, business or anything else. When Bill Shankly came they didn't have a bad side and they had a lot of Baden Powells . . . decent scouts who found good talent like Kevin Keegan and Ray Clemence.

Ralph: I thought every great club is supposed to have a good scouting system. So why didn't Everton find these players?

Dixie: Because the scouts weren't there. But there was a lucky man at Liverpool who got these players.

Ralph: I saw Dave Clements of Everton do Keegan in the first minute of a Goodison derby and he got away with it. Somebody told him to do that.

Dixie: I was captain of Everton for seven years and you don't tell them to do anybody.

Ralph: You told Billy Cook to do Erick Brook of Manchester City in the 1933 Cup Final. You told him to kick him into touch. And he did. That's why you won the game.

Dixie: I didn't tell him to do him. I just said 'try and stop him'. But what a difference in those days. Everton were the football elite of Great Britain, bar none.

Ralph: How the mighty have fallen.

Dixie: Yes. But Liverpool have been lucky to touch for the kids they've got.

Ralph: I think that Keegan is one of the best players we've ever had.

Dixie: I do think that the lad has got a little bit of a swelled head. We are the fellers who stuck out for these people to get his money. We got eight quid a week and six pounds for playing for your country. We stuck out for the player's union to get a rise, which we did. And it went on and on. The first feller to ruin that was Georgie Best. He was getting money too easily. That's what blew his head up. Keegan has come to the top as quickly as Best and threw his shirt down at Wembley when he and Billy Bremner were sent off in the Charity Shield against Leeds.

Ralph: He's not a spoiled brat. He gives everything for 90 minutes. Giles thumped Keegan in the first instance. You can't compare Keegan with Best in terms of maturity.

Dixie: Liverpool did have one player who should have beaten my 60-goal record and that was Tony Hateley. Christ almighty, with the balls he got from Ian Callaghan and Peter Thompson he should have doubled my total. But he was frightened of heading a ball. Callaghan and Thompson, as well as the defender Chris Lawler, are three Liverpool players who have really impressed me. That trio add up to four and a half players in my book. Good wingers can make all the difference to a centre forward and there's one winger I wish Everton had bought a few seasons ago. That's Leighton James of Burnley and Wales. I think he's a smasher, one of the greatest.

I remember watching Liverpool play Inter Milan on television in the 1965 European Cup semi final and the way Ian Callaghan and the other feller were banging over those crosses I'd scored three before half time . . . and I was standing at the bar in a Birkenhead boozer!

Ralph: We do beat these foreign teams. You don't.

Dixie: I don't know . . . we beat five teams in the Canaries when I played.

Ralph: They WERE canaries, too! But getting back to goalscoring, I think John Toshack is underrated. He's great in the air.

Dixie: I've met John and he's a hell of a nice kid. I've met him two or three times. He came over to me from his own table at a dinner in the Adelphi Hotel, sat alongside me and started asking me all sorts of things about the game. I was happy to talk to him. I think there's something in the fact that he's a very tall lad, well over six feet. I was only 5ft 10ins, kept at 12 stone 3 or 4 lb and was as fit as a fiddle. My weight never altered and I felt as if I was bursting with energy.

That's all-important when it comes to timing when you're going up for a ball. I've seen John miss one or two he should have scored, ones I felt I would have got and it could have been down to timing.

Ralph: Toshack was the reason Liverpool won the UEFA Cup in 1973. Shankly left him out one night when the first leg of the final against Borussia Moenchengladbach was abandoned through a waterlogged pitch at Anfield. Shankly played Toshack the next night and he destroyed the Germans. They had no answer to him in the air.

Dixie: I see now that Bob Paisley keeps telling his players off at Liverpool. It's so strong the papers can't print it! But I have to say that Mersey derby games are a great thing for the supporters. You can go right back in time and you won't find one real incident of fighting either on or off the pitch.

Yes, the supporters will argue and swear at each other but they'll end up in the boozer talking about the match on a scale that doesn't happen in any other city.

Ralph: It's something inbred in this city for so long. Mind you, when I die I want my ashes scattered at Goodison in a derby game. I want the wind to blow them in the eyes of the Everton players when they're attacking! It would be even better if we're winning 2–1, with Everton about to take a last minute penalty, and the ashes blow in the kicker's eyes. I'd pay to have that done!'

The humour between Dixie and Liverpool fans lasted throughout his life. Tommy McKinley of Liverpool FC Pensioners Club recalled: 'I was situated in the betting shop close to where Dixie's son Ralph had a pub called 'The Nonpareil'. This particular day there had been a spate of phoney fivers circulating in the city and I had copped for one. I warned Ralph of the serial number of the phoney and he wrote it down and placed it on top of the till. Later, Bill came in and served behind the bar.

'I warned him about the forgeries and he said: "They won't get past me, no chance. I can smell them." "OK, Bill" I said "Give us four pints and have a gill yourself." For a laugh, I passed him the phoney fiver.

'Back came four pound notes and some change. After a few minutes I said to Bill: "How many fivers have you in the till, Bill?" He looked and replied: "One, Tommy." I said: "No, Bill. How many genuine ones have you got? That one is phoney!"

'He studied it, called me a Liverpudlian so-and-so and burst out laughing with the rest of us. I replaced the phoney for a genuine one and we all had another drink. He was just as magnificent off the field as he was on it.'

Jerry Thompson, a driving force shortly after the Second World War behind the formation of the Everton Shareholders and Supporters Federation, recalled: 'I became a personal friend of Bill's and used to drive him to the many functions to which he was invited. I don't think he refused one. When Liverpool Supporters Club were making a presentation to Roger Hunt, after Roger had broken the club's goal record, Bill agreed to say a few words. He pulled out a blue and white scarf, which he wrapped around his neck, and a blue and white bobble hat for his head. The booing and cat calls were tremendous but it was not long before Bill had the audience laughing and applauding. Finally, he left the stage to a tremendous standing ovation. Perhaps many people do not realise that he could easily have earned his living as a comedian.'

Players who arrived at Goodison long after Dixie's departure were reminded of his deeds and stature by trainer Harry Cooke, the man who had tended Dean throughout his Everton career. Just like new recruits at Liverpool went through the ritual of posing for pictures shaking hands with the revered Billy Liddell, new Everton signings had a different kind of welcome, as Ireland winger Tommy Eglington revealed. 'Harry used to keep bits of Dixie preserved in jars and he used to show them to the players. There were pieces of cartilage and bits of bone. Whenever we went on a long train journey to away games Harry would talk about "Billy" all the way there and all the way back so we were left in no doubt about how great a player he was.'

In November 1976, two months before his 70th birthday, Dixie suffered a thrombosis and underwent life-saving surgery. However, within a fortnight, on November 25, he had to have a second operation for the amputation of his right leg. It was the 17th major act of surgery he had undergone in his eventful life but, typical of the man, within five days of losing his leg he was able to get out of bed for short periods and, with assistance, hobble on crutches and deliver the quip: 'I've been in more theatres than Morecambe and Wise.'

Another great name of British comedy, Dickie Henderson, heard about Dixie's operation and on a television show sent best wishes for his speedy recovery and recalled how his father, a close friend of Dean, had introduced him as a child to the great centre forward. Dixie never indulged in self-pity and his indomitable character and spirit was evident when former Everton captain and England centre half Brian Labone visited him at his bedside at Birkenhead General Hospital. 'Bill's old team-mate Gordon Watson and I went to see him shortly after the operation,' Labone recalled. 'We were told he'd had a major blood transfusion and it was red lights and tread softly. So we tip-toed into Bill's room expecting to see him lying there quietly attached to all sorts of tubes and monitors. But instead we found him watching the racing on a portable telly and a bottle of brown ale at the side of his bed. And when he saw us he said: "That so-and-so Piggott's just let me down for a treble!"'

On Christmas Eve that year the hospital allowed Dixie to go home to spend the festive season with daughter Barbara and the family. The following year his hometown Birkenhead named a street 'Deansway' in his honour. Barbara was moved to say in the ensuing days after Dixie had lost his leg: 'I have had many reasons to be proud of my dad but never more so than in the last few weeks. His spirit, his humour and his strength have made me feel very fortunate to be his daughter.'

Joe Mercer felt similar emotions about his long-time friend. 'They've had to take Dixie's leg off but they haven't touched his spirit. That's indestructible,' observed Joe, who accompanied Dixie to the hospital to be fitted for an artificial leg and recounted: 'We walked into the room and it was full of chaps who had limbs missing. Dixie weighed it up then quipped: 'I see Tommy Smith's been let loose in here!''

Dixie told Barbara he wanted a leg similar to the one worn by RAF hero Douglas Bader. 'But dad, they told you that Bader was a lot younger than you,' she said, drawing the reply: 'Listen, love, I might be 70 but I feel 27.' They were right. The Dixie spirit was unquenchable.

Cheers! Whitbread Brewery executives toast Dixie after they had presented him with a tankard following the amputation of his right leg in 1976 (copyright unknown)

CHAPTER TWELVE

# Dean's Choice and Legacy

Comparisons are never more odious than in football. Selecting all-time teams can be a minefield of opinion, experience and even raw prejudice. Such an exercise also, of course, depends on the life span of the person pencilling in the names on the fantasy team sheet. When I asked Dixie Dean in May 1973 to choose his best-ever Everton side it comprised a majority of pre-Second World war players, many of whom had been his colleagues in those golden Goodison eras of the late 1920s and early 1930s and others who went on to help land the championship in 1938–39, the year after his departure. It can be mere hypothesis to speculate on whether a player of such immense stature as that brilliant Welsh goalkeeper Neville Southall, for instance, would have wrested Dixie's vote as his last line of defence from the amazingly consistent record-breaking Ted Sagar. Neither did any of that superb Everton midfield trio of Howard Kendall, Alan Ball or Colin Harvey make Dixie's line-up, although the team he picked does seem to ripple with talent, with Tommy Lawton only making the bench! Without any false modesty Dixie named himself at centre forward in his side, which he selected in the two-three-five formation in which they played: Ted Sagar; Ben Williams, Warney Cresswell; Cliff Britton, Tommy (T.G.) Jones, Joe Mercer; Sam Chedgzoy, Jimmy Dunn, Dixie Dean, Tommy Johnson, Alec Troup. Reserves: Billy Cook, Tommy White, Tommy Lawton. However, having named himself in his all-time best Everton team, Dixie balanced things by picking Lawton in a side he picked from his contemporaries from all clubs and had this to say about the man who succeeded him at

217

Goodison and followed in his goal-laden footsteps as England's centre forward:

> The way Tommy was shaping at Everton he would have had a lot more caps but for the War. He was strong and good with his head and his feet. There's no getting away from the fact that the kid was a great centre forward.
>
> There were three similar players who I rated. There was Tommy, Nat Lofthouse at Bolton and Jackie Milburn at Newcastle. But Tommy was the top. He was the best. There's no getting away from that fact.
>
> Before them you've got to mention Hughie Gallacher, who was one of the trickiest little players you've ever seen. One day at Anfield he beat the full backs, drew Elisha Scott out of his goal, took the ball right up to the goal-line, turned round with his back to the Kop and back-heeled the ball into the net. Then he turned round and bowed to the crowd. You can imagine the noise that came off the Kop that day! That was Hughie all over. He was always up to his tricks. But he was also a very crafty player. Another fine centre forward was Georgie Camsell, a good, big strong northern kid, and you couldn't leave Pongo Waring out. He'd be among the best, too. I also admired John Charles. He was good at centre forward or centre half. In fact he could play anywhere that lad. Bob Latchford was another player I liked. I'd put Bob sixth or seventh on my list of great centre forwards.
>
> If I was picking my best team I'd have Elisha Scott in goal. He'd be the only Liverpool player in it. The others weren't good enough then! My full backs would be Roy Goodall of Huddersfield Town and my Everton team-mate Warney Cresswell. As the half backs I'd have Willis Edwards of Leeds at right half, that great Everton and Wales centre half T.G. Jones in the middle and another Evertonian, Joe Mercer, at left half.
>
> T.G. was the best all-round player I've ever seen. He had everything. No coach could ever coach him or teach him anything. He was neater than John Charles, for instance, and could get himself out of trouble just by running towards the ball

then letting it run between his legs, knowing a team-mate would be in a position to take it. Up front I'd have Scottish international Alex Jackson on the right wing (he's in my team a long way ahead of Stanley Matthews), Georgie Brown of Huddersfield Town inside him, Tommy Lawton at centre forward, Billy Walker of Aston Villa, who captained England and would captain my team at inside left, and Cliff Bastin of Arsenal at outside left.

As a substitute I'd have Joe Smith of Bolton Wanderers, who was a real good goal-getter. He scored 38 First Division goals in 1920–21 and later managed Blackpool. The best team I ever saw was the Everton team I played for in 1932 and 1933 which won the League and then the Cup. You didn't have to tell them to give you the ball or pass it or cross it. It was just like George Gershwin's Rhapsody In Blue. That's what it was. Nobody was told 'do this or do that'. We just went out there and played. We knew what we had to do. We never talked about the other team's players. There was no need. We knew how we were going to play and it was up to the other side to start worrying. Not us.

The one great difference between the game then and now is the use of wingers. In my Everton days we had the likes of Ted Critchley, Sam Chedgzoy, Albert Geldard, Alec Troup, Jimmy Stein and Jackie Coulter. What a great collection that was! . . . You don't see wingers like that now. In fact, when you see someone running down the wing he's probably a full back. In my day the job of the wingers was to get on their bike down the wing and send the ball in hard. My job was to get on the end of it and either put the ball in the net if it was possible or head it to one of the other lads . . . In today's football that doesn't happen. When the ball goes wide everyone drops back and then it's passed all over the place without getting very far. Our football was direct and I think that's good football. The crowd go to see goals and that's what they want to see . . . People say football is faster today. Not in my book. They stop the ball too often today and some of the things I see in games makes me weep. We enjoyed playing and the supporters enjoyed watching because every team had great characters and great players. I don't think anyone enjoys themselves as much now . . . Apart from Everton, I'd say the Arsenal team of George Male, Eddie Hapgood, Herbie Roberts and company was one of the best. They had about nine internationals in the team . . . The hardest team I ever saw was Huddersfield and they were probably the best next to that Everton team. They were at their greatest just as I was starting with Everton and their forward line was out of the bag! It included Alex Jackson, who was a really great Scottish player, Clem Stephenson, Georgie Brown and left winger Billy Smith . . . Soon after the War, we saw Wolves come into the limelight and old Matt Busby straightened Manchester United out. He put them into winning ways, which was not surprising considering the way he could play himself. He was a great player and he enjoyed his days at Anfield with Liverpool.

Briefly putting aside his characteristic banter about his great Anfield antagonists, Dixie added:

When Liverpool got to the European Cup Final against Borussia Moenchengladbach in Rome I wanted them to win it. If they'd have been playing Everton it would have been different. But you always want to see your own clubs win things. I've had a good innings against Liverpool. I've made them cry a bit. So I can't grumble. Why should I worry? Liverpool had an upset when Kevin Keegan cleared off to Hamburg but they did well to get this lad Kenny Dalglish. He's a very good player.

What then, is Dean's own place in history, his position in the pantheon of the sport Pele called 'the beautiful game'? Sir Matt Busby, one of the great figures of British football and, as Dixie said, the man who revived Manchester United, believed the Everton icon was unique. In his book *Soccer At The Top*, Busby wrote:

'Who could ever have seen Bill Dean and not seen greatness? My first sight of him was when I first arrived in Manchester to join City as a boy of 17. He was playing for Everton against

Manchester United at Old Trafford. He confirmed what I had heard. He scored a hat trick. So this was English football. So this was Dixie Dean. Oh dear! However close you watched him his timing in the air was such that he was coming down before you got anywhere near him. And he hit the ball with his head as hard and as accurate as most players could kick it. Defences were close to panic when corners came over and though he scored a huge tally of goals with headers he was an incredibly unselfish and amazingly accurate layer-off of chances for others. He was resilient facing the big, tough centre halves of his day – and I cannot think of one centre half today to match up with that lot. It was often the unstoppable force against the immovable object – and he was a thorough sportsman. Dixie scored a record 60 League goals in 39 games in 1927–28 plus three in the FA Cup. There cannot be another Dixie Dean any more than there can be another anybody else. If there could be, the new Dixie would still score a great pile of goals. He would out-jump, out-time, out-head any defender or any number they could pack into the area. As a header of the ball only Denis Law and, less often since he was more at the back than the front, Jack Charlton have come within a mile of Dixie.'

Dean's friend and former team-mate Joe Mercer, who also made a distinguished contribution to English football as a player and manager, insisted in a 1980 interview that Dixie would have been a goal machine in any era:

'He'd have scored a lot, even today. Present day tactics may have cut out his source of supply but once that ball came across to him he would have put it in the net. Don't forget, he was hot stuff on the ground as well, with either foot. He never missed the simple goals. He was like Jimmy Greaves in that respect. Give me a man who can score the simple goals and there's a great player.

'People say Dixie would not have been able to score 60 goals in a season today. Don't be so sure. If he had men who played to his strengths he'd have knocked them in, alright. In many ways,

Dixie was the complete centre forward because he never seemed to have an off-day and on the field he never did silly things. He never got into trouble with referees, he just got on with the game. He was pushed, kicked, pulled and battered. He never retaliated. Mind you, he used to kid his opponents. Some of the things he said really got them going!

'Off duty he lived life to the full. In his younger days he made people like George Best and Malcolm Allison seem like choir-boys! But on the field he had a perfect temperament because he loved playing football above everything. For him, life was fun. It was a laugh a minute stuff and the dressing room was like a pantomime. He was the captain and led the way when there was some fun to be had. But he led by example, not by order, and was never ever big headed or conceited . . . I've spoken to many men who played with and against Bill – including Warney Cresswell, "Tosh" Johnson, Cliff Britton, Herbie Roberts and Cliff Bastin – and without exception they rated him the greatest. When a professional says that about another professional he's played with or against it's a supreme tribute. I can't think of any other player since the Dean era who would be recalled and talked about as Dixie is so many years after he had finished playing . . . He believed in attacking football and went out there to score goals. He lifted players and never knocked them down with criticism. He was a wonderful influence on youngsters. Dixie Dean was a man of character and personality. He put as much back into football as he took out, so different from many of the top liners today. In all my days in sport I've known two men whose characters and instincts were just flawless, who were perfect in temperament. One was Dixie, the other was Denis Compton.

'They each had a marvellous freedom of action and a total lack of edge. They were bloody untouchables. Football will never see Dixie's like again. In a game full of characters he was the greatest of them all.

'My father played for Tranmere just before Dixie arrived there and when I went to Goodison Dixie was like a father to me and

the other young players. I worshipped him and became his
unofficial batman. He was a tremendous influence on me and the
other kids at the club, including Tommy Lawton. This was the
lad who, after all, had been bought to take his place but nobody
heaped more praise and advice on Tommy than Dixie did. In my
opinion he was a better centre forward than Tommy. In fact, he
was world class, like Pele or Di Stefano. He was in that elite
category, greater than anyone I have known. He had everything
. . . a beautiful physique, superb feet, wide shoulders, a powerful
neck, skill and knowledge. To watch Dixie rising for a ball is a
memory that will last forever. He was like some great salmon
leaping from the water. So much grace and power. There will
never be another. He was unique.'

The eminent British football administrator Sir Stanley Rous, who
rose from referee, to FA secretary to the presidency of football's
world governing body FIFA, hailed Dean as 'incomparable'.

He added: 'Attack was our natural game in the 1930s. It was a
golden decade for the attacking English style of forward play. We
bred a succession of great centre forwards, with the great William
Ralph 'Dixie' Dean the finest centre forward I have ever seen.'

The exploits of Dean and Lawton ignited an Everton centre forward
tradition, the torch being passed on to several notable post-war
strikers. Graeme Sharp, whose 159 senior goals in 447 appearances
put him second behind Dixie in Everton's all-time scoring list, leads a
selection of Dean's successors in appraising his feats and his
Goodison legacy:

'Unfortunately, I never met Dixie. I joined Everton a month after
he had passed away. I was aware back home in Scotland of the
legend of Dixie Dean but after moving to Goodison I soon
realised the remarkable esteem in which he is held by the
supporters. There is a great pride and tradition in the No 9 jersey
at Everton and stories of Dixie have been handed down from one
generation of fans to another. People still talk about his
attributes, his power in the air and what a strong character he

was. You can appreciate what a fantastic folk hero he was in the 1920s and '30s and no wonder his neck muscles were strong when he used a medicine ball to play head tennis with Tommy Lawton! People like Dave Hickson, Joe Royle and Bob Latchford have also worn the Everton centre forward's jersey so it was a great honour and pleasure for me to follow in their footsteps in a path trod by the great Dixie Dean.

'It took me 11 years to build my goal total. But Dixie's record and goalscoring feats are incredible . . . 383 goals in all for Everton and 60 in the League in one season. It's a privilege to come a distant second to a player who is one of football's immortals.'

Dave Hickson, who scored 111 goals in 243 senior outings during two spells at Everton during the 1950s, said:

'I signed for Everton as a 16-year-old amateur in 1946 and I'd heard about Dixie when I was going to school. To follow in his footsteps was just a dream come true, really, and a great honour . . . I saw him play only in charity games but I joined the Cheshire Army Cadets based at Little Sutton after I'd signed for Everton and, lo and behold, Dixie was the manager of our football team. Dixie – or Bill as he insisted on being called – was based in Chester. I played quite a few games for the team and got to know Bill quite well. We played all over the country and in the end Bill helped me get into the England Army Cadets side. He was a nice man and a down to earth person. One of the lads. He used to give me special coaching sessions, including heading tuition when he would chat about some of the goals he'd scored. And when I got into the Everton first team I still used to see him . . . I went to see him in hospital when he had his leg amputated and I kept in contact with him until the day he died. He was known throughout the world for his goalscoring ability . . . During my Everton career I was always aware of his record and his fantastic feats. Even though we knew nobody could emulate Bill he was an inspiration to centre forwards, like me, who came later. I never looked on what Bill had done as a burden on those who followed him. You have to think positively.

'People have asked whether he could play in today's football. My view is that if you have ability like Bill had you can adapt. The training methods were different in Bill's day but I'm certain a man of his talent would have adapted to today's demands. He was very proud of the fact that he was never booked or sent off, even though he was very competitive and got kicked so much by defenders. That was a fantastic achievement and his record was in contrast to mine because I was sent off three times. I'm not proud of that but I think I really got to love the game too much, if that's possible. I was wrapped up in it that much and, it was just over enthusiasm. It was the way I was. I couldn't change. Without doubt Bill is the greatest Everton player of all time. His legend will live forever. One other man I greatly admired was Joe Mercer, another fine Everton player, and Bill was always THE man as far as Joe was concerned. Bill's was always the first name on Joe's lips. If Joe thought that then it was good enough for anybody. Dixie was a man you could listen to because he was such a great player who had done it all. I always played 100 per cent. It might not have come off every time. But I always had that feeling that Dixie had once worn that No 9 jersey. I don't think Bill ever fully realised just how good or popular he was. He was known all over the world. He was brilliant. There will never be anyone like him.'

Bob Latchford, scorer of 138 goals in 289 senior outings for Everton between 1974 and 1981, declared:

'Dixie Dean is one of the game's legends – and rightly so – not only at Everton but throughout football. To score 60 League goals in a season, plus all his others for Everton and England, stands alone as a feat that I think will be unequalled. He was a great man whose feat will stand the test of time. I can't see anyone coming close to it, certainly not in my lifetime. It's difficult to say whether it's more or less possible today. I certainly don't think it's become any easier. The tempo of the game, the fitness and athleticism of the players and the way football is played today, I can't see anybody coming close to his record. To think that someone like Alan Shearer would have to double their best goal tally for a season to match Dixie's output beggars belief. To be honest, it beggars belief Dixie ever did it in the first place. I scored 30 League goals for Everton in 1977–78, to win a £30,000 *Daily Express* prize which was shared around the squad. It was the first time anyone had done that in the top division for six years. I was the second player in the 1970s after Francis Lee to score 30 League goals and the next time it happened was in the 1980s when Ian Rush, Gary Lineker and Clive Allen got 30 or more. So to score 30 is hard, to get 40 or over would be unbelievable, 60 is next to impossible . . . I met Dixie on a few occasions and we posed for a few pictures together. He was a very likeable man and always had a good word to say to you. He was very pleasant. A gentleman. He gave me a few basic tips by telling me how he headed the ball. He would say: "Keep your eye on the ball and meet it on your forehead." Just to have been in the company of a genuine legend of the game was a great privilege. For his feats he's got to be the greatest Everton player of all time and one of the greatest in the entire history of English football. His death showed his status. The reaction of Everton and Liverpool fans and the whole country showed how much they appreciated and respected him. Merseyside opened its heart at his funeral, at which I was a pall bearer. It was a very emotional day with thousands of people turning out to pay their last respects. The man will be remembered for what he did and what he was, a legend.'

Tony Cottee, like Latchford at £350,000, was once Britain's most expensive player at £2.3 million. He scored 99 goals in 240 Everton first team appearances between 1988 and 1994 and said of the Dean factor:

'I was delighted to get into Everton's all-time top 10 scoring list which, of course, Dixie Dean heads. I only just scraped in but I made it! When you play for any club as a forward you always

hope to achieve things like that. It was an honour to follow in the
No 9 tradition of Dixie and for me it was wonderful to get onto
a list that includes such good players and great goalscorers as
Graeme Sharp and Bob Latchford, never mind Dixie. I think
Dixie Dean's achievements are truly phenomenal. I know you
can always look back and ask questions about the standard of
football and how Dixie would have handled the game today. The
ball in those days was like a rock and you only have to think of
those old, heavy boots! Another big difference was the quality
of the pitches. Even the pitches in the 1970s were rubbish
compared to the modern surfaces. So in Dixie's day the pitches
must have been mud heaps. When you take all that into account
you have to say what a wonderful achievement it was to get 60
League goals. You can't knock records and to get 60 League
goals in a season is just unbelievable. In any standard of football,
non league or even a Sunday pub side, to score that many is
bloody hard! I can't see anyone touching it. I don't know what
the pace of the game was like in the 1920s and 1930s. But if you
look at clips of football in the 1960s, '70s and '80s today's game
is so much faster. So perhaps the equivalent of Dixie's record
today is someone getting 40 League goals. But even though we
have great goalscorers you can't even see that happening. And
while Dixie's 1927–28 record was phenomenal he wasn't a one-
season wonder. He scored an amazing number of goals right
through his career for Everton and England. What he has done
will not be pushed under the carpet and forgotten. He will still be
remembered in another 50 years and beyond. The legend of
Dixie Dean will never die.'

Wing half Gordon Watson played in Everton teams with both Dean
and Lawton and said:

'Dixie was the best centre forward I've ever seen. Tommy
Lawton was very close behind him. But I'd choose Dixie every
time as the better of the two. If Dixie was a 100 per cent player,
Tommy was 99 per cent. Dixie had that little bit more will to

score goals. He was very committed and his legs were always black and blue. Yet he was never booked. Tommy was in the same category. I don't think you could put a price on Dixie today. For a start, nobody would be stupid enough to sell him! If they had him they'd keep him. He was that good. He had everything.

'You had to see him to believe it. I was privileged to play with him. He was perfect with his head. I don't know how he could jump like he did. He could leap higher than the goalkeeper could reach. The only two who came near him in that department were Tommy Lawton and Jimmy McGrory, who played for Celtic and Scotland. But Dixie was terrific also on the ground. He could use both left and right foot. His left was the weaker but he could still use it. And he would also do his share of defensive duties, too. If we conceded a corner Dixie would be there or thereabouts in the goalmouth to help out. I and a lot of the players used to live in Goodison Avenue, close to the ground, and Dixie used to come in each morning wearing plimsolls, grey flannels, football stockings and a big polo neck sweater like the ferry men have.

'He'd just take his trousers off and that was him . . . he'd be ready to train. He'd go out there and work really hard. He didn't need the trainer to stand and watch him. And when he'd had enough he'd come in. He used to say to us: "Never, ever forsake your training. Work hard at it."

'He had such enthusiasm. That's why he was such a great man. He used to pump it into you before you went out. When you went onto the pitch with Dixie you felt like playing. You wanted to play. He was a leader and a fine captain. He was great with youngsters and marvellous with school kiddies, never refusing his autograph to anybody. People used to arrive with children and while they were waiting for Dixie they'd go for a drink in the Winslow pub opposite the ground and leave the kids outside. But when Dixie came out of the ground he'd sign autographs for every single one of them before he left. He was like a pop star and when he got married it brought traffic to a standstill. But he didn't like us players calling him Dixie. If someone did he'd remind them very sharply: "Bill's the name, not Dixie." Sometimes just his expression was enough. So we called him Bill.

'In my opinion there will never be another Dixie. Wherever he is he'll still be heading them in! He's the best centre forward of any century. I'm biased but his record proves it. It speaks for itself.'

# CHAPTER THIRTEEN

# *A Dixie Lament*

His colleagues and opponents alike have testified that one of the qualities that separated William Ralph Dean from the rest, something that formed a potent weapon in his considerable football armoury, was his perfect temperament. They talk of his icy precision when he was hunting a goal, his total disregard of opponents ganging up to try to stop him by fair means or foul and his stoical acceptance of injuries sustained in his scoring cause. In January 1978 my late colleague Bob Azurdia had a fascinating discussion with Dixie in a series of BBC Radio Merseyside interviews which provided a revealing insight into the Dean psyche and emphasised his remarkable single-minded approach, in which his own sense of enjoyment was sublimated for the great enjoyment of the masses who idolised him from the terraces. This is how the exchange went:

Azurdia: Did you ever feel excited, have a great sense of occasion?
Dean: No. That's just it. That's what I couldn't make out. It always seemed to me there was always somebody else helping me, having a go alongside me. I never really had a sense of the occasion or felt very excited. It seemed to me that this other person, or whoever it was, was just saying: 'Now that's it. You've done it. It's all over now. You've finished.'
Azurdia: Did you never feel excited or never feel a sense of occasion the moment when you won the Cup, the moment when you knew you were League champions, the moment when the ball hit the back of the net?

Dean: No. The spectators go there to see goals. That's the main thing. If that was all they wanted, good enough they'd get it. And they did get it. Oh, no there was nothing else there for me except there was a net at each end and a ball blown up.

Azurdia: But you got a sense of satisfaction at scoring goals?

Dean: Oh, yes. That was it.

Azurdia: Satisfaction but no great excitement?

Dean: Never any excitement whatsoever. None at all.

It was a surprising admission from a man who thrilled millions during his bountiful career and who, given today's massive global media network, would have been a universal superstar. Dixie had star quality throughout his life. Indeed to his dying day he had a special presence and charisma. I can vouch for that because I took him, as one of my guests, to Goodison Park for the Merseyside derby game at which he passed away.

On Saturday, March 1, 1980 that year's Everton and Liverpool club annuals, which I had written and produced with photographer Harry Ormesher, were launched at a lunch staged by the publishers at what was then Liverpool's Holiday Inn in Paradise Street. The date was specially picked because it was the day of the 122nd League meeting of Everton and Liverpool, to be staged that afternoon at Goodison and among the top table guests I invited to attend the lunch and then go on to the game were Bill Dean and Bill Shankly, the manager who had transformed Anfield fortunes and made Liverpool great before his shock resignation in 1974. Dixie, with only one leg, was in a wheelchair but the impact his arrival had on the 50 guests in the hotel's New York Suite was almost tangible. Autograph books were proffered, anecdotes of his football exploits, handed down from fathers and grandfathers, were re-told to the great man. The clamour and buzz he generated was of pop star proportions.

I sat between Dixie and Shanks for that meal, talking football with the two legends at what was to be the last supper for the greatest Evertonian of them all. To be present that day I will recall forever as a poignant privilege. I still have the lunch menu, signed to me in blue by Dean and red by Shankly, as a cherished possession. Dixie asked

Shankly to autograph his own lunch menu, explaining with a smile: 'It's for my nurse, Bill.'

As he ate what proved to be the last meal of his life, roast beef and Yorkshire pudding, Dixie revealed an astonishing fact. I asked him how long it had been since he had attended a Mersey derby. 'I've never been to one as a spectator,' he replied. 'The last derby I went to I played in!'

He also produced from his wallet a picture of himself and Liverpool centre half Tom 'Tiny' Bradshaw running out of the players' tunnel side by side for a derby game in the 1930s. 'We used to shoulder charge each other and we went in really hard,' he said. 'But we always smiled at each other when we did it.' Then Shankly rose to the microphone and, with an uncanny relevance to the events that were to unfold that afternoon and with that magnetic Scottish delivery and timing which made him such a compelling orator, said of the man just an arm's length from him:

'We have in our midst today, ladies and gentleman, a man who was the greatest at what he did. You can't say that about many people in history, whatever branch of life you're talking about. But you can say that about Dixie Dean. Oh, yes. His record of goalscoring is the most amazing thing under the sun. Nobody will ever come near to equalling his fantastic feat of scoring 60 League goals in a season. I played against him a few times when I was with Preston. He was a big, cocky, confident man, arrogant in his approach to the game. That is the hallmark of a great player and Dixie was the greatest centre forward there will ever be. Nobody who's ever been born could head a ball into the net like him. When he connected it frightened people. You couldn't stop him scoring. He belongs in the company of the supremely great . . . like Beethoven, Shakespeare and Rembrandt. He is super-charged with emotion, awareness and sensitivity and, despite his afflictions, he can laugh.'

As Shankly was spellbinding his audience, though, a tear fell down Dixie's cheek. It was a moving, cameo moment which, for me, remains frozen in time. As another guest, that superb former Everton centre half and captain Brian Labone, put it: 'Shanks gave us a wonderful eulogy to Dixie which, very sadly, became his obituary.'

Dixie, Shankly and I then travelled by taxi to Goodison for the match, which I was covering for the *Daily Express*. It was an ill-tempered contest in which Bob Paisley's Liverpool beat Gordon Lee's Everton 2–1. Towards the end of the game Dixie collapsed and was taken from his seat in the main stand down to the player's gymnasium where he was examined by a doctor and pronounced dead before an ambulance arrived. He had suffered a heart attack. So, at the age of 73, and 55 years to the month since he had joined Everton, the greatest player in the Goodison club's illustrious history had gone. Could there have been a more appropriate occasion and venue for Dixie's final curtain than a Mersey derby on the very stage on which his deeds rendered him a sporting immortal? He would have said not. His long-time friend Joe Mercer, who was also at the game, wiped away tears as he observed: 'That is typical of Dixie. He was always one for the big occasion. He's gone from us now but he was bigger and better than life.'

Brian Labone recalled: 'A rumour went round the ground that something had happened to Dixie and then the news broke that he had passed away. Everyone was so shocked that a legend had gone. He was unique yet he remained an ordinary man. You heard all sorts of stories about Bill. That he'd have 10 pints in the Winslow pub opposite the ground and then go out and get a hat trick. Or that he'd sleep at Goodison and then go out and score four. Those tales are part of the Dixie legend and I never used to believe any of them. But I think there may have been more than a grain of truth in some of them because he was an exceptional, larger than life character to his dying day.' Liverpool manager Paisley, destined to become a legend himself, reacted to Dixie's death when he declared outside his team's Goodison dressing room: 'Dixie lived and breathed Everton and he was respected throughout the football world. I cringe when I think of what anyone would have to pay for a player like him at today's prices. I knew him and I am a better man for knowing him. We will never see his like again.'

Paisley's opposite number that fateful afternoon, Gordon Lee, reflected: 'As a player and a person Dixie helped Everton to greatness. Each generation throws up a player, a Stanley Matthews, a Tom Finney, someone who embodies public belief in what the footballer should be. Dixie Dean was one of that select band. During his playing days, European competition was largely unknown but how he would have relished taking on centre halves from the Continent while wearing his beloved Everton blue.'

Dixie's son Geoff recalls how he learned of his father's death: 'I had a pub in mid-Wales at the time and that's where I heard the news. Obviously, I was extremely choked and then Joe Mercer, a big mate of my dad's, came on television with tears streaming down his face. I burst into tears myself. It's amazing to think it was the first derby game my dad had been to since he played in one. I think he wanted to be remembered as a player, not as a spectator. When Peter Eastoe scored Everton's goal late on in the game my dad threw his arms up and that's when he had his heart attack.

'I think having his leg amputated some years earlier must have weakened his heart. But if he could have chosen somewhere to leave this world I've no doubt his choice would have been Goodison. It used to really sadden my dad if he thought Everton had a poor team and I'm so sorry he missed all those glory years under Howard Kendall not too long after his death. He'd have been thrilled to see Everton winning the championship, FA Cup and their first European trophy, the Cup Winners Cup.'

Geoff's sister Barbara revealed that she had a premonition of her father's death: 'My last memory was helping getting him ready to go to the lunch and then the derby match at which he died. I got him all spruced up, polished his one shoe and dropped him off at the hotel. But as I got him out of the car and put him in his wheelchair I noticed that he'd still got his slipper on! In the rush to get out of the house we'd left the shoe behind. I always like him to look nice but this slipper had drops of tea and bits of biscuit on it. So I ran to the toilet with the slipper and wiped it with some tissue. My Dad wasn't bothered, though. It was obviously more comfortable for him to have a slipper on than wear a shoe.

'It sounds strange to say it but I actually think he knew it was his last day. As I turned to leave the hotel he shouted to me, put his thumb up and said: 'Don't worry I'll be alright.'

'So, quite honestly, when I heard the news of what had happened it wasn't a shock to me. That's strange but true. I definitely think he knew. Goodison was where he would have chosen to die and in fact, I think he stage managed it! Joe Mercer said exactly the same thing. My dad was one for the occasion and for doing things in style.'

The following Friday, March 7, Birkenhead came to a standstill for Dixie's funeral service at St James' Church in the north end of the town, where he had been baptised and married, less than half a mile from his childhood home.

Outside, in Laird Street the flag flew at half mast over the tiny school William Ralph Dean attended before and during the First World War. Youngsters whose fathers were not even old enough to have seen Dixie in action were amongst crowds paying homage to the memory of the game's finest centre forward.

Also present to pay his respects was Jimmy Goodchild, who played in the same school team as Dixie and was himself tipped for stardom before a broken leg shattered his prospects. Instead he became a shipbuilder. 'Bill was always a lovely man,' said Jimmy. 'He was full of jokes, tales and generosity. There will never be another Bill Dean.'

Bill Shankly, whose own death 18 months later stunned the nation, captured the mood of the people at the church and thronging the streets to say goodbye to Dixie when he said: 'Today there is no red and blue, no black and white, no Protestants and Catholics . . . just mourning for a great footballer.'

The entire Everton first team squad and Johnny King, manager of Dixie's first League club Tranmere, were among a 700 congregation as Dixie's coffin was borne into the church by four pallbearers, comprising a quartet of former Everton players . . . Brian Labone, Bob Latchford, Mick Lyons and Gordon West. Joe Mercer read a lesson while the vicar, the Reverend Gordon Dickenson, said: 'Dixie Dean has had a tremendous influence on many young men over the years. He was kind and lovable, helpful to others, ready to tell a joke and anecdote, especially when speaking about the game he loved. He was a gentleman both on the field and off, and was never sent off or reprimanded. It is not only players who can keep his memory alive but those thousands of supporters who, by following his example of goodness, can continue to enjoy their football. What I commend to you, and especially those who knew him personally or followed his fortunes throughout the years, is that you have a memory of Dixie Dean. But it must be used as an inspiration. There is no better tribute to anyone and their memory that you keep alive in your lifetime that which you admired most in theirs.'

The massive public salute to Dixie's memory was a moving experience for the Dean family. 'I'll never forget the amazing turn out in Birkenhead for my dad's funeral,' his daughter Barbara recalled. 'After we left the church the streets were lined with people all the way to Landican Crematorium. There were old men with flat caps mingling with schoolchildren. My dad would have been pleased and proud about that. We received a huge number of letters, cards, flowers and sympathy messages and our family was deeply moved by the regard and affection so many people clearly had for dad.'

In a private ceremony Barbara scattered her father's ashes along the centre line at Goodison Park where memories of Everton's finest performer endure. The club commissioned Merseyside sculptor Tom Murphy to produce a life-size statue of Dixie, fittingly unveiled by his son Geoff. The statue will go with them if and when Everton move to a new stadium.

'Dixie Dean was our greatest player of all time and one of the greatest players this country has ever seen,' said Everton owner and vice-chairman Bill Kenwright. 'It is vital we revel in our famous past. We must celebrate it and that is why we commissioned the statue of the fabulous Dixie.'

The concept was not new. Dr David France, instigator of the 'Gwladys Street's Hall of Fame' and inspiration of the founding of the charitable Everton Former Players' Foundation, of which he is a trustee, recounted:

'My grandfather brainwashed me with tales of William Ralph Dean. He believed that Everton had treated him shabbily towards the end of his career and claimed to have written to Theo Kelly suggesting that the club erect a monument to the greatest goalscorer in the history of the game, similar to that constructed in Trafalgar Square to honour Lord Nelson. The great man's statue would be taller with one foot for every goal he scored for the Toffees in the League. His preferred site was adjacent to the old practice pitch behind the Park End Stand. Being a bit of a scientist, my grandfather had calculated that at 3.00 p.m. on the third Saturday of every August the orientation of the sun would cast a dark silhouette of the 349-foot statue across Stanley Park – over the boating lake and across the Victorian greenhouse to finish exactly at the halfway line at Anfield. Thus reminding Kopites that they would live in the shadow of Dixie Dean and Everton for another season!'

Years of campaigning by the media and public for Everton to erect a statue to Dixie finally became reality when a magnificent, imposing bronze cast of the club's finest player was unveiled at the Park End of Goodison, at the corner of Spellow Lane and Walton Lane, the end of the ground where he rose into immortality by heading his 60th League goal of the 1927–28 season.

The 8ft 2in statue, which on its base stands almost 10 feet and weighs more than a ton, depicts Dixie running out for a match as captain carrying a football which is laced through 16 eyes. The detail of the boots and the ball is uncanny and the facial expression captures Dixie's determined approach to the sport in which he performed heroically.

It is another triumph for Huyton-born sculptor Tom Murphy whose other distinguished work includes the Bill Shankly statue at Anfield and the Merseyside monuments to John Lennon, John and Cecil Moores, Johnny Walker RN and the city of Liverpool's memorial to the wartime Blitz at St Nicholas's Church.

The unveiling of the Dean statue was performed by Dixie's middle son, Geoff, on Friday, May 4, 2001, the day before the 73rd anniversary of the Everton legend setting that unassailable 60-goal record, a total the entire Everton team have matched only once since the club's last championship season in 1987!

Dean's incredible feat is commemorated by sixty circles in the railings at the sides and back of the open statue, which stands opposite the gates of Stanley Park but will accompany Everton if and when they move to a new stadium.

The ceremony proved that the very name of Dixie is still a crowd-puller with police having to control traffic because of the number of people who gathered to see the drapes removed from the figure.

Yet what they did not know was that the image of Dixie was the third that Murphy had fashioned. 'The first was a prototype of Dixie as the dominant figure flanked by two other players but Everton didn't like it so it was decided that I would sculpt a solo figure,' Murphy recalled. 'Just when I had this completed I felt the position of the upper arms wasn't right. But when I loosened one of the main bolts to make adjustments the whole thing toppled over and I had to start all over again.

'Strangely, I had been having a few problems with it and I wasn't totally happy. So maybe it was fate that it fell over. Perhaps even Dixie gave it a kick! When I started again it took me longer to complete than any sculpture I've done. You are never totally satisfied with your work but I'm delighted by the public reaction to the Dixie statue. They say a sculpture should look good from six angles. I hope it does and I hope it symbolises Dixie's spirit and character.

'I used a photograph of him as a starting point but I wanted to give the work maximum gravitas and capture Dixie's totally committed, resolute approach which had a devastating effect on opponents. That is why one of his fists is clenched. The upper torso was also very important because Dixie had powerful, broad shoulders which I'm told he helped develop by carrying milk crates as a boy.

'His shoulders were a big factor in his brilliant heading ability and a part of his physique which is not noticeable in some pictures of him which were taken when his muscles were relaxed. The pose of the statue is powerful. Dixie is switched on, ready for action.

'I had no pictures of the boots Dixie wore so I didn't know which of the many possible ways he used to tie them up. I looked at contemporary photographs from the period and chose one particular style, which he probably used at one time or another.'

Murphy's sculpting was cast in bronze by Chris Butler at his foundry at Llanrhaeadr near Oswestry and the total cost of the statue is estimated at £75,000, a small price to pay to posterity in tribute to a player who would be priceless even in today's climate of ever-rising transfer fees. Inscribed on the base of the statue is a legend to a legend which reads:

*William Ralph Dixie Dean 1907 to 1980*
*377 goals in 431 games including a record 60 League goals*
*in season 1927-28*
*Footballer    Gentleman    Evertonian*
*Sculpture by Tom Murphy*

Dixie's eldest son William, who had flown back to Britain from his home in Australia specially to be at the opening ceremony, and youngest son, Ralph, were unable to attend the statue unveiling due to illness. But three generations of the Dean family did attend, including Dixie's daughter Barbara, his grand-daughter Melanie and his great grand-children Daniel and Scarlet.

Also present were a few long-time Evertonians who were at Goodison to see Dixie set the 60-goal record on that golden day in 1928. They included Bert Dowell, President of Everton Shareholders Association, who enthused: 'Dixie was the finest player ever to wear the blue shirt. There will never be another and it is fitting that the club have erected a statue in his honour.'

The assembled throng at the unveiling ceremony heard Everton owner and deputy chairman Bill Kenwright deliver a moving, off-the-cuff speech in which he proclaimed: 'Fellow Evertonians, this is a long, long overdue day in the history of this football club.

'The word legend is a much abused and over-used word in our game, a game in which the pay packet seems to rule these days, when ego seems to rule and there is little of the hero in some people who wear shirts up and down the country. I'm not saying in all of them, not by any means. But in some of them.

'Today we salute probably the greatest hero of all time. If you ask Evertonian why their dads, why their grandads, why their brothers became Evertonians, why they are proudest of all to be Evertonians, one name will invariably be the name quoted: our beloved William Ralph "Dixie" Dean.

'The 1927–28 season is one of the greatest years in Everton history. It was Dixie's season. Everton's season. We won the League and our No 9 was doing things no footballer had ever done before or has ever done since. Dixie went into the last four games that season requiring 10 goals to reach 60 in the League. By the last match he still needed three goals.

'In 1978 I cancelled my honeymoon to see Super Latch (Bob Latchford) get 30 League goals for the season. I cried tears of joy that day. So what Everton's stadium must have been like 73 years ago tomorrow when Dixie had to score three times to reach that extraordinary 60 would have been something to behold.

'I have seen some great, great days at this football stadium, the happiest days of my life and some of the saddest. But if anyone ever said to me what is the moment you would like to see as an Evertonian it would be Dixie 'the salmon' going up to meet Alec Troup's corner and connecting with that miraculous header to score his 60th League goal in 1928.

'Many, many Premiership teams don't score that many in an entire season today! Dixie was a great leader on the pitch, the hero of Goodison, a colossus among men. An inspiration to his team-mates. He was a God to them. And he was terrifying to the opposing team. I think there's one "never" in football that's a truism . . . Dixie Dean's record will never, ever be beaten.

'His memory will never be forgotten by Evertonians. In fact, it will never be forgotten by people who love football all over the world. Today we celebrate the greatest goal machine in the history of football.

'I would like to think that all the Everton centre forwards I've known and worked with over the years – from Dave Hickson to Alex Young, Bob Latchford, Joe Royle, Graeme Sharp and the two big fellows now (Duncan Ferguson and Kevin Campbell) – are today celebrating football's greatest ever centre forward.

'There will never be another one and I'm very proud to be here today to salute Dixie Dean, Evertonian, and to ask his son, Geoff, to cut the tape and unveil this magnificent statue, which has been created and designed superbly by Tom Murphy.'

After cutting the tape to remove the drapes from the statue to loud cheers from the crowd, a clearly emotional Geoff told them: 'Bill has said it all, really. I'd just like to say that my dad was as good a father as he was a footballer.'

When Dixie's eldest son William, saw the statue he said: 'It is a marvellous, imposing tribute to my dad and it's good to know that wherever Everton go in the future the statue will go with them and continue to have pride of place.

'Australia recently mourned the passing of the great Don Bradman and I often likened his dedication to my dad's. People say they were both naturally gifted sportsmen. But they helped make their talent blossom by their sheer hard work from an early age and right through their wonderful careers. They are the perfect examples to aspiring youngsters and if the statue of my dad can act as an inspiration it will be worth its weight in gold, never mind bronze.'

The decision to erect a statue to Dixie was widely applauded. Kevin Ratcliffe, the Wales defender who became the most successful captain in Everton history by leading them during their glittering era in the 1980s, enthused: 'Other clubs have commissioned statues to the likes of Sir Matt Busby, Jackie Milburn, Bill Shankly and Billy Bremner and a statue of Dixie at Everton was long overdue. Whatever Everton's problems nobody can ever criticise the stature of the club's tradition, history and heritage. Dixie is the great legend of Goodison and the statue is a wonderful way for his memory to be commemorated.'

And Everton's most successful manager, Howard Kendall, declared: 'When I was on Everton's Millennium Giants panel the one player whose claims we didn't argue about or even debate was Dixie Dean, the legend of legends. Memories of his deeds will be handed down the generations. He will never be forgotten and a statue of him was long overdue.'

Visiting directors, dignitaries and guests at Goodison are reminded of Dixie's feats by his portrait outside the Everton boardroom bearing the legend:

'Dixie Dean stands supreme as the greatest scoring machine of all time. His 60 First Division goals in 39 games in season 1927–28 remains an untouchable League record. He scored 349 goals in 399 League games for the Blues as well as plundering 28 goals in 32 FA Cup ties. His Goodison Park career record was a phenomenal 377 goals in 431 appearances between 1925 and 1938. Dean died at his beloved Goodison in March 1980 after the final whistle of an Everton v Liverpool derby match.'

Also, a Goodison lounge has been named after Dixie, containing many mementoes of his career, while his first League club Tranmere opened a similar room at Prenton Park to mark their links with the scoring genius.

Visitors on Goodison's stadium tours can hear clips of Dixie talking, taken from my audio cassette album entitled 'A Sporting Portrait of Dixie Dean', which is on sale at the Everton Megastore, while a plaque on the site of St Domingo Methodist Church, the birthplace of the Everton club in 1878, commemorates Dixie's 60-goal record set in May 1928.

The *Liverpool Echo* run an annual Dixie Dean Memorial Award for sportsmanship and character in professional football, inaugurated immediately after his death, with Joe Mercer and Bill Shankly members of the first judging panel and Ian Callaghan the first recipient.

When England hosted the European Championships in the summer of 1996 Dixie Dean was the only pre-Second World War British player among five whose portraits were chosen by pundits and public to feature on a special set of Football Legends postage stamps to mark Euro 96. The other four were Bobby Moore, Duncan Edwards, Billy Wright and Danny Blanchflower. 'We invited a team of football writers and experts to draw up a short list of 10 great players,' said the Royal Mail. 'Then the public was invited to vote for their favourite five. Football lovers responded in their thousands. The poll rules stated that no living players could be considered. So masters such as Sir Stanley Matthews, Sir Tom Finney, George Best, John Charles, Sir Bobby Charlton, Denis Law and Kenny Dalglish had to be overlooked. But surely the public's choice of the Famous Five can't be argued with. They were true giants of the game . . . their brilliance made football larger than life for millions in the stand.'

In May 1999, Dixie was one of a magnificent seven former Everton players chosen to be among '100 League Legends' as part of the Football League's centenary celebrations. The others were Joe Mercer, Tommy Lawton, Alex Young, Alan Ball, Gary Lineker and Neville Southall.

Years after Dixie's death and into the 21st century public fascination with him continues. Dixie's son Geoff said: 'I worked in the licensed trade until I was 66. The last premises Pat and I had was 'Dixie Dean's Doubles Bar' in London Road, Liverpool which we ran for more than 13 years until selling it in 2000. Every day someone would reminisce about my dad and his exploits with Everton. Irish visitors also used to drop in and talk about his time with Sligo Rovers and even Liverpool fans would come in for a drink! You'd get a few cranks, too, of course, drawn by my dad's fame. One night, when Pat was serving and I was off duty, a chap came in and, not knowing who Pat was, said: "I'm Dixie Dean's son", "Is that so," said Pat. "Well, if you just wait a minute you can meet your brother. I'll go and get him from upstairs!" With that, the fellow ran out!'.

Dixie's collection of cups, medals and other memorabilia from his remarkable career, which he displayed at the 'Dublin Packet', went with him when he left the pub and after his death was left to various members of his family under the terms of his will. Geoff was left his father's 1933 FA Cup winners medal, a gold inscribed medal to commemorate Dixie scoring 200 league goals in 199 appearances and the Hall of Fame Trophy. He has also had news film of Dixie, including shots of the 1933 Final, converted to video as a souvenir.

At auction at Christie's in October 1991, Dixie's 1927–28 League championship medal was sold for £9,350 – more than three times what Dixie had cost Everton from Tranmere – his 1931–32 championship medal for £3,520, his 1932 FA Charity Shield medal for £3,300, a 1926–27 international medal for £3,080 and his 1928 FA Charity Shield medal for £2,420.

In March 2001, Dixie's son Geoff put the 1933 FA Cup medal up for auction at Christie's who placed on it a reserve price of £8,000. But when the sale took place in London's South Kensington the medal raised a British record price of £18,212 and, fittingly, it was bought by Everton to remain as a permanent part of the club's heritage.

'A medal belonging to our greatest ever player was never going anywhere else but to Everton Football Club,' said deputy chairman Bill Kenwright. 'We are delighted to have secured it. We appointed our agent to get it at whatever cost. Dixie Dean was Everton's and England's greatest ever centre forward, he was captain of the Cup-winning team and it was only right that we secured his medal.'

A spokesman for Christie's said: 'The fee paid was a record for an FA Cup winners medal and exceeded even our expectations.' Geoff, too, was delighted at the outcome. 'It's lovely to know that my dad's medal will be on permanent display at the club and that future generations will see it,' he said. 'The medal represents a very successful era in Everton history and it's great that the medal will symbolise it.'

But William Ralph Dean's greatest legacy was his unrivalled demonstration of the goalscoring art – creating the statistics that seem incredible even in the cold print of the record books – and the swashbuckling manner in which he did it. Just how his feats have echoed down the generations to secure a permanent place in Everton's heritage and tradition was powerfully evident when, in November 1997, Dixie's great grandson, two-and-a-half-year-old Daniel Dean Haslam, received a massive welcoming roar from the Everton faithful when his mother Melanie took him onto the Goodison pitch and watched proudly as he kicked a ball into the net at the same end that his great grandfather had soared to head his record-breaking 60th goal almost 70 years earlier.

Dixie's deeds have inspired a plethora of poems, prose and songs. Foremost among the latter is Gerry Markey's moving 'Ballad of Dixie Dean', available on cassette. Two poems, ironically penned by Liverpool supporters, also capture the magic of Dixie. Ron Byrne wrote this one, entitled *The Goodison Giant – A Kopite's Tribute*:

A long time ago when I was a lad
Folk spoke of a genius Everton had
The greatest goalscorer the world's ever seen

Who went by the name William Ralph Dean
This man was so lethal with a flick of his head
He'd leave goalies flat out as if they were dead
This working class hero was humble and poor
He never bragged of the goals that he scored
No flashy clothes and no trendy car
He'd drink with the Gwladys Street fans in the bar
He never cared much for money or fame
He just loved the Blues and the footballing game
Though I was too young to have seen Dixie play
His feats are remembered and talked of today
I grew up an urchin down old Scotty Road
No shoes on my feet and a small, snotty nose
We kicked cans on the cobbles each kid with one dream
One day we'd be legends, just like Dixie Dean

Another rhyming tribute to Dixie was printed on the order of service at his funeral. Written By Reg Ikin it is entitled *Shades of Dixie*:

Have no regrets for Dixie, the timing was there as before
He left his beloved Goodison still unbeatable his score
This great heart and head had given Everton its all
and the golden goals that flowed when Dixie touched the ball
So when they talk of 'shades of Dixie' and Elisha's blasphemies
or Pastor Jackson's rebukes; then thank God for men as these
They played the game for all its worth, for little pay, and yet
their characters counted a richer worth, one we will never forget

'As a schoolboy the phrase "shades of Dixie" was in common use to express the ultimate excellence in football accomplishment,' said Reg. 'All Liverpool kids are born with a football bent and it was to the team of that name I have been loyal since my earliest days. That does not debar me from giving credit where credit is due and it is a fact that W.R. Dean is special to football. The short poem is my tribute to a very ordinary man off the field and a genius on it.'

Dixie, himself, would have been embarrassed at such sincerely offered superlatives. Perhaps he unwittingly supplied his own epitaph when he told me over that last lunch: 'I just liked to get the job done quickly and without any fuss. The sooner that ball was in the onion bag the happier I was.'

Happiness was something he spread thickly among his adoring terrace gallery. He epitomised Everton's motto 'Nil Satis Nisi Optimum' – nothing but the best satisfies – and it was a message he wanted youngsters to heed and act upon. 'My advice to young players is to take notice of people who try to help them,' said Dixie. 'Always keep your eyes and ears open. Look and listen. And don't be shooting your mouth off. If someone offers you advice say "Yes, thank you" but don't let anything bother you. And whatever else you do make sure you get a ball of your own and practise exactly as I did on the old chapel wall.'

In this television-financed era of centres of excellence, youth academies and football clinics, when we have even witnessed moves to ban games of street football, such a prospect may seem straight from the game's dark ages.

But it is true what they say about Dixie. He was the best. So if a youngster can find a ball and a wall he will be stepping into Dixie's land, a land that echoed to a melody which will be a constant refrain thanks to the deeds of William Ralph Dean.

# CHAPTER FOURTEEN

# *The Statistics*

## DIXIE DEAN'S CAREER RECORD IN SENIOR ENGLISH FOOTBALL

With Tranmere Rovers (League games in Division Three North)

| Season | Appearances | Goals | Totals |
|---|---|---|---|
| 1923–24 | 3 League  0 FA Cup | 0 League   0 FA Cup | 3 apps    0 goals |
| 1924–25 | 27 League  3 FA Cup | 27 League   0 FA Cup | 30 apps   27 goals |
| **Totals** | **30 League  3 FA Cup** | **27 League   0 FA Cup** | **33 apps   27 goals** |

With Everton (League games in former First Division apart from 1930–31 which were in former Second Division)

| Season | Apps | | Goals | | Totals | | INTER-NATIONALS | | INTER LEAGUE | |
|---|---|---|---|---|---|---|---|---|---|---|
| | *League* | *FA Cup* | *League* | *FA Cup* | *Apps* | *Goals* | *Apps* | *Goals* | *Apps* | *Goals* |
| 1924–25 | 7 | 0 | 2 | 0 | 7 | 2 | | | | |
| 1925–26 | 38 | 2 | 32 | 1 | 40 | 33 | | | | |
| 1926–27 | 27 | 4 | 21 | 3 | 31 | 24 | 5 | 12 | | |
| 1927–28 | 39 | 2 | 60 | 3 | 41 | 63 | 5 | 4 | 2 | 6 |
| 1928–29 | 29 | 1 | 26 | 0 | 30 | 26 | 3 | 1 | 2 | 3 |
| 1929–30 | 25 | 2 | 23 | 2 | 27 | 25 | | | | |
| 1930–31 | 37 | 5 | 39 | 9 | 42 | 48 | 1 | 0 | | |
| 1931–32 | 38 | 1 | 45 | 1 | 39 | 46 | 1 | 1 | 1 | 0 |
| 1932–33 | 39 | 6 | 24 | 5 | 45 | 29 | 1 | 0 | | |
| 1933–34 | 12 | 0 | 9 | 0 | 12 | 9 | | | | |
| 1934–35 | 38 | 5 | 26 | 1 | 43 | 27 | | | | |
| 1935–36 | 29 | 0 | 17 | 0 | 29 | 17 | | | | |
| 1936–37 | 36 | 4 | 24 | 3 | 40 | 27 | | | 1 | 0 |
| 1937–38 | 5 | 0 | 1 | 0 | 5 | 1 | | | | |
| **Totals** | **399** | **32** | **349** | **28** | **431** | **377** | **16** | **18** | **6** | **9** |

In addition Dean made two appearances in the Charity Shield, scoring twice against Blackburn Rovers in Everton's 2–1 win at Old Trafford on October 24, 1928 and scoring four in Everton's 5–3 win over Newcastle United at St James' Park on October 12, 1932 giving him a grand total of 383 Everton goals in 433 senior games for the club.

Dean's total of goals in season 1927–28 reached a century. In addition to his record-setting 60 League goals and three in the FA Cup he also scored four for England, six for the Football League, eight in FA Trial games, nine on an FA tour and a further 10 in friendly and charity games including the Blackpool Hospital Cup and Fleetwood Disaster Match. His 100 goals came in 56 matches.

With Notts County (League games in Division Three South)

| Season | Appearances | | Goals | | Totals | |
|--------|-----|-----|-----|-----|-----|-----|
| 1937–38 | 3 League | 0 FA Cup | 0 League | 0 FA Cup | 3 apps | 0 goals |
| 1938–39 | 6 League | 0 FA Cup | 3 League | 0 FA Cup | 6 apps | 3 goals |
| **Totals** | **9 League** | **0 FA Cup** | **3 League** | **0 FA Cup** | **9 apps** | **3 goals** |

Grand total (club and representative matches):
Appearances: 497      Goals: 440

## Dean's Hat Tricks

Dixie Dean scored 43 hat tricks at club and representative level during his career in senior football, including a record 37 for Everton. These are his hat trick games, with his total given in the matches in which he scored more than three:

### With Tranmere Rovers

1924–25 – October 25, 1924:   Tranmere 4 Harlepools United 3 (Div 3 North)

February 14, 1925:   Tranmere 4 Barrow 1 (Div 3 North)

March 7, 1925:   Tranmere 3 Rochdale 1 (Div 3 North)

### With Everton

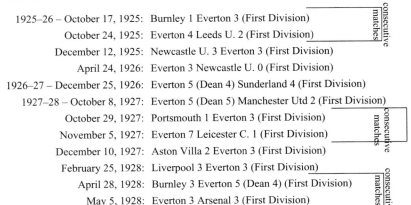

1925–26 – October 17, 1925: Burnley 1 Everton 3 (First Division)

October 24, 1925: Everton 4 Leeds U. 2 (First Division)

December 12, 1925: Newcastle U. 3 Everton 3 (First Division)

April 24, 1926: Everton 3 Newcastle U. 0 (First Division)

1926–27 – December 25, 1926: Everton 5 (Dean 4) Sunderland 4 (First Division)

1927–28 – October 8, 1927: Everton 5 (Dean 5) Manchester Utd 2 (First Division)

October 29, 1927: Portsmouth 1 Everton 3 (First Division)

November 5, 1927: Everton 7 Leicester C. 1 (First Division)

December 10, 1927: Aston Villa 2 Everton 3 (First Division)

February 25, 1928: Liverpool 3 Everton 3 (First Division)

April 28, 1928: Burnley 3 Everton 5 (Dean 4) (First Division)

May 5, 1928: Everton 3 Arsenal 3 (First Division)

1928–29 – August 25, 1928:  Bolton 2 Everton 3 (First Division)

September 1, 1928:  Everton 4 Portsmouth 0 (First Division)

December 22, 1928:  Everton 5 Newcastle U. 2 (First Division)

December 29, 1928:  Everton 3 Bolton W. 0 (First Division)

January 1, 1929:  Everton 4 Derby County 0 (First Division)

*consecutive matches*

1929–30 – September 28, 1929:  Portsmouth 1 Everton 4 (First Division)

1930–31 – November 22, 1930:  Everton 5 Stoke City 0 (Second Division)

December 6, 1930:  Everton 6 (Dean 4) Oldham 4 (Second Division)

December 27, 1930:  Everton 9 (Dean 4) Plymouth 1 (Second Division)

January 24, 1931:  Crystal Palace 0 Everton 6 (Dean 4) (FA Cup 4)

February 7, 1931:  Charlton Athletic 0 Everton 7 (Second Division)

February 28, 1931:  Everton 9 (Dean 4) Southport 1 (FA Cup 6)

1931–32 – September 19, 1931:  Liverpool 1 Everton 3 (First Division)

October 10, 1931:  Sheffield United 1 Everton 5 (First Division)

October 17, 1931:  Everton 9 (Dean 5) Sheff. Wed. 3 (First Division)

*consecutive matches*

November 14, 1931:  Everton 7 (Dean 5) Chelsea 2 (First Division)

November 28, 1931:  Everton 9 (Dean 4) Leicester 2 (First Division)

December 26, 1931:  Everton 5 Blackburn Rovers 0 (First Division)

March 19, 1932:  Everton 4 Huddersfield Town 1 (First Division)

April 16, 1932:  Everton 6 West Ham United 1 (First Division)

1932–33 – October 12, 1932:  Newcastle U. 3 Everton 5 (Dean 4) (Charity Shield)
                              (At St James Park)

March 8, 1933:  Everton 6 Leicester City 3 (First Division)

1934–35 – December 29, 1934:  Everton 5 Tottenham H. 2 (First Division)

1935–36 – April 25, 1936:  Everton 4 Birmingham 3 (First Division)

1936–37 – November 7, 1936:  Everton 4 West Bromwich 2 (First Division)

## Dean's England hat tricks

May 11, 1927: Belgium 1 England 9 (Brussels)

May 21, 1927: Luxemburg 2 England 5 (Luxemburg)

## Dean's Football League representative hat tricks

September 21, 1927: Football League 9 (Dean 4) Irish League 1 (at Newcastle)

Hat tricks totals:   For Tranmere Rovers:   3

                    For Everton:   37

                    For England:   2

          For Football League:   1

                 GRAND TOTAL:   43

## Dean's Representative Record

### For England

February 12, 1927: v Wales (Wrexham) Drew 3–3 (Dean 2)
April 2, 1927: v Scotland (Hampden Park) Won 2–1 (Dean 2)
May 11, 1927: v Belgium (Brussels) Won 9–1 (Dean 3)
May 21, 1927: v Luxemburg (Luxemburg) Won 5–2 (Dean 3)
May 26, 1927: v France (Paris) Won 6–0 (Dean 2)
October 22, 1927: v Ireland (Belfast) Lost 0–2
November 28, 1927: v Wales (Burnley) Lost 1–2
March 31, 1928: v Scotland (Wembley) Lost 1–5
May 17, 1928: v France (Paris) Won 5–1 (Dean 2)
May 19, 1928: v Belgium (Antwerp) won 3–1 (Dean 2)
October 22, 1928: v Ireland (Goodison Park) Won 2–1 (Dean 1)
November 17, 1928: v Wales (Swansea) Won 3–2
April 13, 1929: v Scotland (Hampden Park) Lost 0–1
March 28, 1931: v Scotland (Hampden Park) Lost 0–2
December 9, 1931: v Spain (Highbury) Won 7–1 (Dean 1)
October 17, 1932: v Ireland (Blackpool) Won 1–0

## TOTAL: Appearances 16, Goals 18

### For Football League

September 21, 1927: v Irish League (Newcastle) Won 9–1 (Dean 4)
March 10, 1928: v Scottish League (Ibrox Park) Won 6–2 (Dean 2)
September 22, 1928: v Irish League (Belfast) Won 5–0 (Dean 2)
November 7, 1928: v Scottish League (Villa park) Won 2–1 (Dean 1)
November 7, 1931: v Scottish League (Celtic Park) Lost 3–4
October 21, 1935: v Scottish League (Goodison Park) Won 2–0

## TOTAL: Appearances 6, Goals 9

## Dean's Roll of Honour

### *With Everton*

League championship medals 1927–28 and 1931–32
FA Cup winners medal 1933
Second Division championship medal 1930–31
FA Charity Shield winners medals 1928 and 1932
Central League championship medal 1937–38
'Sunday Pictorial' Trophy for 60 League goals in 1927–28
Lewis's Medal to commemorate 200 League goals in 199 appearances
England caps 16, Goals 18
Football League representative appearances 6, Goals 9

### *With Sligo Rovers*

League of Ireland runners-up medal 1938–39
Football Association of Ireland Cup runners-up medal 1938–39

### *In Retirement*

Hall of Fame Trophy 1971
Football Writers Association inscribed silver salver 1976

### *Posthumously*

Inaugural inductee in National Football Museum Hall of Fame 2002.

### *Dixie Dean's scoring record against Liverpool:*

February 6, 1925: Everton 3 Liverpool 3 (Dean 1)
February 25, 1928: Liverpool 3 Everton 3 (Dean 3)
September 7, 1929: Liverpool 0 Everton 3 (Dean 2)
January 4, 1930: Everton 3 Liverpool 3 (Dean 2)
September 19, 1931: Liverpool 1 Everton 3 (Dean 3)
January 19, 1932: Everton 1 Liverpool 2 (FA Cup) (Dean 1)
October 1, 1932: Everton 3 Liverpool 1 (Dean 2)
February 11, 1933; Liverpool 7 Everton 4 (Dean 2)
September 15, 1934: Everton 1 Liverpool 0 (Dean 1)
March 6, 1935: Liverpool 2 Everton 1 (Dean 1)
September 19, 1936: Everton 2 (Liverpool 0 (Dean 1)

He also played in another six games against Liverpool without scoring, giving him a Mersey derby haul of 19 goals in 17 outings against Liverpool

# Bibliography

*Albert Geldard*, Albert Geldard and John K. Rowlands, Countryside Publications, 1990

*The Daily Express A–Z Of Mersey Soccer*, John Keith and Peter Thomas, Beaverbrook Newspapers, 1973

*Dixie Dean*, Nick Walsh, Macdonald and Jane's, 1977

*Dixie Dean Of Tranmere Rovers*, Gilbert Upton, Upton Publishing, 1992

*Everton: A Complete Record*, Ian Ross and Gordon Smailes, Breedon Books, 1985

*Everton: The Official Centenary History*, John Roberts, Mayflower Granada Publishing, 1978

*The Fabulous Dixie*, Phil Thompson, Quarry Publications, 1990

*Football Is My Business*, Tommy Lawton with Roy Peskett, Sporting Handbooks, 1946

*Gwladys Street's Hall of Fame*, David H. France, Skript Publishing, 1998

*History Of The Everton Football Club*, Thomas Keates, Thomas Brakell, 1929

*In Reserve: Tranmere Rovers In The Cheshire County League*, Gilbert Upton, Upton Publishing, 2000

*Soccer At The Top*, Matt Busby, Weidenfeld and Nicolson, 1973

*A Sporting Portrait Of Dixie Dean* audio album Volumes 1 and 2, John Keith, Mastersound, 1997

*Tranmere Rovers: A Complete Record*, Gilbert Upton and Steve Wilson, Upton and Wilson Publishing, 1997

*My Twenty Years of Soccer*, Tommy Lawton, Heirloom Modern World Library, 1955

# *Appendix*

The iconic status of William Ralph Dean, the fabulous Dixie, continues to be powerfully illustrated, almost mocking the passage of time, underlining his fellow Everton and England centre forward Tommy Lawton's view that he is football's legend of legends.

When Everton achieved, in 2002–2003, the unique feat of playing 100 seasons in the top flight of English football it was to their greatest star that they turned to spearhead celebrations of that proud distinction.

Some 65 years since he last kicked a ball in the service of the club, and more than two decades after his death, Everton commissioned an imposing colour mural of Dixie, only yards from his giant bronze statue, which graces the approaches to Goodison Park.

Nothing could have been more appropriate because that season, which saw a renaissance of the club's playing fortunes under the leadership of their exciting new manager David Moyes, ended with another anniversary of a unique achievement . . . Dixie's fantastic, unassailable record of 60 League goals, which he completed 75 years earlier with a dramatic hat trick against Arsenal on May 5, 1928.

The power of Dean's celebrity was emphasised, too, outside the confines of sport. When BBC Radio Merseyside and the *Liverpool Echo* staged a 2003 public poll to find 'The Greatest Merseysider' from any walk of life, Dixie outstripped current football stars such as Michael Owen and Everton prodigy Wayne Rooney.

Indeed, he was in the vanguard of the voting along with Lennon and McCartney and Ken Dodd, the master of mirth who eventually triumphed with Dean fourth, the highest-placed sporting hero.

Given that Dixie's professional playing days ended before the Second World War his place in the public's heart is another fulsome tribute to the impact he and his deeds had on the forefathers of the present generation who, clearly passed on the Dean legend like an unquenchable torch.

Everton's affection for their greatest ever player, symbolised by a special kit badge featuring Dixie's silhouette surrounded by the words 'Everton: 100 Years Top Flight Football', was reflected also in their inspired decision to have a Dean mural in a year that also commemorated the club's 125th birthday, having been founded in 1878.

'As part of our ongoing celebrations during this historic season we decided to commission a huge Everton mural in a position as close to Goodison Park as we could and we felt that the end house in Goodison Road was the ideal location,' said a club spokesman.

'Terry Smith, who lives in the property, was happy to oblige with a season's "loan" of the outside wall of his house on which the mural could be painted.

'Dixie Dean was an obvious choice as the subject of the mural. Dixie is an Everton icon if ever there was one! It was decided that he should hold others in the palm of his hands – but who to choose provoked much discussion.

'Eventually, we decided to honour that magnificent 1970 championship-winning midfield trio of Howard Kendall, Colin Harvey and Alan Ball not just for the enormous parts they played in bringing the title to Goodison in that wonderful year but for the unforgettable standard of their play.

'With the design having been established it was then merely a matter of transferring the image from a piece of A3 paper to the side of a house!

'Our stadium manager Alan Bowen approached the club's decorating contractors who put us in touch with mural expert Mark Garrod of Hunts Cross, Liverpool. He was happy to carry out the task and both from a professional and football-fan aspect he's satisfied with the result.

'It was something different to reflect Everton's heritage in a unique season and no other club in the Premiership has anything similar.'

Mural artist Mark admitted: 'I'm a Crystal Palace supporter but I've got a soft spot for Everton and I thought the mural was a great idea. I was up there for four days painting it and it was quite cold.

'I began on a Monday, lost one whole day through rain, and finished it on the Friday, the day before the home game against West Brom. I'd done murals before but I'd say this was my biggest project and most people were made up with it.'

Terry, whose house was the 'canvas' for the mural, declared: 'The club asked me if I would mind having the mural on my house. I jumped at the chance. My great-grandfather was a chairman of the supporters club and the whole family are Evertonians.

'The neighbours loved the mural and it's been great that the tourists have come to take pictures of it. It's been a real celebration.'

The celebration of Dixie has even extended to the Santiago Bernabeu Stadium, home of the world's greatest club Real Madrid . . . although not in the way it was planned!

Everton supporters Ernie Hird, Kevin Burns and Alan Sherlock of Bootle, Merseyside journeyed to the Spanish capital with a small bronze statue, which they mistakenly believed to be that of a young Dixie Dean, to present to Real to mark their centenary in 2002.

In fact, no miniatures of Dixie have been made and the statue now on display in a glass case in the Bernabeu trophy room, alongside figures of Real legends Ferenc Puskas and Alfredo di Stefano, is that of an unknown, unnamed Everton player!

'We thought the statue was that of a young Dixie Dean but it's still a nice one and I can't go back and tell Madrid it's not Dixie,' said Ernie, who with his friends raised funds for charity by auctioning reciprocal gifts given to them by Real.

There was no confusion, however, about Dean's place among the inaugural inductees of players and managers in the Hall Of Fame at Preston's National Football Museum in November 2002.

A selection panel of twenty judges, including football knights Sir Bobby Charlton and Sir Bobby Robson, Gary Lineker, Alan Hansen and Mark Lawrenson, named Dixie in their original selection of 23 players who had made 'a lasting contribution to the British game and played in its leagues.'

Dean's fellow luminaries in the Museum's Hall of Fame, which is situated at Preston North End's Deepdale stadium, include Sir Stanley Matthews, Sir Tom Finney, Sir Matt Busby, Bob Paisley, Sir Alex Ferguson, Kenny Dalglish and John Charles.

The publication of the hardback edition of this book in 2001 prompted a remarkable public response with a batch of readers coming forward to reveal their own memories of and anecdotes about Dixie.

Some people even dug into their own treasured archives to hand me material, much of it yellowing with age, featuring the great man and his exploits.

Former *Liverpool Echo* sports sub editor and *Daily Mirror* sportswriter Dave Horridge contributed a collection of wonderful stories about Dixie.

Dave related: 'Joe Wiggall, a lovely man who wrote under the *Echo* pen name of *Stork*, told me that Dixie was such a clever player. When a cross came in and defenders were in close attendance he would appear as if he was ready to jump for the ball.

'The defenders would rise but Dixie, instead of jumping, would stoop to head the ball and, on many occasions, score. Joe also told me that he'd seen Dixie walk into Goodison, place the ball on the centre spot and kick it into the net . If you think it's easy just try it some time!

'That great Everton and Scotland full back Alex Parker told me that one day during Alex's playing days in the 1960s he was talking to Dean in the dressing room when, the club secretary Bill Dickinson came in and asked Dixie: "Who are you?"

'Dixie replied: "Ask who I am when I've left. And when you know who I am go out and take a look at that big stand and think to yourself that I built it!"

'Then there was the marvellous story about Dixie from Bill Shankly. Shanks told me that when he was playing for Preston he and a few team-mates went to watch an Everton game at Goodison.

'He said that when he got into the stand he could see the ball being crossed into the goalmouth and Dixie Dean jumping to meet it. "I showed the steward my ticket," said Shanks "and when I sat down Dixie was still in the air! His ability to hang there was uncanny."

'I did a series of interviews with Dixie for the Mirror prior to his testimonial match in 1964 and he told me that during his playing days he was contacted by a woman who lived in the Everton Valley area.

'She told him that her husband was an Evertonian and a great fan of his but whenever Everton lost he would turn violent and beat her up. So after one home game, which Everton lost, Dixie went to the house.

'He asked the woman where her husband was and she told him he was getting drunk in the local pub and that when he came in he would knock seven bells out of her.

'Amazingly, Dixie said he'd wait with her until the husband came home. When, finally, he did return in an alcoholic haze he was stunned to find Dean waiting for him.

'Dixie told him that he was very concerned that he was beating up his wife and said: "I want you to promise you'll stop doing that." According to Dixie he never heard from the woman again so presumably his intervention had succeeded.'

Dixie, of course, liked to enjoy himself in off-duty moments and stories abound of his social life. Apparently after one enjoyable night out with a friend Bob McCrystal, including a prolonged appearance at the *Lisbon* bar, one of Dixie's favourite haunts, the pair ran out of patience in trying to find a taxi home.

On finding an unoccupied cab near the Pier Head they 'borrowed' it and set off home. But as they reached Islington they came to a full stop. The vehicle they had commandeered was a horse-drawn taxi – and the animal collapsed and died in the middle of the road!

The story goes that when the police arrived and discovered it was Dixie they burst into gales of laughter and ordered a vehicle to take the pair home.

Gilbert Upton, that noted Tranmere historian, archivist and supporter, believes that a story related to him by one of the Birkenhead club's former players might solve the mystery of why Dixie did not make a heavily advertised appearance as a guest for his first professional club in a wartime Football League North match at Prenton Park on Christmas Day 1942, referred to on page 188.

'Ronnie Hodgson, a wartime player for Tranmere, told me that he had heard from within the club that on the day of the game Dixie met his great friend and fellow England international Tom "Pongo" Waring in the nearby Prenton Park Hotel,' said Gilbert.

'The pair had both started their careers at Tranmere and were very close pals. According to Ronnie the talk within the club was that their Yuletide reunion extended to preclude Dixie from turning out in the match.

'But Dixie would have been pleased with the result in his absence. Watched by a 3,000 crowd, Tranmere won 3–2 against a Liverpool team that included Willie Fagan and Cyril Done.'

Internationally renowned football journalist Brian Glanville offered an anecdote that captures perfectly Dixie's acerbic humour. Said Glanville: 'After England's 7–1 hiding of Spain in December 1931 the much vaunted Spanish goalkeeper Ricardo Zamora said to Dean at London's Cafe Royal: "Tonight I am nothing in Madrid." To which Dean replied: "Well, you're not very much here, either."'

That humour was also to the fore when Dixie was confronted by the landlady as he went to collect an Everton team-mate from his digs. 'Mr Dean,' she said sternly. 'I've had such a shock. I was tidying your friend's bedroom when I found this in the bin,' she added, holding up a copy of the *News of the World*.

'And inside I found this thing,' she said in horrified tones, with the offending object dangling from her gloved hand. To which Dixie responded by putting a comforting arm around her and saying: 'Now, now . . . you mustn't believe everything you see in the papers!'

The caring aspect of Dean's personality shines through time and again when those who came into contact with him recall their experiences. A classic example was cited by Fred Williams who grew up with Dixie in Birkenhead.

'He was five years older than me and occasionally I used to kick a ball around with him,' said Fred. 'I lived in Penrith Street with my widowed mother and times were tough. Near our house was a coal yard called Daddy Wilsons.

'My mother used to send me to get a big bag of coal at a cost of threepence a bag. On my way one day I lost that precious threepenny bit. I dared not face my mum who would have given me a good hiding for losing it.

'Then I met Dixie, who was on his way to Tranmere. "What's wrong, Fred?" he asked. I told him I'd lost my mum's coal money. Dixie then put his hand in his pocket, gave me a shilling and said: "Here, get your mum a cart of coal."

'My mum got a big shock when she got a full hundredweight of coal and I guess Dixie saved me from a beating. That's the kind of human being Dixie was. He was a wonderful man.'

Tommy Lawton, perhaps now linking up with his fellow England and Everton centre forward Dixie in a celestial forward line, would have attested powerfully to that sentiment.

Lawton, who died in November 1996, declared:

'I'm not one of those people who always tell you things were better in the old days but I don't mind how many times I say it – Dixie was the greatest of all centre forwards, head and shoulders above anybody else I have seen in that position.

'He was also a great character and, unfortunately, characters are going out of the game. Off the field he was one of the boys and used to enjoy his beer and night out as much as anybody.

'Dixie was a great man who became my friend, my teacher and who was, from the days when I was a toddling schoolboy, my idol.

'He simply oozed personality and nothing seemed to ruffle him. I've seen him with his ankles and back kicked black and blue – but I've never seen him without a smile.

'He was a pal to everyone and everybody came alike to him. Dixie lived near the Everton ground and it was nothing to see him walking to Goodison in a pair of old flannel trousers and a sweater with bedroom slippers on his feet!

'In those days when a match was on there used to be hundreds of unemployed men outside the ground, waiting for the gates to be opened twenty minutes from the end so they could go in to see the final stages of a game they couldn't afford to pay to see.

'More than once I saw one of those unfortunate men approach Dixie on his way to the ground and ask: 'Have you got a ticket, please, Dixie?' Always, his reply would be the same. 'Just a minute, lad,' he'd reply as he'd cheerfully slap the man on the back.

'Then he'd go to the office and get a ticket – and if he'd had his ration of complimentaries he'd buy one. Then he'd give it to the unknown fan outside and say to him: "There you are, pal. Now go and enjoy yourself." That was Dixie Dean the man – and I mean "man" in its real sense.

'He helped me a great deal in my early days at Everton. He'd spend hours with me, teaching me his tricks and giving me tips. There was never any bitterness, even though he knew I'd been signed to take his place eventually. In fact he went out of his way to help me.

'Dixie was a great and glorious player and I'm proud to say I played alongside him and that he was my friend. The greatest compliment anyone could pay me was to compare me with him.

'There have been many good centre forwards. There have been quite a few very good centre forwards but there has been only one REAL centre forward and that is the incredible William Ralph Dean. He is unforgettable, irreplaceable and one of the game's immortals.'

In 'The Good Companions' J.B. Priestley wrote of football supporters 'cheering together, thumping one another on the shoulders, swapping judgments like lords of the earth, having pushed through a turnstile into another altogether more splendid kind of life, hurtling with conflict and yet passionate and beautiful in its art.'

Dixie Dean was part of that splendid kind of life and his art was passionate and beautiful at the heart of the conflict.

# *Index*